Know the Bible Now

Edward A. Engelbrecht

Dawn Mirly Weinstock

Gail E. Pawlitz

Sarah J. Steiner

CONCORDIA PUBLISHING HOUSE · SAINT LOUIS

Library of Congress Cataloging-in-Publication Data

Names: Engelbrecht, Edward, author.

Title: Know the Bible now / Edward A. Engelbrecht, Dawn Mirly Weinstock, Gail
   E. Pawlitz, Sarah J. Steiner.

Description: St. Louis : Concordia Publishing House, 2016. | Includes index.

Identifiers: LCCN 2015030342 | ISBN 9780758644480

Subjects: LCSH: Bible--Introductions.

Classification: LCC BS475.3 .E54 2016 | DDC 220.6/1--dc23 LC record available at http://lccn.loc.gov/2015030342

1 2 3 4 5 6 7 8 9 10   25 24 23 22 21 20 19 18 17 16

Contents

Bible Book Summaries

Foreword

Biblical literacy seems to be at an all-time low today. One can no longer assume that a reference even to a major scriptural event will be understood by the general public.

Fifty years ago, when I first started teaching ancient history at Western Michigan University, any mention I made of a familiar person or event in Scripture was readily understood by nearly all the students. Now the same reference provokes glassy-eyed stares from much of the class. And this problem is not limited to the young, to non-Christians, or to the laity. The horror stories abound and include the clergy. One survey found that only three of ten British clerics could name all Ten Commandments!

Such biblical illiteracy makes the task of sharing or defending the faith—obligatory for every Christian—even more difficult. How do we share our beliefs without understanding their source? How can Christians mount a defense against all the trash being loaded upon the faith today in our media, magazines, radio and TV, novels, Internet blogs, and sensationalist books when they are not quite sure what they are trying to defend?

Even in the context of a local congregation, some may feel intimidated at assuming any leadership in Bible study due to the massive amount of material in the Scriptures. This may well be the case for new converts who have not had a Christian upbringing.

Know the Bible Now is a genuine antidote to biblical illiteracy, and a welcome solution to the problems illiteracy raises. The editors and publisher have not used the "Read the Bible in A Year" approach through the familiar listings of daily devotional segments of Holy Writ. Instead, they have responded to authorities in the field of education, who tell us that the literary vehicle most likely to draw attention and to effortlessly enter the memory is the story. Accordingly, they have chosen the 120 greatest stories in the Old and New Testaments to engage the reader.

When using the term *story* in this context, of course, we must always remember that the meaning is "historical account," not fictional fairy tale for bedtime reading to children. The stories in Scripture give us the true record of how humanity has responded to God and His revelation in the most colorful and diverse ways.

Visual imagery is another powerful tool for communication, learning authorities insist. For example, witness the use of icons on computer screens that the mind absorbs more quickly than wordage. For that reason, *Know the Bible Now* is filled with illustrations, including pictorial art, infographics, charts, maps, explanatory sidebars, and many other visual aids, all in full color. The art, in particular, has a photographic quality that sets it above the usual imagery found in Sunday School leaflets, while the "Did you know?" segments offer fresh insights that even theologians will admire.

Another unique feature in these pages are the brief but powerful summaries of the various biblical books, which will enable the reader to "see the forest as well as the trees." This wider view reveals the overall divine plan behind the Old and New Testaments.

All of these aids are designed to render the massive amount of material in that religious library we call the Bible much more intelligible and memorable for the reader. *Know the Bible Now*, then, is no unfounded claim or a publisher's hype, but sober truth.

Whoever reads this book will be rewarded with a more comprehensive understanding of Holy Scripture. Readers will see how it all fits together in a masterpiece of creative unity, as revealed by its ultimate Author. The Bible thus equips any Christian with the working instructions for life here on earth—the Law, as well as the great good news about the life to come, the Gospel. For this reason, I commend these pages to all lay Christians, as well as any clergy and even theologians who may have neglected personal Bible study.

—Paul L. Maier

Preface

Give me life, O LORD, according to Your
Word! . . . I am Your servant; give me
understanding, that I may know Your
testimonies! *Psalm 119:107, 125*

The Bible is a grand, mysterious book—and for many of us,
a bit intimidating. Unless you grew up in Sunday School or
read Bible stories with your family at home, the Bible may feel
like a closed book. Where do you start? What's most important to
know? How does one prepare to hear the Bible preached in church,
discussed in classes, or shared with one's family?

Know the Bible Now is based on the proven practice—centuries
old—of learning the Bible through study of its key stories. The 120
Bible stories in this book are based on the English Standard Version
and provide the perfect bridge into reading the full Bible with
clear understanding. Yet *Know the Bible Now* also includes 75 pages
of cutting-edge infographics to summarize key points about the
books of the Bible and their teachings. Together, they present easy
access to God's life-giving Word.

Because many events and books of the Bible overlap one another
in time, the presentation of stories and book summaries is roughly
chronological. This should help the reader gain a broad sense of
when things happened without troubling over too many details. For
a thorough study of biblical chronology, we recommend Andrew E.
Steinmann's *From Abraham to Paul: A Biblical Chronology* (St. Louis:
Concordia, 2011).

—Rev. Edward A. Engelbrecht
Bible Resources Senior Editor
Concordia Publishing House

The Bible as Story

The Bible Is

| The story of God's promised salvation | *Know the Bible Now* describes both ways of seeing the Bible—through its great, ongoing story and through facts about the many books and persons through whom the story is told. | A collection of books God inspired |

Creation
The Promise
The Fathers
The Exodus
The Tribes
The Kingdom
The Exile
The Return
The Promise Fulfilled
The Mission
The End

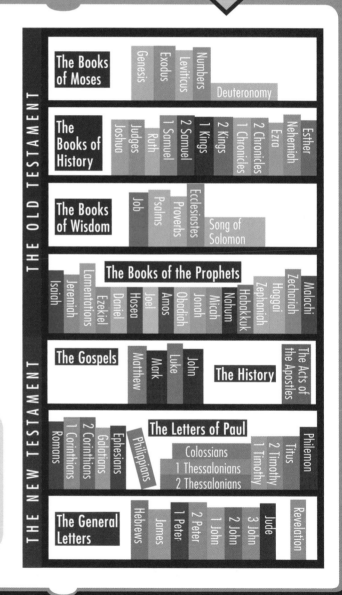

THE OLD TESTAMENT

The Books of Moses
Genesis, Exodus, Leviticus, Numbers, Deuteronomy

The Books of History
Joshua, Judges, Ruth, 1 Samuel, 2 Samuel, 1 Kings, 2 Kings, 1 Chronicles, 2 Chronicles, Ezra, Nehemiah, Esther

The Books of Wisdom
Job, Psalms, Proverbs, Ecclesiastes, Song of Solomon

The Books of the Prophets
Isaiah, Jeremiah, Lamentations, Ezekiel, Daniel, Hosea, Joel, Amos, Obadiah, Jonah, Micah, Nahum, Habakkuk, Zephaniah, Haggai, Zechariah, Malachi

THE NEW TESTAMENT

The Gospels
Matthew, Mark, Luke, John

The History
The Acts of the Apostles

The Letters of Paul
Romans, 1 Corinthians, 2 Corinthians, Galatians, Ephesians, Philippians, Colossians, 1 Thessalonians, 2 Thessalonians, 1 Timothy, 2 Timothy, Titus, Philemon

The General Letters
Hebrews, James, 1 Peter, 2 Peter, 1 John, 2 John, 3 John, Jude, Revelation

Understanding Bible References

The following diagram illustrates how a common Bible reference to John 3:16 breaks down.

Book Title	Chapter Number	Verse Number
John	3:	16

Using the Bible's table of contents, look up the book John, then chapter 3, and finally verse 16.

The Bible Is Two Major Teachings

2

THE GOSPEL is the promise that the heavenly Father would send the Savior of the world: Jesus, who rescues us from our sins and gives new and eternal life. In the Bible, all the passages that describe or refer to the blessings God promises and gives us through Jesus may be called Gospel.

1

THE LAW is the rules we should obey. In the Bible, God's Law commands the good works we should do. It also threatens punishments for the sins we should not do. All the passages or stories that speak in these ways are examples of Law.

Scholars of the Bible have distinguished a total of 613 commands or prohibitions in the Books of Moses, which are commonly called the Law of Moses.

These TWO teachings are the TWO basic ways God works in people's lives, found throughout the Bible. God defines Himself through these two teachings in Exodus 34:6–7. The Gospel of John also begins with this distinction (John 1:17).

With these **basic truths**, you are ready to start reading the story of salvation and exploring the books of the Bible. As you read a story, learn about the book where it is found or take the approach that best works for you or for the group with which you are studying.

Bible reference

Bible story

Sample page

God Creates the World

Genesis 1–2

In the beginning, God **created** the heavens and the earth. The earth had no shape. It was empty. Darkness was over the face of the deep. The Spirit of God was hovering over the waters. God said, "Let there be light," and there was light. God separated the light from the darkness. God called the light Day. The darkness He called Night. There was evening and there was morning, the first day.

God said, "Let an expanse separate the waters from the waters." And it was so. God called the expanse Heaven. There was evening and there was morning, the second day.

God said, "Let the waters under the heavens be gathered into one place, and let the dry land appear." And it was so. God called the dry land Earth, and the waters He called Seas. God saw that it was good.

And God said, "Let the earth sprout plants and fruit trees. Let each bring forth seeds, according to its kind." And it was so. The earth brought forth plants and trees. God saw that it was good. There was evening and there was morning, the third day.

God said, "Let there be lights in the heavens to separate the day from the night and to give light upon the earth." And it was so. God made the greater light to rule the day and the lesser light to rule the night, and He made the stars. God saw that it was good. There was evening and there was morning, the fourth day.

God said, "Let the waters swarm with living creatures, and let birds fly above the earth." God created the sea creatures and birds according to their kinds. God saw that it was good. God blessed them, saying, "Be fruitful and multiply." There was evening and there was morning, the fifth day.

God said, "Let the earth bring forth living creatures—livestock and creeping things and beasts of the earth." And it was so. God made the beasts of the earth and the livestock and everything that creeps on the ground according to their kinds. God saw that it was good.

Then God said, "Let Us make man in Our image." So God created man in His own image. He created them male and female. God **blessed** them, saying, "Be fruitful and multiply and fill the earth and have **dominion** over every living thing." And God said, "I have given you plants and trees with seed in its fruit for food." And it was so. God saw everything that He had made, and it was very good. There was evening and there was morning, the sixth day.

God blessed the seventh day and made it **holy**, because on it He rested.

Words to Remember
In the beginning, God created the heavens and the earth.
Genesis 1:1

Creation to the Flood 13

DID YOU KNOW?
- The Hebrew word for create is never used with a subject other than God in the Old Testament.
- Lights (lamps or candles) are used in Christian worship to symbolize God's active faith-creating and faith-sustaining presence among His people.
- Before the flood, plants were sustained by water in the soil itself and by the river that flowed through and out of Eden.

Bible facts

The Bible sometimes includes **special terms** that you may not hear or see in day-to-day English. It sometimes includes words that are more challenging to understand. A number of these words are set in **bold** so they are easier to find and to discuss or explore with a dictionary.

et Us make man in Our image." So God created man in His d them male and female. God **blessed** them, saying, "Be and fill the earth and have **dominion** over every living thing." given you plants and trees with seed in its fruit for food." And erything that He had made, and it was very good. There was s morning, the sixth day.
venth day and made it **holy**, because on it He rested.

While you read and explore, look for facts about the Savior, Jesus. He is the chief character of the Bible, which is all about Jesus and you.

The Old Testament

The Beginning

In the beginning, God created
the heavens and the earth. *Genesis 1:1*

Every book has a beginning, a middle, and an end. The Bible is no different. In fact, the first book of the Bible, Genesis, tells the story of how everything began, including human beings. God spoke and the entire universe was created. Then God created human beings from the dust of the ground. He breathed into the dust He had formed. He created human beings in His image: perfect, without sin, obedient.

But the first people, Adam and Eve, did not trust God. They did not obey His commands. They put themselves first. They sinned when they ate the fruit from the tree in the middle of the garden. As a result, Adam and Eve had to leave the garden. As a result, all of Adam and Eve's children, including us, are born as sinners, experience troubles, and will die.

But the story does not end there. In Genesis 3:15, God makes the very first promise of a Savior. He will repeat this promise throughout the Old Testament: to Noah and Abraham and David and to all who will hear the prophets.

As you read the Bible stories in this section, think about how God takes care of you. He created a unique planet that supports you with air and water and food. God placed you in a family so you can grow and learn, especially about God and your Savior, Jesus. God controls the world, so you do not need to be afraid of wars or natural disasters or even death.

This is the beginning of an amazing book that is all about God's love for you. Each story connects to Jesus Christ, God's Son, who came to earth because God always keeps His promises. Jesus loves you so much that He took the punishment for the sin of Adam and Eve and for all your sins. His death and resurrection are the middle of this book—and when God takes you to heaven, you will live the end of the story forever.

The Days of Creation

Day 1: Light and dark, day and night

Day 2: Sky and water

Day 3: Dry land, bodies of water, trees and plants

Day 4: Sun, moon, planets, and stars

Day 5: Animals that live in the water and birds

Day 6: Animals that live on the earth, man and woman

Day 7: God rested

Making Connections

In the Book of Genesis, God used Moses to write down how He created the world. Moses also tells us about the first sin and the problems it caused: Adam and Eve were afraid of God, they had to leave the garden, their son committed murder, and eventually evil people filled the earth.

But Moses also tells us that God loved the people He created. He promised a Savior who would destroy Satan. He gave Cain a mark that would protect him even though he killed his brother. God saved Noah, his family, and the animals from the flood.

God loves you and protects you too. He kept His promise to send Jesus, your Savior, to bruise Satan's head. God marks you as His special and much-loved child in Baptism. Jesus' disciple Peter said that Baptism was like a flood that washes us clean and makes us a new creation. You can look it up in 1 Peter 3:21.

The apostle Paul wrote a letter to his friends in the city of Corinth. He said, "If anyone is in Christ, he is a new creation" (2 Corinthians 5:17) and "In Adam all die, so also in Christ shall all be made alive" (1 Corinthians 15:22). Thank God that from the very beginning He had a plan for you and that in Christ you are a new creation!

Genesis

God creates all things • c. 1446–1406 BC Genesis written • 1406 BC Israel enters Promised Land

Genesis tells the story of God's promise from Eden, where it was first heard (Genesis 3:15), to the descendants of Abraham and Sarah, to whom God promised, "In you all the families of the earth shall be blessed" (Genesis 18:18; 22:18; 28:14). The book breaks down into **three major sections**.

1. Chapters 1–11: Creation and the nations.

2. Chapters 12–36: The heart of the book; the stories of Abraham, Isaac, and Jacob.

3. Chapters 37–50: The brothers whose descendants will lead Israel.

Nearly a third of the book describes the brothers who would give rise to leading tribes at the time Moses wrote the book. Joseph/ Ephraim becomes the forefather of the leading northern tribe. Benjamin becomes the forefather of Saul, the first king of Israel. Judah becomes the forefather of David and Solomon, the greatest kings of Israel in the Old Testament.

Sin & Law

The curse and death that comes with sin and disobedience; humankind's slavery to evil; families divided by sin

Grace & Gospel

The promise of a Savior; God gives blessings, life, and freedom; God's goodness and covenant promise for the faithful

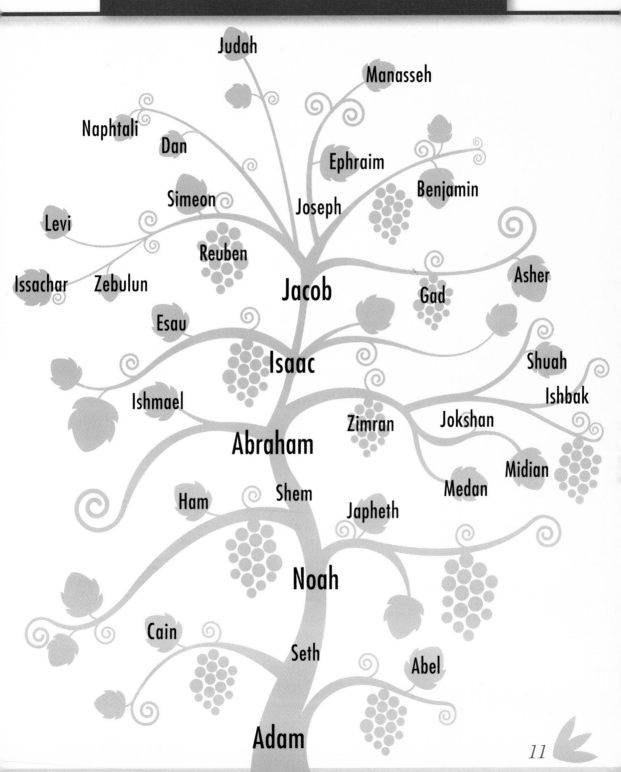

Judah

Manasseh

Naphtali

Dan

Ephraim

Benjamin

Simeon

Joseph

Levi

Reuben

Asher

Issachar

Zebulun

Jacob

Gad

Esau

Isaac

Shuah

Ishmael

Ishbak

Zimran

Jokshan

Abraham

Shem

Midian

Ham

Medan

Japheth

Noah

Cain

Seth

Abel

Adam

God Creates the World

Genesis 1–2

In the beginning, God **created** the heavens and the earth. The earth had no shape. It was empty. Darkness was over the face of the deep. The Spirit of God was hovering over the waters.

God said, "Let there be light," and there was light. God separated the light from the darkness. God called the light Day. The darkness He called Night. There was evening and there was morning, the first day.

God said, "Let an expanse separate the waters from the waters." And it was so. God called the expanse Heaven. There was evening and there was morning, the second day.

God said, "Let the waters under the heavens be gathered into one place, and let the dry land appear." And it was so. God called the dry land Earth, and the waters He called Seas. God saw that it was good.

And God said, "Let the earth sprout plants and fruit trees. Let each bring forth seeds, according to its kind." And it was so. The earth brought forth plants and trees. God saw that it was good. There was evening and there was morning, the third day.

God said, "Let there be lights in the heavens to separate the day from the night and to give light upon the earth." And it was so. God made the greater light to rule the day and the lesser light to rule the night, and He made the stars. God saw that it was good. There was evening and there was morning, the fourth day.

God said, "Let the waters swarm with living creatures, and let birds fly above the earth." God created the sea creatures and birds according to their kinds. God saw that it was good. God blessed them, saying, "Be fruitful and multiply." There was evening and there was morning, the fifth day.

God said, "Let the earth bring forth living creatures—livestock and creeping things and beasts of the earth." And it was so. God made the beasts of the earth and the livestock and everything that creeps on the ground according to their kinds. God saw that it was good.

Then God said, "Let Us make man in Our image." So God created man in His own image. He created them male and female. God **blessed** them, saying, "Be fruitful and multiply and fill the earth and have **dominion** over every living thing." And God said, "I have given you plants and trees with seed in its fruit for food." And it was so. God saw everything that He had made, and it was very good. There was evening and there was morning, the sixth day.

God blessed the seventh day and made it **holy**, because on it He rested.

DID YOU KNOW?

- The Hebrew word for *create* is never used with a subject other than God in the Old Testament.

- Lights (lamps or candles) are used in Christian worship to symbolize God's active faith-creating and faith-sustaining presence among His people.

- Before the flood, plants were sustained by water in the soil itself and by the river that flowed through and out of Eden.

The Fall into Sin

Genesis 2–3

Words to Remember
You are dust, and to dust you shall return.
Genesis 3:19

The **LORD** God planted a garden in Eden, and there He put the man. The tree of life was in the middle of the garden, and the tree of the knowledge of good and evil. God commanded the man, saying, "You may eat of every tree of the garden, but you shall not eat of the tree of the knowledge of good and evil. In the day that you eat of it you shall surely die."

The serpent, who was more **crafty** than any beast that God had made, said to the woman, "Did God actually say, 'You shall not eat of any tree in the garden'?"

The woman said, "We may eat the fruit of the trees. But God said, 'You shall not eat of the tree in the middle of the garden, neither shall you touch it, or you will die.'"

The serpent said, "You will not die. God knows that when you eat from this tree, you will be like God, knowing good and evil."

The woman saw that the tree was good for food and could make one wise, so she took its fruit and ate. She also gave some to her husband, and he ate. Then their eyes were opened, and they knew that they were naked. They sewed fig leaves together and made themselves loincloths.

They heard the LORD God walking in the garden, and the man and his wife hid themselves. But the LORD God called to the man, "Where are you?"

And the man said, "I was afraid, because I was naked, and I hid myself."

God said, "Who told you that you were naked? Have you eaten of the tree?"

The man said, "The woman gave me fruit of the tree, and I ate."

Then the LORD God said to the woman, "What have you done?"

The woman said, "The serpent **deceived** me, and I ate."

The LORD God said to the serpent, "I will put **enmity** between you and the woman, and between your **offspring** and her offspring. He shall bruise your head, and you shall bruise His heel."

To the woman God said, "In pain you shall bring forth children."

And to Adam God said, "Cursed is the ground because of you. By the sweat of your face you shall eat bread until you return to the ground. For you are dust, and to dust you shall return."

The man called his wife's name Eve, because she was the mother of all living. And the LORD God made garments of skins and clothed Adam and Eve.

Then the LORD God drove the man out of the garden. At the east of the garden, God placed the **cherubim**, who held a flaming sword that turned every way to guard the way to the tree of life.

DID YOU KNOW? _____

- Man is called '*adam* (Hebrew) because he comes from the '*admah* (Hebrew for "earth"). Both terms refer to the reddish brown color of clay soil.

- The garden was only a part of the region called Eden.

- The name *Satan* means "adversary."

The Children of Adam and Eve

Genesis 4

Adam and Eve had a son. Eve named him Cain, saying, "I have gotten a man with the help of the LORD." And again, she gave birth to his brother Abel. Now Abel was a keeper of sheep, and Cain a worker of the ground.

In the course of time, Cain brought to the LORD an **offering** of the fruit of the ground. Abel also brought an offering of the firstborn of his flock and of their fat portions. The LORD had regard for Abel and his offering, but for Cain and his offering He had no regard. So Cain was angry, and his face fell.

> ### Words to Remember
> [Eve] bore a son and called his name Seth, for she said, "God has appointed for me another offspring."
> *Genesis 4:25*

The LORD said to Cain, "Why are you angry, and why has your face fallen? If you do well, will you not be accepted? And if you do not do well, sin is crouching at the door. Its desire is for you, but you must rule over it."

Cain spoke to Abel his brother. And when they were in the field, Cain rose up against his brother Abel and killed him.

Then the LORD said to Cain, "Where is Abel your brother?"

Cain said, "I do not know. Am I my brother's keeper?"

The LORD said, "What have you done? The voice of your brother's blood is crying to Me from the ground. Now you are cursed from the ground, which has opened its mouth to receive your brother's blood from your hand. When you work the ground, it shall no longer **yield** to you its strength. You shall be a fugitive and a wanderer on the earth."

Cain said to the LORD, "My punishment is greater than I can bear. Today You have driven me away from the ground. I will be hidden from Your face. I shall be a fugitive and a wanderer on the earth. Whoever finds me will kill me."

Then the LORD said to him, "Not so!" And the LORD put a mark on Cain so no one would attack him. Then Cain went away from the presence of the LORD and settled in the land of Nod, east of Eden.

And Eve gave birth to a son and called his name Seth. She said, "God has given me another offspring instead of Abel because Cain killed him."

To Seth also a son was born, and he called his name Enosh. At that time, people began to call upon the name of the LORD.

DID YOU KNOW?

- God asked Cain where his brother was to give Cain the opportunity to confess his sin.

- God continued to care for Cain even after pronouncing judgment on him, just as He provided clothes for Adam and Eve to show His ongoing care for them after the fall.

- Cain's murder of Abel immediately revealed how the curse of sin and death corrupted God's perfect creation and gift of life.

Noah and the Flood

Genesis 6–9

The LORD saw that the wickedness of man was great in the earth and that all man thought about doing was evil. The LORD was sorry that He had made man, and it **grieved** Him to His heart. So the LORD said, "I will blot out man and animals and creeping things and birds of the heavens, for I am sorry that I have made them." But Noah **found favor** in the eyes of the LORD. And Noah had three sons, Shem, Ham, and Japheth.

God said to Noah, "Make an ark of gopher wood. Cover it inside and out with pitch. Make a roof for the ark, and set the door in its side. Make it with lower, second, and third decks. Behold, I will bring a flood upon the earth to destroy all flesh. But I will make My **covenant** with you. You, your sons, your wife, and your sons' wives shall come into the ark. You shall bring male and female of every sort of animal into the ark to keep them alive with you. Also take with you every sort of food." Noah did all that God commanded.

In the six hundredth year of Noah's life, all the fountains of the great deep burst forth. The windows of the heavens were opened. Rain fell upon the earth forty days and forty nights. But Noah, his family, and the animals were in the ark. And the LORD shut him in. The ark floated on the face of the waters, which covered all the high mountains. All flesh on earth died. Only Noah and those with him in the ark were left.

God remembered Noah and all the animals with him in the ark. He made a wind blow over the earth, and the waters subsided. The ark came to rest on the mountains of Ararat. Finally all the earth was dry. God said to Noah, "Go out from the ark. Be fruitful and multiply on the earth." So Noah and his sons and his wife and his sons' wives and every beast went out from the ark.

Noah built an altar to the LORD and offered burnt offerings. When the LORD smelled the pleasing aroma, He said in His heart, "I will never again curse the ground because of man. Neither will I ever again strike down every living creature as I have done."

God said to Noah and to his sons, "Never again shall there be a flood to destroy the earth. This is the sign of the covenant that I make between Me and you and every living creature that is with you: I have set My bow in the cloud. When I bring clouds over the earth and the bow is seen in the clouds, I will remember My covenant. And the waters shall never again become a flood to destroy all flesh."

DID YOU KNOW?

- The Bible first mentions rain falling at the time of the flood.

- The pitch that Noah used to cover the ark was also used by Moses' mother to make his basket watertight.

- It took one year and eleven days until the earth was dry enough for occupation.

- The deck of Noah's ark was 33,750 square feet—larger than twelve tennis courts lined side by side.

The Patriarchs

God will visit you and bring you up out of this land to the land that He swore to Abraham, to Isaac, and to Jacob. Genesis 50:24

God created man in His image, but because Adam and Eve sinned, now all people sin. Although some of Adam and Eve's children trusted God, eventually only Noah and his family followed God. So God rescued them when He sent the flood to destroy the earth. God also made promises (covenants): that He would save people from Satan through Eve's Offspring, that He would not destroy the world again with a flood, that He would care for His people.

The Bible stories in this section talk about three special people: Abraham, Isaac, and Jacob. God chose Abraham to be the father of His special people. God called Abraham from his home somewhere in present-day Iraq to travel to the land of Canaan (present-day Israel). Because God loved Abraham, He promised to make Abraham's children as many as the stars. But Abraham and his wife, Sarah, had no children for a very long time.

Finally, the child God promised was born to Abraham and Sarah. They named him Isaac. Isaac and his wife, Rebekah, had twins: Jacob and Esau. Jacob had twelve sons. God changed Jacob's name to Israel. The descendants of his sons became the twelve tribes of Israel. And Israel became a great nation under Kings David and Solomon. Today Abraham's physical descendants are the Jewish people who live all around the world. So God kept His promise to Abraham.

But the most important part of God's promise to Abraham was this: "in your Offspring shall all the nations of the earth be blessed" (Genesis 22:18). God was again promising to send the Savior. In Jesus, Abraham's Offspring and Eve's Offspring (Genesis 3:15), we are blessed with forgiveness of sins and salvation. Because of Jesus, God blesses us with His love and He promises to bring us to the new land of heaven when we die. So all Christians are Abraham's children too—and there are as many of us as the stars!

Making Connections

The Bible is full of children of promise. What does this mean? Think of all the times someone asked God for a baby or was promised a baby: Abraham and Sarah (see page 28), Hannah (see page 106), Zechariah and Elizabeth (see page 214), and Mary (see page 216) are the ones we think of most often.

In the waters of Baptism, God makes you a child of promise. He forgives your sins because of Jesus' saving work on the cross. As His special child, God blesses you with gifts: love, joy, peace, patience, kindness, goodness, faithfulness, gentleness, self-control (Galatians 5:22–23). God guarantees that you will inherit eternal life, which only His children can receive. God even fills you with His Holy Spirit, who makes sure you know all this is true (John 16:13).

The Twelve Sons of Jacob

Reuben

Simeon

Levi

Judah (Jesus would come from this son)

Zebulun

Issachar

Dan

Gad

Asher

Naphtali

Joseph

Benjamin

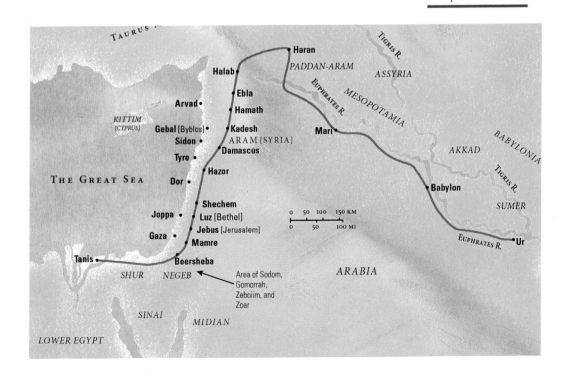

God Calls Abram

Genesis 12–13

The LORD said to Abram, "Go to the land that I will show you. And I will make of you a great nation. I will bless you and make your name great. In you, all the families of the earth shall be blessed."

Abram was seventy-five years old when he took Sarai his wife, and Lot, his brother's son, and all their possessions and set out. When they came to the land of Canaan, the LORD appeared to Abram and said, "To your offspring I will give this land." So Abram built an **altar** to the LORD.

Now there was a famine in the land. So Abram went to Egypt. Before he entered Egypt, he said to Sarai, "You are a beautiful woman. Say you are my sister. Then it may go well with me and my life may be spared." When Abram entered Egypt, the princes of **Pharaoh** saw Sarai. They praised her to Pharaoh, and she was taken into Pharaoh's house. For her sake he dealt well with Abram.

But the LORD afflicted Pharaoh and his house with plagues because of Sarai. So Pharaoh called Abram and said, "What is this you have done to me? Why did you say, 'She is my sister,' so that I took her for my wife? Take her, and go." And Pharaoh's men sent Abram and Sarai away with all that he had.

So Abram returned to the land of Canaan, and Lot went with him. Abram journeyed to the place where he had made the first altar. There Abram called upon the name of the LORD.

Abram was rich in livestock. Lot also had flocks and herds and tents. The land could not support both of them. There was **strife** between the herdsmen of Abram's livestock and the herdsmen of Lot's livestock.

Abram said to Lot, "Let there be no strife between you and me, for we are **kinsmen**. Separate yourself from me. If you take the left hand, then I will go to the right. If you take the right hand, then I will go to the left."

Lot saw that the Jordan Valley was well watered everywhere like the garden of the LORD. So Lot chose all the Jordan Valley. Thus Abram settled in the land of Canaan, while Lot settled among the cities of the valley and moved his tent as far as Sodom.

The LORD said to Abram, "Look from the place where you are, northward and southward and eastward and westward. All the land that you see I will give to you and to your offspring forever. I will make your offspring as the dust of the earth. Walk through the length and the breadth of the land, for I will give it to you."

DID YOU KNOW?

- By calling Abram, an idolater (see Joshua 24:2), out of pagan surroundings and affiliations and setting him apart from the world of false belief, God demonstrated that it is not by works but by grace that we are saved.

- Sarai *is* actually Abram's half sister. They were both fathered by Terah but had different mothers (see Genesis 20:12). In the early ages of the history of the world, God had not forbidden marriages between brothers and sisters.

Abram Rescues Lot

Genesis 13–14

Abram and Lot separated from each other. Abram settled in the land of Canaan, while Lot settled among the cities of the valley. He moved his tent as far as Sodom.

There was a great battle between many kings that took place in the land where Lot had chosen to live. The kings of Sodom and Gomorrah were on the losing side.

Now the place where the battle took place was full of bitumen pits. As the kings of Sodom and Gomorrah fled, some fell into these pits. The rest fled to the hill country. So the enemy took all the possessions of Sodom and Gomorrah, and all their food, and went their way. The enemy also took Lot, who was living in Sodom, and his possessions.

One who had escaped came and told Abram. When Abram heard that his kinsman had been taken captive, he led his trained men (318 of them) in pursuit. At night, he divided his forces against them and defeated the enemy kings. Then Abram brought back all the possessions, and Lot and his possessions, and the women and the people.

After Abram's return from the defeat of the enemy kings, the king of Sodom went out to meet him. And Melchizedek, the king of Salem, brought out bread and wine. (He was priest of God Most High.) And Melchizedek blessed Abram and said,

> "Blessed be Abram by God Most High,
> > Possessor of heaven and earth.
> Blessed be God Most High,
> > who has delivered your enemies into your hand!"

Abram gave Melchizedek a **tenth of everything.**

The king of Sodom said to Abram, "Give me the persons, but take the goods for yourself."

But Abram said to the king of Sodom, "I have lifted my hand to the LORD, God Most High, Possessor of heaven and earth, that I would not take a thread or a sandal strap or anything that is yours."

Words to Remember

Blessed be Abram by God Most High, Possessor of heaven and earth; and blessed be God Most High, who has delivered your enemies into your hand! *Genesis 14:19–20*

DID YOU KNOW?

- Abram and Lot had to separate because their wealth was in their growing herds, so more and more pasture was needed to support them both. Abram allowed Lot, his younger nephew, to choose where he wanted to settle first.

- Bitumen pits are pits of asphalt or tar. The Salt Sea is known for having chunks of asphalt floating in it.

- To lift up or raise the hand is to swear or make an oath.

God's Covenant with Abram

Genesis 15 and 17

The word of the LORD came to Abram in a **vision**: "Fear not, Abram, I am your shield. Your reward shall be very great."

But Abram said, "O Lord GOD, what will You give me, for I continue childless."

The word of the LORD came to him, "Your very own son shall be your **heir**."

And God brought Abram outside and said, "Look toward heaven. Number the stars, if you are able. So shall your offspring be."

And Abram believed the LORD, and He counted it to him as **righteousness**.

When Abram was ninety-nine years old, the LORD appeared to him and said, "I am God Almighty. Walk before Me, and be blameless. My covenant is with you. No longer shall your name be called Abram. Your name shall be Abraham, for I will make you into nations. Kings shall come from you. I will make My covenant between Me and you and your offspring for an everlasting covenant, to be God to you and to your offspring. I will give to you and to your offspring all the land of Canaan for an everlasting possession. I will be their God."

And God said to Abraham, "As for Sarai your wife, you shall not call her name Sarai. Sarah shall be her name. I will bless her, and I will give you a son by her. I will bless her, and she shall become nations. Kings of peoples shall come from her."

Then Abraham fell on his face and laughed. He said to himself, "Shall a child be born to a man who is a hundred years old? Shall Sarah, who is ninety years old, give birth to a child?"

God said, "Sarah your wife shall give birth to your son. You shall call his name Isaac. I will make My covenant with him as an everlasting covenant for his offspring. I will make My covenant with Isaac, whom Sarah shall give birth to at this time next year."

When He had finished talking with him, God went up from Abraham.

Words to Remember

I will establish My covenant between Me and you and your offspring after you . . . to be God to you and to your offspring after you. *Genesis 17:7*

DID YOU KNOW?

- *Abram* means "exalted father." God changed the name to *Abraham* as a sign of the covenant God made with him, promising that Abraham would be the "father of many nations."

- Special appearances of God among human beings are called *theophanies*, which means "manifestations of God." They remind us that God sustains His creation and that His personal, active participation in human history continued after the fall.

Abraham's Visitors

Genesis 18 and 21

The LORD appeared to Abraham as he sat at the door of his tent in the heat of the day. Abraham looked, and three men were standing in front of him. He ran from the tent door to meet them. He bowed himself to the earth and said, "O Lord, if I have found favor in Your sight, do not pass by Your servant. Let a little water be brought, and wash your feet. Rest yourselves under the tree, while I bring bread. After that you may pass on."

So they said, "Do as you have said."

Abraham went quickly into the tent to Sarah and said, "Quick! Knead fine flour and make cakes." And Abraham ran to the herd. He took a calf and gave it to a young man, who prepared it quickly. Then he took curds and milk and the calf that he had prepared and set it before his visitors. He stood by them while they ate.

They said to Abraham, "Where is Sarah your wife?"

And he said, "She is in the tent."

The LORD said, "I will surely return to you about this time next year, and Sarah your wife shall have a son."

Sarah was listening at the tent door. Now Abraham and Sarah were old. So Sarah laughed to herself, saying, "After I am worn out, and my lord is old, shall I have pleasure?"

The LORD said to Abraham, "Why did Sarah laugh and say, 'Shall I indeed give birth to a child now that I am old?' Is anything too hard for the LORD? I will return to you, about this time next year, and Sarah shall have a son."

The LORD visited Sarah as He had said, and the LORD did to Sarah as He had promised. Sarah gave birth to Abraham's son in his old age. She gave birth at the time God said. Abraham called the name of his son Isaac. Abraham was a hundred years old when his son Isaac was born to him.

And Sarah said, "God has made laughter for me. Everyone who hears will laugh over me. Who would have said to Abraham that Sarah would nurse children? Yet I have given birth to his son in his old age."

Words to Remember

Is anything too hard for the LORD?
Genesis 18:14

DID YOU KNOW?

- Because there were so few inns, people placed high importance on hospitality. Abraham recognized that his guests were special and thus honored them by waiting on them rather than sitting with them.

- Abraham and Sarah had great patience—they waited twenty-five years for God to fulfill His promise to make Abraham the father of many nations.

- *Isaac* means "he laughs," reflecting the laughter of Sarah when she at first could not believe that she would bear a son in her old age.

Abraham and Isaac

Genesis 22

God tested Abraham and said to him, "Take your only son Isaac, whom you love, and go to the land of Moriah. Offer him there as a burnt offering on one of the mountains of which I shall tell you."

So Abraham rose early in the morning, saddled his donkey, and took two of his young men and his son Isaac. He cut the wood for the burnt offering and went to the place of which God had told him.

On the third day, Abraham saw the place from afar. Then Abraham said to his young men, "Stay here with the donkey. I and the boy will go over there and **worship** and come again to you." Abraham took the wood and laid it on Isaac, his son. He took the fire and the knife. So they went together.

Isaac said to his father, Abraham, "Behold, the fire and the wood, but where is the lamb for a burnt offering?"

Abraham said, "God will provide for Himself the lamb for a burnt offering, my son." So they went together.

When they came to the place, Abraham built the altar and laid the wood in order. He bound Isaac, his son, and laid him on top of the wood. Then Abraham took the knife to kill his son.

But the angel of the LORD called to him from heaven and said, "Abraham, Abraham! Do not lay your hand on the boy or do anything to him. Now I know that you **fear** God, seeing you have not withheld your only son from Me."

Abraham looked, and behind him was a ram, caught in a thicket by his horns. Abraham offered the ram as a burnt offering instead of his son. So Abraham called the name of that place "The LORD will provide."

The angel of the LORD called to Abraham a second time from heaven and said, "Because you have not withheld your only son, I will surely bless you. I will surely multiply your offspring as the stars of heaven and as the sand that is on the seashore. In your offspring shall all the nations of the earth be blessed, because you have obeyed My voice."

So Abraham returned to his young men. They arose and went home together.

Words to Remember

In your offspring shall all the nations of the earth be blessed, because you have obeyed My voice.
Genesis 22:18

DID YOU KNOW?

- The land of Moriah is where Jerusalem and the temple would later be built.

- One way that faith is strengthened is through trial and hardship. We often fail tests of faith that do not begin to compare to Abraham's, but thankfully, God made an even greater sacrifice by offering His Son to secure forgiveness for our failures.

- Jesus' work for our salvation is pictured in the Old Testament sacrifices.

Isaac and Rebekah

Genesis 24

Words to Remember
Blessed be the LORD, the God of my master Abraham, who has not forsaken His steadfast love and His faithfulness toward my master. *Genesis 24:27*

Now Abraham was old, and he said to his servant, "Go to my country and to my **kindred** and take a wife for my son Isaac."

So the servant took ten camels and all sorts of gifts and went to the city of Nahor. He made the camels kneel by the well at the time when women go out to draw water. He said, "O LORD, please grant me success today. Let a young woman come to whom I shall say, 'Please let down your jar that I may drink.' She shall say, 'Drink, and I will water your camels.' Let her be the one whom You have chosen for Isaac."

Before he had finished speaking, Rebekah came out with her water jar. She was very pretty. The servant said, "Please give me a little water."

Rebekah said, "Drink, my lord. I will draw water for your camels also."

When the camels had finished drinking, the man said, "Please tell me whose daughter you are. Is there room in your father's house for us to spend the night?"

She said, "I am the daughter of Bethuel. We have plenty of room for you to stay."

The man bowed his head and worshiped the LORD. He said, "Blessed be the LORD, who has led me to the house of my master's kinsmen." The young woman ran and told her household about these things.

Laban, Rebekah's brother, went to the man. He said, "Come in, O blessed of the LORD. I have prepared the house and a place for the camels."

The servant told Laban everything that had happened since Abraham sent him to find a wife for Isaac. Laban and Bethuel said, "Take Rebekah to be the wife of your master's son, as the LORD has spoken." When Abraham's servant heard their words, he bowed before the LORD. He gave Rebekah silver and gold jewelry and clothes. He gave costly ornaments to her brother and to her mother. And he and the men who were with him ate and drank, and they spent the night.

In the morning, Rebekah and her young women arose and rode on the camels and followed the man.

Now Isaac had gone out to **meditate** in the field toward evening. And he saw camels coming. Rebekah saw Isaac and said to the servant, "Who is that man, walking in the field to meet us?"

The servant said, "It is my master." So she took her veil and covered herself. The servant told Isaac all that he had done. Then Isaac took Rebekah, and she became his wife, and he loved her.

DID YOU KNOW?

- Abraham was about 140 years old when he sent his servant to find a wife for Isaac.

- Rebekah was Isaac's second cousin.

- Rebekah covered herself with her veil to show modesty and respect.

Jacob and Esau

Genesis 25 and 27

Words to Remember

Isaac prayed to the LORD for his wife, because she was barren. And the LORD granted his prayer. *Genesis 25:21*

Isaac was forty years old when he took Rebekah to be his wife. And Isaac prayed to the LORD, because she was barren. The Lord granted his prayer. When her days to give birth were completed, there were twins. The first came out red, all his body like a hairy cloak, so they called his name Esau. Afterward his brother came out with his hand holding Esau's heel, so his name was called Jacob. When the boys grew up, Esau was a skillful hunter, while Jacob was a quiet man. Isaac loved Esau because he ate of his game, but Rebekah loved Jacob.

Once when Jacob was cooking stew, Esau came in from the field, and he was very tired. Esau said, "Let me eat some stew."

Jacob said, "Sell me your **birthright**." So Esau sold his birthright to Jacob. Then Jacob gave Esau bread and lentil stew.

When Isaac was old and he could not see, he said to Esau, "Go hunt game for me. Prepare delicious food for me to eat, that my **soul** may bless you before I die."

Rebekah was listening. She said to Jacob, "Bring me two young goats. I will prepare delicious food for your father. Then he may bless you before he dies."

But Jacob said, "Esau is a hairy man, and I am a smooth man."

His mother said, "Obey my voice." So Jacob brought the goats to his mother, and she prepared delicious food. Then Rebekah put Esau's clothes on Jacob. She put the goat skins on his hands and on this neck. She gave him the food and the bread.

Jacob went in to his father and said, "I am Esau. I have done as you told me. Eat, that your soul may bless me."

Isaac said, "Come near, that I may feel you." So Jacob went near to Isaac, who felt him and said, "The voice is Jacob's, but the hands are Esau's." Then Isaac said, "Come near and kiss me." Isaac smelled his clothes and blessed him.

As soon as Isaac had finished blessing Jacob, Esau came in from his hunting. He prepared delicious food and brought it to his father. Isaac said, "Who are you?"

He answered, "I am Esau."

Then Isaac trembled violently and said, "Who was it then that I have blessed? Your brother came deceitfully. He has taken away your blessing."

Now Esau hated Jacob because of the blessing. Esau said to himself, "The days of **mourning** for my father are approaching. Then I will kill my brother Jacob."

But Esau's words were told to Rebekah. So she said to Jacob, "Esau plans to kill you. Flee to Laban. Stay with him until your brother's fury turns away and he forgets what you have done to him. Then I will send and bring you from there."

DID YOU KNOW?

- It was contrary to ancient custom and family right for Esau to be subservient to his younger twin, Jacob. By this favor for Jacob, the Lord emphasized that the promise does not come by obligation, rights, or works, but by miraculous, undeserved grace.

- The name for Genesis comes from the book's Greek title and means "birth" or "genealogy," topics that are important to the stories of Genesis and to its structure.

Jacob's Dream

Genesis 27–28

Isaac called Jacob and blessed him and told him, "You must not take a wife from the Canaanite women. Go to the house of your mother's father. Take as your wife one of the daughters of Laban. God Almighty bless you and make you fruitful and multiply you, that you may become a company of peoples. May He give the blessing of Abraham to you and to your offspring, that you may take possession of the land that God gave to Abraham!" So Isaac sent Jacob away.

Jacob went toward Haran. He came to a certain place and stayed there that night, because the sun had set. Taking one of the stones, he put it under his head and lay down to sleep. He dreamed, and there was a ladder set up on the earth. The top of the ladder reached to heaven. The angels of God were ascending and descending on it!

The LORD stood above it and said, "I am the LORD, the God of Abraham your father and the God of Isaac. The land on which you lie I will give to you and to your offspring. Your offspring shall be like the dust of the earth. You shall spread to the west and to the east and to the north and to the south. In you and your offspring shall all the families of the earth be blessed. Behold, I am with you and will keep you wherever you go. I will bring you back to this land. For I will not leave you until I have done what I have promised you."

Then Jacob awoke from his sleep and said, "Surely the LORD is in this place, and I did not know it." And he was afraid and said, "How awesome is this place! This is none other than the house of God, and this is the gate of heaven."

Early in the morning Jacob took the stone that he had put under his head and set it up for a pillar. He poured oil on the top of the stone. He called the name of that place Bethel.

Then Jacob made a **vow**, saying, "If God will be with me and will keep me in this way that I go, and will give me bread to eat and clothing to wear, so that I come again to my father's house in peace, then the LORD shall be my God. And this stone, which I have set up for a pillar, shall be God's house. And of all that You give me I will give a full tenth to You."

Words to Remember

Behold, I am with you and will keep you wherever you go. . . . I will not leave you until I have done what I have promised you. *Genesis 28:15*

DID YOU KNOW?

- The Canaanites derive their name from the son of Ham. Ham dishonored his father, Noah; therefore, Ham's son Canaan was cursed (Genesis 9:18–25). His descendants rejected God's grace.

- Jacob used the stone as a pillar to mark the spot where God appeared to him. He would later build an altar from this stone and others and preach God's name and sacrifice there.

Jacob's Family

Genesis 29–31

Jacob came to the land of the people of the east. He saw a well in the field. Three flocks of sheep were beside it. The stone on the well's mouth was large.

Jacob said to the shepherds, "Do you know Laban the son of Nahor?"

They said, "We know him."

Jacob said to them, "Is it well with him?"

They said, "It is well. See, Rachel his daughter is coming with the sheep!"

As soon as Jacob saw Rachel, he rolled the stone from the well's mouth. He watered the flock of Laban his mother's brother. Then Jacob kissed Rachel and wept. He told Rachel that he was her father's kinsman. She ran and told her father.

Laban ran to meet Jacob. He hugged Jacob and kissed him and brought him to his house. Laban said, "Because you are my kinsman, should you serve me for nothing? Tell me, what shall your wages be?" Now Laban had two daughters: Leah, whose eyes were weak, and Rachel, who was beautiful.

Jacob loved Rachel. He said, "I will serve you seven years for your younger daughter Rachel." So Jacob served seven years for Rachel. They seemed to him but a few days because of the love he had for her.

Then Jacob said to Laban, "Give me my wife, for my time is completed." So Laban made a feast. But in the evening he brought Leah to Jacob.

In the morning, Jacob said to Laban, "Why have you deceived me?"

Laban said, "We do not give the younger before the firstborn. We will give you Rachel in return for serving me another seven years." Jacob agreed, and Laban gave him Rachel to be his wife. Jacob loved Rachel more than Leah.

Jacob's family grew and grew. He had twelve sons: Reuben, Simeon, Levi, Judah, Dan, Naphtali, Gad, Asher, Issachar, Zebulun, Joseph, and Benjamin. He also had a daughter named Dinah. While he lived with Laban, Jacob's flocks and herds grew large too.

Then the Lord said to Jacob, "Return to the land of your fathers and to your kindred. I will be with you."

So Jacob arose and set his sons and his wives on camels. He drove away all his livestock, all his property that he had gained, to go to the land of Canaan to his father, Isaac.

Words to Remember

God remembered Rachel, and God listened to her and opened her womb. She conceived and bore a son and said, "God has taken away my reproach." *Genesis 30:22–23*

DID YOU KNOW?

- Jacob did not have money to pay a bride price, so he offered his labor. Seven years would equal an extravagant amount of money and thus indicated his deep love for Rachel.

- The Hebrew expression saying Leah's eyes "were weak" is unclear. Apparently, her eyes were dull and lacking luster in comparison to Rachel's beautiful eyes.

- Just as Jacob deceived his brother, Esau, the firstborn, so also Laban deceives Jacob regarding a firstborn.

Esau Forgives Jacob

Genesis 32–33

Words to Remember
Your name shall no longer be called Jacob, but Israel, for you have striven with God and with men, and have prevailed.
Genesis 32:28

Jacob sent messengers to Esau. He told them to say, "Thus says your servant Jacob, 'I have lived with Laban until now. I have oxen, donkeys, flocks, and servants. I desire to find favor in your sight.'"

The messengers returned to Jacob, saying, "Esau is coming to meet you. There are four hundred men with him."

Jacob was greatly afraid. He divided the people and the animals into two camps, thinking, "If Esau attacks one camp, then the camp that is left will escape."

Jacob said, "O LORD who said to me, 'Return to your country and to your kindred, that I may do you good,' I am not worthy of the least of all the deeds of **steadfast** love and all the faithfulness that You have shown to Your servant. Please deliver me from the hand of Esau, for I fear that he may attack me."

So Jacob took a present for his brother Esau: goats, ewes, rams, camels and their calves, cows, bulls, and donkeys. He handed these to his servants and said, "Pass on ahead of me. When Esau asks to whom you belong, say, 'They belong to your servant Jacob. They are a present. And he is behind us.'" So the present passed on ahead, and Jacob stayed in the camp.

The same night a man wrestled with Jacob until the breaking of the day. When the man saw that He did not **prevail** against Jacob, He put Jacob's hip out of joint. Then He said, "Let Me go, for the day has broken."

But Jacob said, "I will not let You go unless You bless me."

Then He said, "Your name shall no longer be called Jacob, but Israel. You have struggled with God and with men and have prevailed."

Jacob said, "I have seen God face-to-face, and yet my life has been delivered."

Jacob saw Esau and the four hundred men with him. So he divided the children among Leah and Rachel and the two female servants. He himself went on before them, bowing to the ground seven times, until he came near to his brother. But Esau ran to meet Jacob. He hugged him and kissed him, and they wept. Esau said, "Who are these with you?"

Jacob said, "The children whom God has graciously given your servant."

Esau said, "What do you mean by all these animals that I met?"

Jacob said, "If I have found favor in your sight, please accept my blessing. God has dealt graciously with me." Thus Jacob urged Esau, and he took the present.

Jacob came safely to the city of Shechem, which is in the land of Canaan. He bought the piece of land on which he had pitched his tent. There he built an altar.

DID YOU KNOW?

- Dividing the people and animals was a tactic used by ancient merchants and caravans to ensure that some of their livestock and goods would survive a raid.

- The one who wrestled with Jacob was God. Seeing Him "face to face" means Jacob saw God in His assumed human form.

- In Israelite culture, the name of a person represented the character, or essence, of the person.

Job

2166 BC Abraham born • 2006 BC Jacob and Esau born • 1859 BC Jacob dies in Egypt

The Lord's servant Job endured a **whirlwind** of suffering without understanding why such terrible things happened to him (cf. Job 1:19; 27:20; 37:9; 38:1; 40:6). Along the way, other persons comment on his plight and give lots of advice. Through it all, Job continued to trust in the Lord, who finally delivered him from evil. Like the problem of why good people suffer, Job's story is ancient and may have taken place in the era of the Book of Genesis.

God. Shall a faultfinder contend with the Almighty?

Job. I know my Redeemer lives.

Wife. Curse God and die!

Elihu. God acts justly. Don't question Him.

Friends. If you obey God, He would reward you.

Satan. Job fears God for no reason.

Job's Fortunes	Reversed
Before Suffering →	**After Suffering**
Wife	Wife
7 sons	7 new sons
3 daughters	3 new daughters
7,000 sheep	14,000 sheep
3,000 camels	6,000 camels
500 yoke of oxen	1,000 yoke of oxen
500 female donkeys	1,000 female donkeys

In the ancient Near East, the elders of a community would typically hold court in a city gate, dressed in fine robes (Job 29:7, 14). Parties in dispute would approach the elders, explain their case, and seek a wise ruling. Instead of supporting Job's case, his friends support the suit against him. Job realizes that he needs an arbiter, a redeemer, to rescue him from condemnation. God Himself ultimately comes to Job's aid. In this way, Job's story points forward to the role of Jesus as our Redeemer.

Job's Arbiter and Redeemer

Job 9:33–35	My Arbiter
Job 13:15–16	My Salvation
Job 14:13–14	My Renewal
Job 16:19–21	My Witness
Job 19:24–27	My Redeemer

Joseph's Dreams

Genesis 37

Now Israel loved Joseph more than any other of his sons. And he made him a robe of many colors. But when his brothers saw that their father loved Joseph more, they hated him and could not speak peacefully to him.

Joseph had a dream, and when he told it to his brothers, they hated him even more. He said, "Hear this dream that I have dreamed: Behold, we were binding sheaves in the field. My sheaf stood upright. Your sheaves gathered around it and bowed down to my sheaf."

His brothers said to him, "Are you indeed to rule over us?" So they hated Joseph even more for his dreams and for his words.

Then he dreamed another dream and told it to his brothers. Joseph said, "Behold, the sun, the moon, and eleven stars were bowing down to me."

When he told it to his father and to his brothers, his father said, "Shall I and your mother and your brothers bow ourselves to the ground before you?" And his brothers were jealous, but his father remembered the saying.

Now his brothers went to pasture their father's flock near Shechem. Israel said to Joseph, "See if it is well with your brothers and with the flock. Bring me word." So Joseph went after his brothers and found them at Dothan.

They saw Joseph from afar. Before he came near to his brothers, they planned how to kill him. They said to one another, "Here comes this dreamer. Let us kill him and throw him into one of the pits. Then we will say that a fierce animal has eaten him, and we will see what will become of his dreams."

When Reuben heard it, he said, "Throw him into this pit, but do not lay a hand on him." He wanted to rescue him. So when Joseph came to his brothers, they stripped him of his robe of many colors. And they threw him into a pit.

Then they sat down to eat. They saw a caravan of Ishmaelites on their way to Egypt. Judah said, "Let us sell Joseph to the Ishmaelites." They lifted Joseph out of the pit and sold him for twenty **shekels** of silver. The Ishmaelites took Joseph to Egypt.

When Reuben returned and saw that Joseph was not in the pit, he tore his clothes. Then he killed a goat and dipped Joseph's robe in the blood. They brought it to their father and said, "We found this. Please tell us whether it is your son's robe."

Jacob said, "It is my son's. Joseph is without doubt torn to pieces." Then Jacob tore his clothes, put on **sackcloth**, and refused to be comforted.

DID YOU KNOW?

- In Genesis, God used dreams especially to reveal His will. But today we ought not expect God to reveal Himself in dreams, since we have God's will recorded in the Bible for us.

- Joseph's dream was fulfilled years later in Egypt when his family bowed down to him (Genesis 42:6).

- Joseph traveled about sixty-seven miles before finding his brothers.

- The pits referred to here were cisterns that were dug to collect rain water. At this time of year, the pits would be dry.

Joseph in Egypt

Genesis 39–41

Words to Remember
The LORD was with Joseph and showed him steadfast love.
Genesis 39:21

Potiphar, an officer of Pharaoh, bought Joseph and put him in charge of all that he had. But Potiphar's wife said to Joseph, "Lie with me." Joseph refused.

One day, she caught Joseph by his clothing, saying, "Lie with me." But he left his clothing in her hand and fled. She called to the men of her household and said, "He came to lie with me, and I cried out. He left his clothing and fled."

Joseph's master was angry and put him into prison. But the LORD was with Joseph and showed him steadfast love. The keeper of the prison put Joseph in charge of all the prisoners. The cupbearer of the king and his baker were put in the prison too. One night, they both dreamed, but they were sad because there was no one to **interpret** the dreams.

Joseph said, "Do not interpretations belong to God? Please tell me the dreams."

So the cupbearer said, "There was a vine with three branches with clusters of grapes. I pressed the grapes into Pharaoh's cup and gave it to Pharaoh."

Joseph said, "In three days, Pharaoh will restore you to your office. Only mention me to Pharaoh, so I can get out."

The chief baker said, "There were three cake baskets on my head. In the top one were baked foods for Pharaoh. But the birds were eating from it."

Joseph said, "In three days, Pharaoh will hang you on a tree. And the birds will eat the flesh from you."

On the third day, everything happened as Joseph had said.

After two years, Pharaoh dreamed that he was standing by the Nile. Out of the Nile seven plump cows came and fed in the grass. Then seven thin cows came out of the Nile and ate the seven plump cows. Pharaoh dreamed a second time that seven thin ears of grain swallowed up seven plump ears. So Pharaoh sent for all the magicians and wise men, but no one could interpret the dreams.

The cupbearer told Pharaoh about Joseph. Pharaoh sent for Joseph and told him his dreams. Joseph said, "God has **revealed** what He is about to do. There will be seven years of plentiful harvest followed by seven years of famine. Let Pharaoh select a wise man to store up grain for the years of famine."

Pharaoh chose Joseph. He said, "All my people shall do as you command."

Joseph stored up grain. When the famine came, he sold grain to the Egyptians. Moreover, all the earth came to Egypt to Joseph to buy grain, because the famine was severe over all the earth.

DID YOU KNOW?

- *Pharaoh* is an Egyptian royal title meaning "the great house." It originally applied to the king's palace, but was later applied to rulers of Egypt.

- Joseph was seventeen years old when sold into slavery, around twenty-eight when he interpreted the dreams of the cupbearer and baker, and thirty when freed from jail.

- Joseph became the highest ranking official, master in the royal palace and also throughout Egypt. However, supreme authority remained with Pharaoh.

Joseph Forgives His Brothers

Genesis 42–45

Jacob learned there was grain for sale in Egypt. So he sent ten of his sons to buy grain. But Jacob did not send Benjamin, Joseph's brother.

Joseph sold grain to all the people, so Joseph's brothers bowed before him. Joseph recognized them, but they did not recognize him. Joseph remembered the dreams. He said, "You are spies."

Words to Remember

Do not be distressed or angry with yourselves because you sold me here, for God sent me before you to preserve life. *Genesis 45:5*

They said, "No, your servants have come to buy food. We are twelve brothers. The youngest is with our father, and one is no more."

Joseph said, "You are spies. If you are honest, let one brother remain. The rest will take grain and bring your youngest brother to me." Joseph bound Simeon before their eyes. Then Joseph had their bags filled with grain and their money placed in the sacks. He gave them food for the journey.

The brothers left. When they came to Jacob, the brothers told him everything. As they emptied their sacks, their money was inside. They were afraid.

When they had eaten the grain, Jacob said to them, "Go buy us a little food."

But Judah said, "The man warned us, saying, 'You shall not see my face unless your brother is with you.' Send Benjamin with me. If I do not bring him back to you, then let me bear the blame forever."

Israel said, "Take some of the choice fruits of the land. Take double the money. Take your brother. May God Almighty grant you **mercy** before the man."

When Joseph saw Benjamin, he said to his steward, "Kill an animal and make ready. The men are to dine with me at noon." When Joseph came home and saw Benjamin, he said, "God be gracious to you!" Then he hurried out and wept. He came back and they ate. Benjamin was given five times more than his brothers.

Joseph commanded the steward, "Fill the sacks with food. Put each man's money in his sack. Put my silver cup in the sack of the youngest." The next day, the men left. Now Joseph said to his steward, "Follow the men."

When the steward overtook the brothers, he searched, and the cup was found in Benjamin's sack. When Judah and his brothers came to Joseph's house, Judah said, "Your servant became a pledge of safety for the boy. Therefore, please let your servant remain instead of the boy. Let the boy go back with his brothers."

Joseph said, "I am your brother, whom you sold into Egypt. Do not be distressed or angry because you sold me here. God sent me before you to **preserve** life. He has made me ruler over all the land." And he kissed his brothers and wept upon them.

DID YOU KNOW?

- Joseph's brothers did not recognize him because twenty-two years had gone by, and he was wearing Egyptian royal garb and speaking a foreign language.

- Joseph gave five times as much food to Benjamin in order to test his brothers and to learn whether they would be jealous of or abandon their youngest brother, as they had Joseph after Jacob's generosity.

- Joseph's forgiveness of his brothers pictures Jesus' mercy on us.

Jacob's Blessing

Genesis 45–49

Words to Remember
I am God, the God of your father. Do not be afraid to go down to Egypt, for there I will make you into a great nation. *Genesis 46:3*

When Pharaoh heard that Joseph's brothers had come, he said to Joseph, "Say to your brothers, 'Come to me. I will give you the best of the land of Egypt.'"

So Joseph gave his brothers wagons and food for the journey. They came to the land of Canaan and told Jacob, "Joseph is ruler over all Egypt."

Israel said, "I will go and see him before I die."

So Israel came to Beersheba. He offered sacrifices to God. And God spoke to Israel in visions of the night and said, "Do not be afraid to go to Egypt. There I will make you into a great nation."

The sons of Israel carried Jacob their father, their little ones, and their wives in the wagons that Pharaoh had sent. They also took their livestock and their goods, which they had gained in the land of Canaan.

Joseph prepared his chariot and went to meet Israel his father in Goshen. He presented himself to him and wept on his neck a good while. Israel said, "Now let me die, since I have seen your face and know that you are still alive."

So Israel settled in the land of Egypt, in the land of Goshen. And they gained possessions in it. They were fruitful and multiplied. When the time drew near that Israel must die, he called his son Joseph and said, "Do not bury me in Egypt, but let me lie with my fathers." Joseph promised.

After this, Joseph took his sons Manasseh and Ephraim to Jacob. And Jacob said, "Bring them to me, please, that I may bless them." Then Jacob blessed Joseph and Joseph's sons.

Then Jacob called his sons and said, "Gather together, that I may tell you what shall happen to you in days to come." And he blessed Reuben, Simeon, and Levi. To Judah he said, "The scepter shall not depart from Judah, nor the ruler's staff from between his feet. To him shall be the obedience of the peoples." And Jacob blessed Zebulun, Issachar, Dan, Gad, Asher, Naphtali, Joseph, and Benjamin each with the blessing suitable to him.

Then Jacob commanded his sons, "Bury me with my fathers in the cave that is in the field of Ephron the Hittite, in the land of Canaan. There they buried Abraham and Sarah his wife. There they buried Isaac and Rebekah his wife. There I buried Leah."

When Jacob finished commanding his sons, he drew up his feet into the bed and breathed his last and was gathered to his people.

DID YOU KNOW?

- Most people assumed gods had power only in certain places, but the Lord showed that He is the God of all the earth, present with His people wherever they are.

- Before blessing Joseph's sons Ephraim and Manasseh, who were born in Egypt to an Egyptian mother, Jacob adopted them (Genesis 48:5), giving them full status as children of Israel.

- Jacob's blessing of Judah—the forefather of King David and of the Messiah—foretells Jesus' kingly role.

Moses and the Return to Canaan

The LORD is my strength and my song,
and He has become my salvation. *Exodus 15:2*

God promised Abraham, Isaac, and Jacob that He would make their offspring into a great nation. But Abraham had only one son, Isaac. Isaac had two sons. Then Jacob had 12 sons. How could so few children become a great nation? There were troubles too. For example, God asked Abraham to sacrifice Isaac. Isaac's sons couldn't get along. And Jacob's sons sold Joseph, their brother, into slavery.

But God was always at work to keep His promises. He provided Abraham with a ram for the sacrifice. God brought Isaac's son Jacob safely back to Canaan, and Jacob's brother Esau forgave him for "stealing" Isaac's blessing. God made the slave Joseph into a ruler in Egypt who would help Jacob and his family survive a famine.

The next Bible stories are about salvation (deliverance). God had made Jacob's descendants into a large nation, but the Egyptians oppressed (held down) the Israelites. They worked as slaves and their male babies were killed.

The Israelites cried out to God for help. God heard their prayers and acted to save His people. His plans started with a baby boy named Moses. Nearly 2,000 years later, *the* plan of salvation would start with the birth of a baby boy named Jesus.

You probably know many of the Bible stories in this section: the plagues, crossing the Red Sea, and Jericho's tumbling walls. But did you know these stories are all connected to Jesus and the plan of salvation He carried out for you? You are plagued by the devil, sin, the world, and the angel of death, but Jesus' blood covers you with the gift of forgiveness that He won on the cross. You crossed through the waters of Baptism and God delivered you from the devil's kingdom. Because you are one of God's special people, He will break down the walls of death and bring you safely to the promised land of heaven. So you can say with Moses, "I will sing to the LORD, for He has triumphed gloriously" (Exodus 15:1).

Making Connections

The plagues must have been scary. Although God protected the Israelites, they would have seen dead cattle and fields eaten by locusts. They would have heard Egyptians crying because their oldest sons died during the final plague.

Now imagine standing at the edge of the Red Sea with Pharaoh's army behind you and all that water in front of you. Can God really get you to the other side? Yes, He can. His pillar of cloud and fire guarded the Israelites as they walked safely across on dry ground.

Today you might be scared by threatening weather, or an accident that hurts someone you love, or a family member fighting in a war far away. You might be standing on the edge of big changes.

Jesus, God's Son, knows all about big changes. He left heaven and came to earth to be your Savior. Because Jesus loved you enough to take your sins to the cross, you know He loves you enough to bring you safely across the scary places to be with Him in the promised land of heaven. Jesus truly is the "Lord who saves" (the meaning of His name).

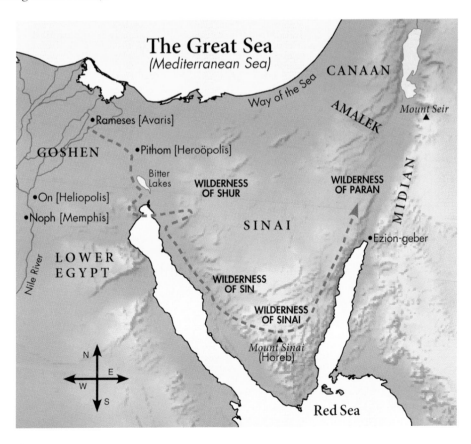

God takes Israel to be His people.

Exodus

1526 BC Moses born • c. 1446 BC Exodus written • 1406 BC Israel enters Promised Land

The ten plagues of Egypt were part of God's plan to rescue Israel and to punish the Egyptians for enslaving them. As the plagues kept coming, Pharaoh grew more and more aware that something miraculous was taking place. But he also resisted God's demands by hardening his heart until the tenth plague took his firstborn son.

Sin & Law

Plagues against unrepentant Egypt; God gives the Ten Commandments and requires an oath to fulfill the Law

Grace & Gospel

God remembers and fulfills His promises to the patriarchs; atonement through sacrifice

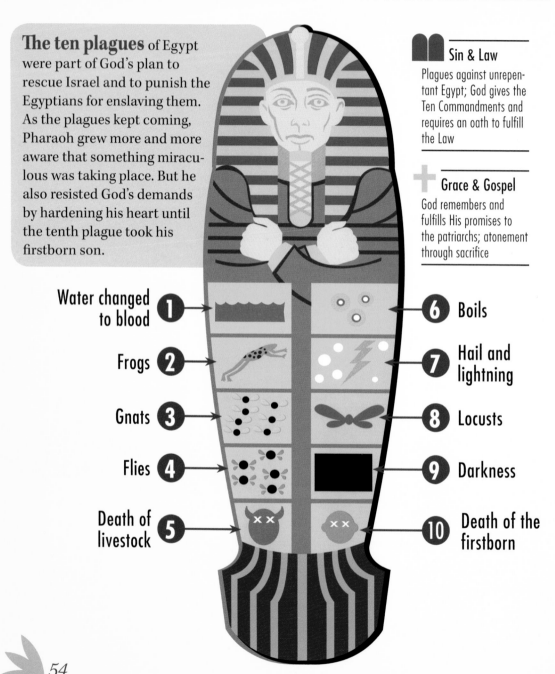

Water changed to blood **1**

Frogs **2**

Gnats **3**

Flies **4**

Death of livestock **5**

6 Boils

7 Hail and lightning

8 Locusts

9 Darkness

10 Death of the firstborn

Tabernacle in the Desert

The items gathered for the tabernacle provided more than just building materials. Many of the items carried spiritual significance for the early Israelites and were part of the Lord's message to His people.

The Materials of the Tabernacle

Materials	Uses	Notes on Culture and Symbolism
Gold	Ark; table; lampstand; clasps; gold hooks; frames and crossbars; ephod; chains for breastpiece; bells; plate; altar of incense	Symbol of wealth and authority (Genesis 41:42); used for money and for making precious items, such as idols.
Silver	Bases for curtain frames; curtain hooks	Represented wealth (Proverbs 3:13–14); used for money and making idols.
Bronze	Clasps; altar utensils; curtain bases; basin	Represented strength (Deuteronomy 33:25); used for weapons and tools (Genesis 4:22; 1 Kings 14:27).
Blue yarn	Curtain decoration; courtyard curtain; ephod; breastpiece; robe; cord	The coast of Canaan was known for the production of blue and purple dyes, which derived from mollusk shells and were expensive to produce. Therefore, these colors were associated with wealth and royalty.
Purple yarn	Curtain decoration; courtyard curtain; ephod; breastpiece	
Scarlet yarn	Curtain decoration; courtyard curtain; ephod; breastpiece	Color derived from the body of the female cochineal insect. This strong dye is known for its staining power. Scarlet became a symbol of sin (Isaiah 1:18). However, in Moses' day, scarlet wool was used in ritual cleansing from sin and sickness (Leviticus 14:1–7, 48–53). The color probably represented the cleansing power of blood.
Fine linen	Curtains; courtyard curtains; ephod; breastpiece; tunic; turban; undergarments	The term for fine linen comes from the word for "white." Linen was the clothing of authority (Genesis 41:42). White cloth also suggested purity and refinement.
Goats' hair	Curtains	An animal of sacrifice. The curtains made from its hair enclosed the tabernacle.
Rams' skins	Tent roof	An animal of sacrifice. The scarlet dye may have symbolized the blood of the sacrifices, which covered the sanctuary.
Goatskins or dugong skins	Tent roof	The dugong is a slow-moving sea mammal, 7–11 feet long, from the Red Sea. It is valued for its meat, oil, and waterproof hide. Goatskins were also used (Exodus 26:14).
Acacia wood	Ark; table; curtain frames; crossbars; altar; altar of incense	A hardwood tree that grows in desert valleys. Such trees were more plentiful in ancient times, growing in groves. The wood is still used for cabinetmaking today.
Olives	Oil for the lampstand	As a fuel, food, and medicine, olive oil was one of the staple resources of the ancient Near East. It symbolizes plenty (Genesis 8:11; Deuteronomy 32:13; 33:24).
Spices	For incense and anointing oil	Spices provided a necessary perfume in the desert climate of the ancient Near East. As incense, the spices would help to cover up the smell of the animals and smoke that were found in the court of the tabernacle each day.
Onyx stones	Shoulder pieces	A precious stone made of fine-grained silica in black-and-white layers. Artists carved through the layers to produce sharp black-and-white contrasts, ideal for lettering.
Gems	Breastpiece	Precious stones covered the heart of the high priest, who bore them before God. They showed how God regarded the tribes of Israel as precious.

The Birth of Moses

Exodus 1–2

A new king ruled Egypt. He did not know Joseph. He said, "The people of Israel are too many and too mighty for us. If war breaks out, they may fight against us and escape." Therefore the Egyptians set taskmasters over the people of Israel to **afflict** them with heavy burdens. But the more they were **oppressed**, the more they multiplied. So the Egyptians ruthlessly made the people of Israel work as slaves.

Then the king of Egypt said to the Hebrew midwives, "When you serve as midwife to the Hebrew women, if it is a son, you shall kill him. If it is a daughter, she shall live." But the midwives feared God and let the male children live. So God dealt well with the midwives. And the people multiplied and grew very strong.

Now a man from the house of Levi took as his wife a Levite woman. The woman gave birth to a son. She hid him three months. When she could hide him no longer, she made a basket of bulrushes. She sealed it with bitumen and pitch. She put the child in it and placed it among the reeds by the river bank. His sister stood at a distance to know what would be done to him.

The daughter of Pharaoh came down to bathe at the river. She saw the basket among the reeds. She sent her servant woman, and she took it. When she opened it, she saw the child, who was crying. She took pity on him and said, "This is one of the Hebrews' children."

Then his sister said to Pharaoh's daughter, "Shall I find a Hebrew woman to nurse the child for you?"

Pharaoh's daughter said, "Go."

So the girl went and called the child's mother. Pharaoh's daughter said to her, "Take this child and nurse him for me. I will give you your wages." So the woman took the child and nursed him.

When the child grew up, she brought him to Pharaoh's daughter. He became her son. She named him Moses, "Because," she said, "I drew him out of the water."

When Moses had grown up, he saw an Egyptian beating a Hebrew, one of his people. Seeing no one, Moses struck down the Egyptian and hid him in the sand. When Pharaoh heard of it, he tried to kill Moses. But Moses fled from Pharaoh and stayed in the land of Midian.

> **Words to Remember**
> When the child grew older, she brought him to Pharaoh's daughter, and he became her son. She named him Moses, "Because," she said, "I drew him out of the water." *Exodus 2:10*

DID YOU KNOW? _____

- The new king did not know Joseph because his death took place around three hundred years earlier.

- The Hebrew word used for Moses' "basket" is the same as that for Noah's ark.

- Moses' mother is paid from Pharaoh's treasury to nurse her own son. Moses may have grown up knowing his Hebrew heritage since he was nursed by his own mother.

God Calls Moses

Exodus 2–4

The people of Israel groaned because of their slavery and cried out for help. God heard their groaning and remembered His covenant with Abraham, Isaac, and Jacob.

Now Moses was keeping the flock of his father-in-law. He led his flock to Horeb, the mountain of God. And the angel of the LORD appeared to him in a flame of fire out of the middle of a bush. The bush was burning, yet it was not consumed.

God called from the bush, "Moses! Take your sandals off, for the place on which you are standing is holy ground. I am the God of your father, the God of Abraham, the God of Isaac, and the God of Jacob." Moses hid his face, for he was afraid to look at God. Then the LORD said, "I have seen the affliction of My people. I have come down to deliver them out of the hand of the Egyptians and to bring them to a land flowing with milk and honey. I will send you to Pharaoh that you may bring My people, the children of Israel, out of Egypt."

Moses said, "If the people of Israel ask me Your name, what shall I say?"

God said, "Say to the people of Israel, 'I AM has sent me to you.' This is My name forever. They will listen to your voice. You and the **elders** of Israel shall go to the king of Egypt and say, 'Please let us go a three days' journey into the wilderness, that we may sacrifice to the LORD our God.' But the king of Egypt will not let you. So I will stretch out My hand and strike Egypt with all the wonders that I will do. After that he will let you go."

Then God commanded Moses to throw his staff on the ground. It became a snake, and Moses ran from it. The LORD said, "Take it by the tail." So Moses caught it, and it became a staff. God also gave Moses leprosy and cured him. He told Moses to do these **signs** before the people when he spoke to them.

But Moses said, "I am slow of speech and of tongue."

The LORD said, "I will teach you what you shall speak."

But Moses said, "Please send someone else."

Then the anger of the LORD was kindled against Moses. He said, "Your brother, Aaron, is coming out to meet you. He shall speak for you to the people."

So Moses took his wife and his sons and the staff of God and went back to Egypt. Aaron met Moses at the mountain of God. Then Moses told Aaron all the words of the LORD and all the signs that He had commanded him to do. Aaron spoke to the people and did the signs. The people believed, and they worshiped.

DID YOU KNOW?

- God's Old Testament covenant name, the LORD (which God revealed to Moses on Mount Sinai), is referred to as the tetragrammaton. *Tetra* means "four" in Greek, and *grammaton* refers to the letters of the alphabet. *Tetragrammaton*, therefore, refers to a four-letter name that Bible translators render "YHWH," "Yahweh," or "Jehovah." In many English Bibles, the tetragrammaton appears as "the LORD."

- Horeb is the mountain that is elsewhere called Sinai.

- Moses may have had a speech impediment.

Moses and the Plagues

Exodus 5–10

Words to Remember

I am the LORD, . . . and I will redeem you with an outstretched arm and with great acts of judgment. *Exodus 6:6*

Moses and Aaron said to Pharaoh, "Thus says the LORD, 'Let My people go.'"

But Pharaoh said, "Who is the LORD, that I should obey His voice? I will not let Israel go." So Pharaoh made their tasks even harder for the people of Israel.

But the LORD said to Moses, "Say to the people of Israel, 'I am the LORD your God. I will bring you into the land that I swore to give to Abraham, to Isaac, and to Jacob.' Aaron shall tell Pharaoh to let the people go. But I will **harden** Pharaoh's heart. The Egyptians shall know that I am the LORD, when I stretch out my hand against Egypt and bring out the people of Israel."

Moses and Aaron did as the LORD commanded them. They went to Pharaoh. Aaron cast down his staff, and it became a serpent. The magicians of Egypt did the same by their secret arts. But Aaron's staff swallowed up their staffs. Still Pharaoh's heart was hardened.

The LORD told Moses and Aaron to strike the water of the Nile with the staff. The water turned into blood. But the magicians did the same by their secret arts. So Pharaoh's heart remained hardened.

The LORD sent frogs and gnats to cover the land. He sent great swarms of flies into the house of Pharaoh and throughout all the land of Egypt. But Pharaoh hardened his heart and did not let the people go.

The LORD killed the animals of the Egyptians but protected the animals of the people of Israel. And He caused boils to break out on man and beast throughout all the land of Egypt. But the LORD hardened the heart of Pharaoh.

The LORD rained hail upon the land. It struck down everything in the field in all the land of Egypt. Only in the land of Goshen, where the people of Israel were, was there no hail. Yet Pharaoh hardened his heart and did not let the people go.

The LORD brought such a dense swarm of locusts that the land was darkened. The locusts ate all that the hail had left. Not a green thing remained. But the LORD hardened Pharaoh's heart.

Moses stretched out his hand toward heaven, and there was pitch darkness in all of Egypt three days. The people of Israel had light where they lived. But the LORD hardened Pharaoh's heart. He would not let the people go.

Then Pharaoh said to Moses, "Get away from me. Take care never to see my face again. On the day you see my face you shall die."

Moses said, "As you say! I will not see your face again."

DID YOU KNOW?

- The Lord hardened Pharaoh's heart only after the sixth plague. Prior to that, Pharaoh hardened his own heart against the Lord and continued to do so. By hardening Pharaoh's heart, the Lord confirmed Pharaoh in his persistent unbelief.

- The plagues showed that God was true to His Word. Signs provided assurance, gave testimony and warning, and encouraged faith.

The Passover

Exodus 11–13

The LORD said to Moses, "Yet one plague more I will bring upon Pharaoh and upon Egypt. Afterward he will let you go. Speak now to the people."

So Moses said, "Thus says the LORD: About midnight I will go out in Egypt. And every firstborn in Egypt shall die, from the firstborn of Pharaoh to the firstborn of the cattle. There shall be a great cry throughout all of Egypt. But not a dog shall growl against any of the people of Israel, either man or beast, that you may know that the LORD makes a distinction between Egypt and Israel."

The LORD said to Moses and Aaron, "This month shall be the first month of the year. Every man shall take a lamb for his household. If the household is too small for a lamb, then he and his neighbor shall share. Your lamb shall be without **blemish**, a male a year old. All Israel shall kill their lambs at twilight. Put some of the blood on the doorposts and the lintel of the houses in which they eat it. They shall eat the flesh that night, roasted on the fire. They shall eat **unleavened bread** and bitter herbs. None of it shall remain until morning. Eat it with your belt fastened, your sandals on your feet, and your staff in your hand. Eat it in haste. It is the LORD's **Passover**. For I will pass through the land that night and strike all the firstborn in Egypt, both man and beast. When I see the blood, I will pass over you. You shall keep this day as a feast to the LORD forever."

Then Moses called all the elders of Israel and said, "Kill the Passover lamb. And when you come to the land that the LORD will give you, as He has promised, you shall keep this service. And when your children say to you, 'What do you mean by this service?' you shall say, 'It is the **sacrifice** of the LORD's Passover. For He passed over the houses of the people of Israel when He struck the Egyptians.' "

At midnight the LORD struck down all the firstborn in the land of Egypt. And Pharaoh summoned Moses and Aaron by night and said, "Go, serve the LORD. Take your flocks and your herds, and be gone, and bless me also!"

About 600,000 men on foot, besides women and children, and very much livestock, left Egypt. God led the people toward the Red Sea. And the LORD went before them by day in a pillar of cloud, and by night in a pillar of fire to give them light.

Words to Remember

And the LORD went before them by day in a pillar of cloud to lead them along the way, and by night in a pillar of fire to give them light. *Exodus 13:21*

DID YOU KNOW?_____

- God intended the Passover to point ahead to—or foreshadow—Jesus, the perfect Lamb of God, who would sacrifice His life to deliver all people from slavery to sin and death.

- Israel was to eat unleavened bread because leavening was a symbol of sin. Abstaining from leaven symbolized the new life cleansed from the sinful nature.

- Commentators calculate that there were more than two million Israelite men, women, and children.

Crossing the Red Sea

Exodus 14–15

When the king of Egypt was told that the people had fled, he said, "What is this we have done, that we have let Israel go from serving us?" The LORD hardened the heart of Pharaoh. He pursued the people of Israel. All Pharaoh's horses and chariots and his horsemen and his army overtook the people of Israel as they were camped at the sea.

> **Words to Remember**
> The LORD is my strength and my song, and He has become my salvation. *Exodus 15:2*

When Pharaoh drew near, the people of Israel feared greatly. They cried out to the LORD. They said to Moses, "What have you done to us in bringing us out of Egypt?"

Moses said, "Fear not. Stand firm. See the **salvation** of the LORD, which He will work for you today. The LORD will fight for you."

The LORD said to Moses, "Lift up your staff, and stretch out your hand over the sea and divide it. Then the people of Israel may go through the sea on dry ground." Then the angel of God who was going before the **host** of Israel went behind them. The pillar of cloud came between the host of Egypt and the host of Israel.

Then Moses stretched out his hand, and the LORD drove the sea back by a strong east wind all night. God made the sea dry land, and the waters were divided. The people of Israel went into the middle of the sea on dry ground. The Egyptians went in after them. And the LORD in the pillar of fire and of cloud threw the Egyptian forces into a panic. The Egyptians said, "Let us flee from before Israel, for the LORD fights for them."

Then the LORD said to Moses, "Stretch out your hand over the sea, that the water may come back." So Moses stretched out his hand, and the waters returned and covered the chariots and the horsemen. Of all the host of Pharaoh, not one of them remained. Thus the LORD saved Israel.

Then Moses and the people of Israel sang this song to the LORD:

> "I will sing to the LORD, for He has triumphed gloriously.
> The horse and his rider He has thrown into the sea.
> The LORD is my strength and my song,
> and He has become my salvation....
> You have led in Your steadfast love the people whom You have **redeemed**.
> You have guided them by Your strength to Your holy abode....
> The LORD will reign forever and ever."

DID YOU KNOW?

- Pharaoh and the Egyptians would not admit that God had forced them to let Israel go.

- Salvation does not depend on anything humans do or avoid doing; it is a gift from God. Israel did not need to save itself from the Egyptian army.

- God used the pillar of cloud to protect Israel, providing them with light while leaving the Egyptians in darkness.

God Provides Manna and Quail

Exodus 16

The people of Israel came to the wilderness of Sin. The whole congregation grumbled against Moses and Aaron. They said, "Would that we had died by the hand of the LORD in Egypt. There we sat by the meat pots and ate bread to the full. You have brought us into this wilderness to kill this whole assembly with hunger."

Then the LORD said to Moses, "Behold, I am about to rain bread from heaven."

So Moses and Aaron said to all the people of Israel, "At evening you shall know that it was the LORD who brought you out of the land of Egypt. In the morning you shall see the glory of the LORD."

And the LORD said to Moses, "I have heard the grumbling of the people of Israel. Say to them, 'At twilight you shall eat meat. In the morning you shall be filled with bread. Then you shall know that I am the LORD your God.'"

In the evening, quail came up and covered the camp. In the morning, dew lay around the camp. And when the dew had gone, there was a fine, flake-like thing, fine as frost on the ground.

Moses said, "It is the bread that the LORD has given you to eat. The LORD has commanded: 'Gather as much as you can eat according to the number of persons in your tent.'" And the people of Israel did so. And Moses said, "Let no one leave any till the morning." But they did not listen. Some left part of it till the morning, and it bred worms and stank. Moses was angry.

On the sixth day they gathered twice as much bread. And Moses said, "This is what the LORD has commanded: 'Tomorrow is a day of solemn rest, a holy Sabbath to the LORD. Bake what you will bake and boil what you will boil. All that is left over lay aside to be kept till the morning.'" So they laid it aside as Moses commanded. It did not stink, and there were no worms in it.

Moses said, "Eat it today, for today is a Sabbath to the LORD. Six days you shall gather it, but on the seventh day, which is a Sabbath, there will be none."

Now the house of Israel called its name **manna.** It was like coriander seed. It was white. The taste of it was like wafers made with honey. The people of Israel ate the manna 40 years, till they came to the border of the land of Canaan.

Words to Remember

And the LORD said to Moses, "I have heard the grumbling of the people of Israel. Say to them, 'At twilight you shall eat meat, and in the morning you shall be filled with bread. Then you shall know that I am the LORD your God.'"
Exodus 16:11–12

DID YOU KNOW?

- One month had passed since the Israelites left Egypt. They would likely have traveled no more than ten miles per day.

- God used manna to teach Israel at least three lessons: (1) They were to rely on Him (gathering manna one day at a time). (2) They were to obey Him (not hoarding the manna). (3) They were to have special regard for the Sabbath (seventh-day exception to gathering).

- The bread God provided daily for the Israelites foreshadows the gift of Jesus as the bread of life.

God Gives the Law

Exodus 19–20

Words to Remember

If you will indeed obey My voice and keep My covenant, you shall be My treasured possession among all peoples. *Exodus 19:5*

The people of Israel came into the wilderness of Sinai and camped before the mountain, while Moses went up to God. The LORD called to him, "Tell the people: You have seen what I did to the Egyptians. If you will keep My covenant, you shall be My treasured possession. You shall be to Me a kingdom of priests and a holy nation."

Moses called the elders of the people and told them all the LORD had commanded. The people answered together, "All that the LORD has spoken we will do."

The LORD said to Moses, "Go to the people and **consecrate** them. On the third day the LORD will come down on Mount Sinai." So Moses consecrated the people.

On the morning of the third day, there were thunders and lightnings, a thick cloud on the mountain, and a very loud trumpet blast. All the people in the camp trembled. Then Moses brought the people to meet God at the foot of the mountain. The LORD had descended on it in fire. The whole mountain trembled greatly. The LORD called Moses to the top of the mountain, and Moses went up.

And God spoke all these words, saying,

"I am the LORD your God, who brought you out of the land of Egypt, out of the house of slavery.

"You shall have no other gods before Me. You shall not make for yourself a carved image. You shall not bow down to them or serve them. I am a jealous God, visiting the **iniquity** of the fathers on the children to the third and the fourth generation of those who hate Me, but showing steadfast love to thousands of those who love Me and keep My commandments.

"You shall not take the name of the LORD your God in vain.

"Remember the Sabbath day, to keep it holy. For in six days the LORD made heaven and earth and rested on the seventh day.

"Honor your father and your mother, that your days may be long in the land that the LORD your God is giving you.

"You shall not murder.

"You shall not commit adultery.

"You shall not steal.

"You shall not bear false witness against your neighbor.

"You shall not **covet** your neighbor's house.

"You shall not covet your neighbor's wife or servants or animals or anything that is your neighbor's."

DID YOU KNOW?

- The Law shows us our sin and our need for the Savior.

- The New Testament Book of Galatians tells us that God gave the covenant of Sinai to help the people mature and to prove to His people that they could not obey, so that they would cling in faith to the coming Savior, the One who could and would obey the Law of God in their place and die the death they deserved because of their sins.

God's Covenant with the Israelites

Exodus 32–34 and 40

Moses was delayed coming down from the mountain. So the people said to Aaron, "Make us gods." He received the gold from their hand and made a golden calf. And the people offered burnt offerings.

The LORD said to Moses, "Your people have turned aside out of the way that I commanded them. Let Me alone, that I may consume them."

But Moses **implored** the LORD, and the LORD **relented** from the disaster that He had spoken of bringing on His people.

The LORD said to Moses, "Go up to the land of which I swore to Abraham, Isaac, and Jacob, saying, 'To your offspring I will give it.' Go up to a land flowing with milk and honey. But I will not go with you, for you are a **stiff-necked** people." When the people heard this, they mourned.

Moses said to the LORD, "If I have found favor in Your sight, please show me Your ways. Consider, too, that this nation is Your people."

The LORD said to Moses, "I will make all My goodness pass before you. But man shall not see Me and live. While My glory passes by I will put you in a cleft of the rock. I will cover you with My hand until I have passed by. You shall see My back."

So Moses rose early in the morning and went up on Mount Sinai. The LORD passed before him and proclaimed, "The LORD, the LORD, a God merciful and gracious, slow to anger, and abounding in steadfast love and faithfulness."

Moses bowed his head and worshiped. He said, "If I have found favor in Your sight, O Lord, please **pardon** our sin. Take us for Your inheritance."

The LORD said to Moses, "Behold, I am making a covenant. Before all your people I will do marvels. All the people shall see the work of the LORD, for it is an awesome thing that I will do with you. Observe what I command you this day. Write these words, for I have made a covenant with you and with Israel." When Moses came down from Mount Sinai, his face shone because he had been talking with God.

The LORD spoke to Moses, saying, "You shall build the **tabernacle** of the tent of meeting. Put in it the ark of the testimony, the table, the lampstand, and the golden altar for **incense**. Set the altar of burnt offering before the door of the tabernacle. Place the basin between the tent and the altar. Put water in the basin."

This Moses did. Then the cloud covered the tent of meeting, and the glory of the LORD filled the tabernacle. The cloud of the LORD was on the tabernacle by day and fire was in it by night throughout all their journeys.

Words to Remember

The LORD, the LORD, a God merciful and gracious, slow to anger, and abounding in steadfast love and faithfulness. *Exodus 34:6*

DID YOU KNOW?

- A yoked or haltered animal might tighten its neck muscles to resist having its head turned to go a new direction. Like a farm animal that refused to be guided, Israel was "stiff-necked," refusing to follow God's new direction for them.

- God intended the tabernacle to be a picture of heaven on earth. He lived among His people in the tabernacle and provided the cloud to protect and lead them.

> You shall be holy, for I the Lord your God am holy.

Leviticus

1446 BC Exodus from Egypt • c. 1445 BC Events of Leviticus • 1406 BC Israel enters Promised Land

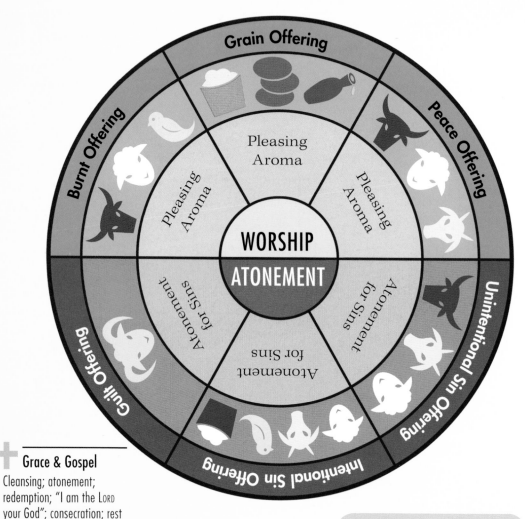

Grace & Gospel

Cleansing; atonement; redemption; "I am the Lord your God"; consecration; rest

Sin & Law

Uncleanness; sin requires blood sacrifices; diseases resulting from sin; walking in God's statutes and commands

Purpose: To teach Israel how to worship and live as the Lord's holy people,

Priestly Garments

HIGH PRIEST'S GARMENTS	NOTES
Holy garments Exodus 28:2	General term for all the garments that follow.
Breastpiece Exodus 25:7; 28:4, 15–30	Twelve precious stones engraved with the names of Israelite tribes.
Urim and Thummim Exodus 28:30	Held in a pouch behind the breastpiece.
Ephod Exodus 25:7; 28:4, 6–14	Style was gold, blue, purple, and scarlet yarns worked into fine linen.
Shoulder pieces Exodus 25:7; 28:7	Two onyx stones attached to the ephod; names of Israelite tribes engraved on the onyx.
Chains (gold) Exodus 28:14	Running from the shoulder plates to the breastpiece.
Robe (blue) Exodus 28:4, 31–35	Blue, with pomegranates and bells attached at the hem.
Pomegranates Exodus 28:33	Attached to the hem of the robe, alternating with the bells (see below).
Bells (gold) Exodus 28:33	Attached to the hem of the robe (see above).
Coat (fine linen) Exodus 28:4, 39	Woven in checker pattern to be tear resistant.
Turban (fine linen) Exodus 28:4, 39	The design as it appeared in later history was based on the shape of a plant.
Plate (gold) Exodus 28:36	Etched with "Holy to the LORD." Attached to the turban with blue cord.
Sash (embroidered) Exodus 28:4, 39	Cf. ephod styling.

In Leviticus 8, Aaron was consecrated as the first high priest.

Numbers

1446 BC Exodus from Egypt • c. 1445 BC First census of tribes • 1406 BC Israel enters Promised Land

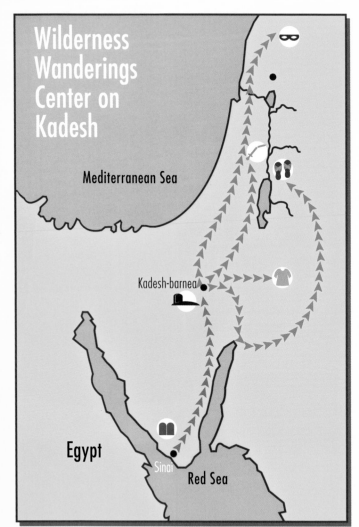

Wilderness Wanderings Center on Kadesh

Mediterranean Sea

Kadesh-barnea

Egypt

Sinai

Red Sea

Tables of Commandments
Sinai to Kadesh, 11 days

Mask
Spies sent out

Broken Sword
Failed conquest

Grave Miriam buried

Sandals
Israel had to walk around
Edom's territory

Garment
Priesthood passes from
Aaron to Eliezer

 Sin & Law
Duties; uncleanness; punishment
for complaining; rebellion; cursing

 Grace & Gospel
Redemption; "I am the LORD your God"; consecration; purification; atonement; blessing

Wilderness Growth and Losses

During the wanderings, Moses conducted **two censuses** of Israel's population. The chart below illustrates the changes experienced by the different tribes.

First Census Numbers 1–4	Tribes	Second Census Numbers 26	% Change (Rounded)
46,500	Reuben	43,730	- 6%
59,300	Simeon	22,200	- 62.5%
45,650	Gad	40,500	- 11%
74,600	Judah	76,500	+ 2.5%
54,400	Issachar	64,300	+ 18%
57,400	Zebulun	60,500	+ 5.4%
40,500	Ephraim	32,500	- 19.75%
32,200	Manasseh	52,700	+ 63.6%
35,400	Benjamin	45,600	+ 28.8%
62,700	Dan	64,400	+ 2.7%
41,500	Asher	53,400	+ 28.7%
53,400	Naphtali	45,400	- 15%
TOTAL 603,550	**ISRAEL**	**601,730**	- 0.3%

JOSEPH: 72,700 → 85,200

Although most of the tribes experienced a less than 20 percent change in population during the wilderness wanderings, the tribe of Simeon was devastated, losing 62.5 percent. This was likely due to persistent unfaithfulness, as specifically described in the idolatry of Baal of Peor (25:4–5). The tribes of Judah and Dan remained the largest, though the combined strength of the tribes of Joseph (Ephraim and Manasseh) eclipsed that of Judah, assuring that they would become key players in Israel's future. The strength of Judah and Joseph reflects the blessings Jacob pronounced over them in Genesis 49.

The Twelve Spies

Numbers 13–14

The LORD spoke to Moses, saying, "Send men to spy out the land of Canaan, which I am giving to the people of Israel. From each tribe send a man." From the tribe of Judah went Caleb. From the tribe of Ephraim went Hoshea, whom Moses called Joshua.

Moses said, "See what the land is. See whether the people are strong or weak, few or many. See whether the cities are camps or strongholds. Be of good courage. Bring some of the fruit of the land." It was the season of the first ripe grapes.

So they spied out the land. They cut a branch with a single cluster of grapes, and they carried it on a pole between two of them. They also brought pomegranates and figs. At the end of 40 days, they returned to all the congregation in the wilderness. They showed them the fruit of the land. They told Moses, "We came to the land to which you sent us. It flows with milk and honey. This is its fruit. However, the people are strong. The cities are fortified and very large."

But Caleb said, "Let us go at once and occupy it. We are able to overcome it."

Then the men who had gone with him said, "We are not able to go up against the people. They are stronger than we are. The land devours its inhabitants. All the people that we saw in it are of great height. We seemed like grasshoppers to them."

The whole congregation said, "Our wives and our little ones will become a prey. Would it not be better for us to go back to Egypt?"

Joshua and Caleb tore their clothes and said, "If the Lord delights in us, He will bring us into this land and give it to us. Only do not rebel against the Lord. And do not fear the people of the land. The Lord is with us."

The Lord said to Moses, "How long will they not believe in Me, in spite of all the signs that I have done among them? I will strike them and disinherit them."

But Moses said to the LORD, "Please pardon the iniquity of this people, according to the greatness of Your steadfast love."

The LORD said, "I have pardoned, according to your word. But none of the men who have seen My glory and My signs that I did in Egypt and in the wilderness shall see the land, except Caleb and Joshua. But your little ones, who you said would become a prey, shall know the land that you have rejected. You shall bear your iniquity 40 years."

When Moses told these words to all the people of Israel, the people mourned.

Words to Remember
The LORD is with us; do not fear them.
Numbers 14:9

DID YOU KNOW?

- The Book of Numbers details Israel's forty-year journey through the wilderness on their way to the Promised Land. It includes all of the events that happened after their year-long stay at Mount Sinai after the exodus.

- The spies carried the cluster of grapes on a pole between them because extraordinarily large clusters could weigh as much as twelve pounds.

- Joshua and Caleb tore their clothes as a warning to the Israelites that their action was equivalent to blasphemy.

Water from a Rock and Fiery Serpents

Numbers 20–21

The people of Israel came into the wilderness of Sin. Now there was no water for the congregation. And the people quarreled with Moses and said, "Why have you brought the assembly of the LORD into this wilderness? Why have you made us come up out of Egypt to bring us to this evil place? There is no water to drink."

Words to Remember
And the LORD said to Moses and Aaron, "Because you did not believe in Me, to uphold Me as holy in the eyes of the people of Israel, therefore you shall not bring this assembly into the land that I have given them." *Numbers 20:12*

Then Moses and Aaron went to the entrance of the tent of meeting and fell on their faces. The glory of the LORD appeared to them. The LORD spoke to Moses, saying, "Take the staff, and assemble the congregation. Tell the rock before their eyes to yield its water. So you shall bring water out of the rock for them and give drink to the congregation and their cattle."

Moses and Aaron gathered the assembly before the rock. He said to them, "Hear now, you rebels: shall we bring water for you out of this rock?" And Moses lifted up his hand and struck the rock with his staff twice. Water came out abundantly. The congregation drank, and their livestock.

The LORD said to Moses and Aaron, "Because you did not believe in Me, therefore you shall not bring this assembly into the land that I have given them."

They journeyed to Mount Hor. And Aaron died there on the top of the mountain. When all the congregation saw that Aaron had **perished**, all the house of Israel wept for Aaron 30 days.

From Mount Hor they set out by the way to the Red Sea. The people became impatient. The people spoke against God and against Moses, "Why have you brought us up out of Egypt to die in the wilderness? There is no food and no water, and we **despise** this worthless food."

Then the LORD sent fiery serpents among the people. They bit the people, so that many people of Israel died. The people came to Moses and said, "We have sinned. We have spoken against the LORD and against you. Pray to the LORD, that He take away the serpents from us."

So Moses prayed for the people. And the LORD said to Moses, "Make a fiery serpent. Set it on a pole. Everyone who is bitten, when he sees it, shall live."

Moses made a bronze serpent and set it on a pole. If a serpent bit anyone, he would look at the bronze serpent and live.

DID YOU KNOW?

- Moses' words "shall we" indicate that he and Aaron were claiming credit for the miracle, not attributing it to God. Instead of letting God's Word reveal its power, Moses sought to make his contribution to the miracle by striking the rock twice, failing to sanctify God before the people.

- In the Old Testament, God tied promises to physical objects, such as the serpent on the pole, to strengthen the faith of His people. These signs revealed His kindness and His understanding of His children's needs.

- Healing was not magical but depended on faith in God's promise.

You shall love the Lord your God.

Deuteronomy

1446 BC Exodus from Egypt • 1407/06 BC Moses' farewell address • 1406 BC Israel enters Promised Land

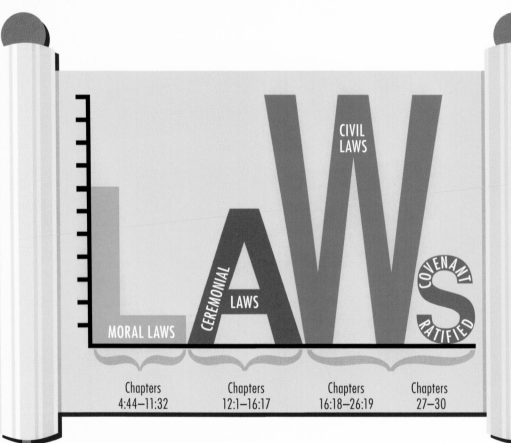

CIVIL LAWS

CEREMONIAL LAWS

COVENANT RATIFIED

MORAL LAWS

| Chapters 4:44–11:32 | Chapters 12:1–16:17 | Chapters 16:18–26:19 | Chapters 27–30 |

Deuteronomy exhibits the three types of laws the Lord gave to Israel as well as the ceremony of covenant renewal by which Israel promised to keep the Law and the Lord promised to bless Israel. The book is a series of sermons that Moses delivered before his death. Moses gave more attention to civil laws to prepare Israel for settling in the Promised Land.

The following chart shows three different types of laws in the Old Testament and comments on how they changed in the New Testament.

EXAMPLES OF LAWS			
Types of Law	Moral Law	Ceremonial Law	Civil Law
Examples	The Ten Commandments (Exodus 20; Deuteronomy 5)	Festivals like Passover (Exodus 12)	Cutting trees down (Deuteronomy 20:19)
Changes	The moral law stayed the same. Jesus and the apostles continued to teach the same moral law in the New Testament.	Jesus transformed Passover into the Lord's Supper (Matthew 26; 1 Corinthians 11).	The civil laws in the Books of Moses were especially for Israel when they settled the Promised Land. In the New Testament, the Lord teaches us to obey the just laws of the nation where we live (Romans 13).

Sin & Law

Devoted to destruction; hard-hearted; laws of the covenant; snare of idolatry; cursing

Grace & Gospel

Redemption; "I am the LORD your God"; inheritance; righteousness by God's Word; promises of the covenant; God's love and calling; atonement; faithfulness; blessing

The Death of Moses

Deuteronomy 18, 31, and 34

Moses said, "When you come into the land that the LORD your God is giving you, you shall not learn to follow the **abominable** practices of those nations. You shall be blameless before the LORD your God. The LORD your God will raise up for you a **prophet** like me from among you, from your brothers. It is to Him you shall listen. And the LORD said to me, 'I will put My words in His mouth. He shall speak to them all that I command Him. Whoever will not listen to My words that He shall speak in My name, I Myself will require it of him.'"

Words to Remember

It is the LORD who goes before you. He will be with you; He will not leave you or forsake you. Do not fear or be dismayed. *Deuteronomy 31:8*

So Moses continued to speak these words to all Israel. And he said, "The LORD has said to me, 'You shall not go over this Jordan.' The LORD your God Himself will go over before you. He will destroy these nations before you."

Then Moses summoned Joshua and said in the sight of all Israel, "Be strong and courageous. You shall go with this people into the land that the LORD has sworn to their fathers to give them. It is the LORD who goes before you. He will not leave you or forsake you. Do not fear or be dismayed."

The LORD said to Moses, "Call Joshua and present yourselves in the tent of meeting, that I may **commission** him." Moses and Joshua presented themselves in the tent of meeting. And the LORD appeared in the tent in a pillar of cloud. The LORD commissioned Joshua and said, "Be strong and courageous. You shall bring the people of Israel into the land that I swore to give them. I will be with you."

Then Moses went to Mount Nebo, which is opposite Jericho. The LORD showed Moses all the land. And the LORD said, "This is the land of which I swore to Abraham, to Isaac, and to Jacob, 'I will give it to your offspring.' I have let you see it with your eyes, but you shall not go over there."

So Moses the servant of the LORD died in the land of Moab. God buried him in the valley in the land of Moab. Moses was 120 years old when he died. His eye was undimmed. He was still strong. The people of Israel wept for Moses 30 days.

And Joshua was full of the spirit of wisdom, for Moses had laid his hands on him. The people of Israel obeyed Joshua and did as the LORD had commanded Moses.

There has not arisen a prophet since in Israel like Moses, whom the LORD knew face-to-face. None did all the signs and the wonders that the LORD sent him to do in the land of Egypt.

DID YOU KNOW?

- *Deuteronomy* means "second law," in part because the Ten Commandments are repeated in chapter 5.

- Moses' burial by the Lord has been interpreted to mean that his lifeless body was immune to decay (cf. Jude 9).

- Although Moses disqualified himself from entering the Promised Land because of his disobedience, God allowed him to see firsthand the fulfillment of all Scripture, for Moses and us, at Christ's transfiguration (Matthew 17:1–8).

24 chapters

Be strong and very courageous.

Read in 1 hour, 50 minutes

Joshua

1407/06 BC Moses' farewell • c. 1406–1400 BC Conquest under Joshua • 1399–1375 BC Deaths of Joshua and the elders

Purpose: To record how the Lord fulfilled His promise to give Canaan as an inheritance to Israel.

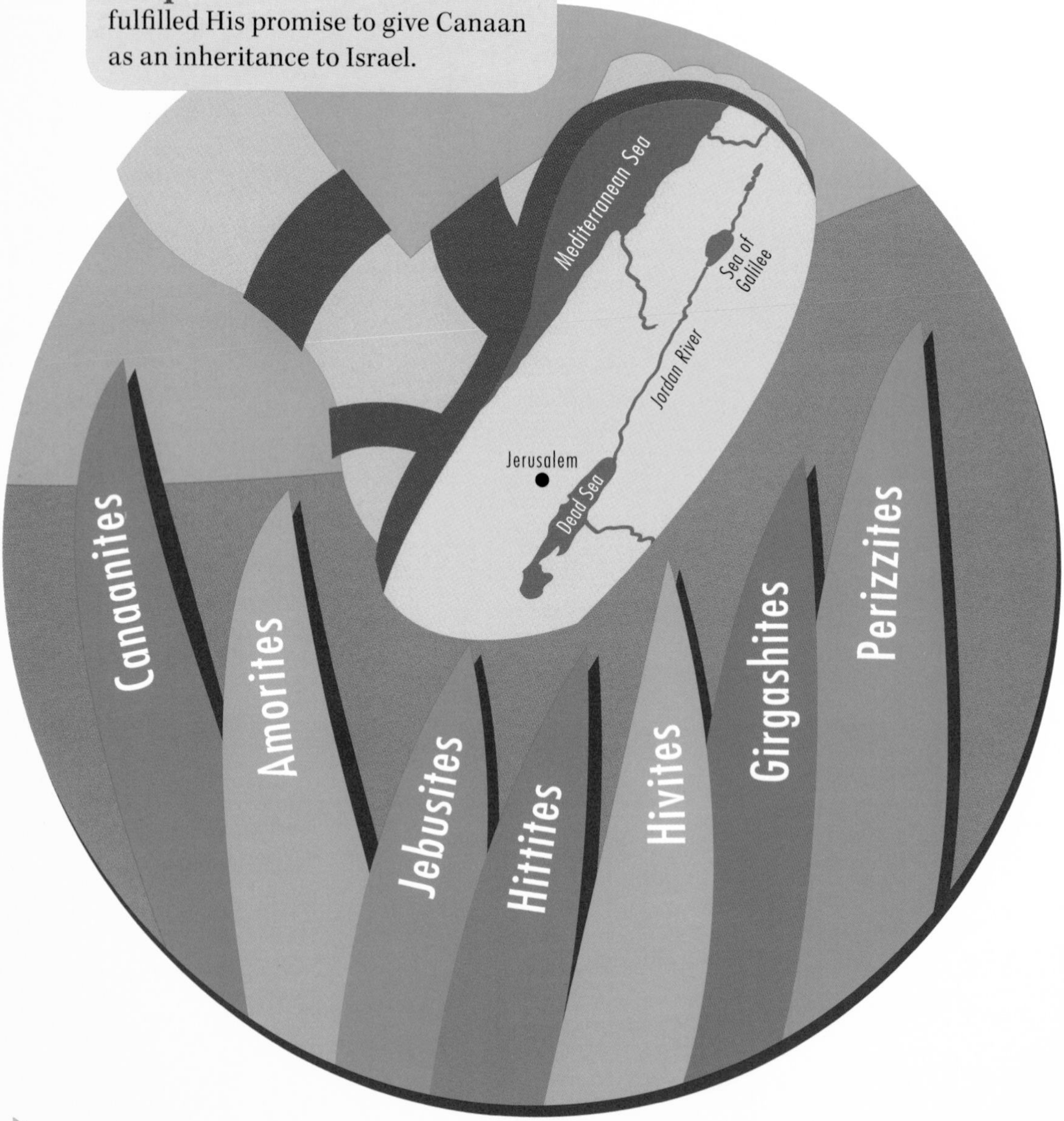
Mediterranean Sea
Sea of Galilee
Jordan River
Jerusalem
Dead Sea
Canaanites
Amorites
Jebusites
Hittites
Hivites
Girgashites
Perizzites

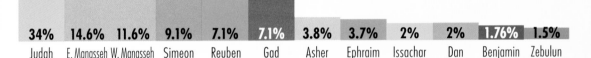

34%	14.6%	11.6%	9.1%	7.1%	7.1%	3.8%	3.7%	2%	2%	1.76%	1.5%
Judah	E. Manasseh	W. Manasseh	Simeon	Reuben	Gad	Asher	Ephraim	Issachar	Dan	Benjamin	Zebulun

The bar graph below illustrates the amount of land each tribe received as described in Joshua 13–19. This fulfilled God's promises to the patriarchs and placed His people at the junction of three continents: Asia, Africa, and Europe.

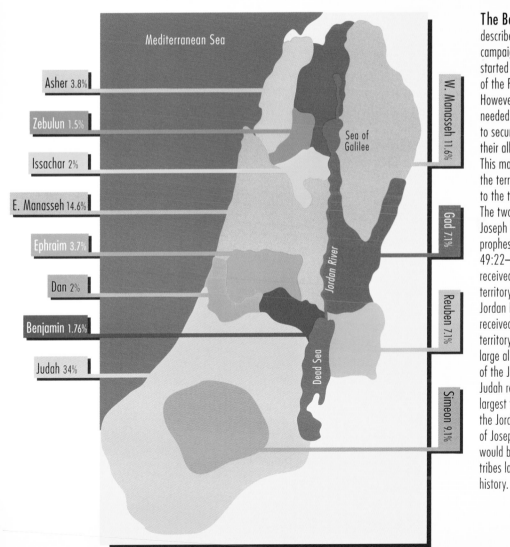

The Book of Joshua describes the military campaigns that started the conquest of the Promised Land. However, each tribe needed to continue to secure and settle their allotted territory. This map illustrates the territories allotted to the tribes of Israel. The two tribes of Joseph fared well, as prophesied in Genesis 49:22–26. Ephraim received the central territory west of the Jordan River. Manasseh received much more territory due to the large allotment east of the Jordan River. Judah received the largest territory west of the Jordan. The tribes of Joseph and Judah would become leading tribes later in Israel's history.

Rahab Hides the Spies

Joshua 1–2

After the death of Moses, the LORD said to Joshua, "Just as I was with Moses, so I will be with you. This Book of the **Law** shall not depart from your mouth, but you shall meditate on it day and night. Be careful to do according to all that is written in it. Be strong and courageous. Do not be frightened. Do not be dismayed. The LORD your God is with you wherever you go."

Joshua sent two men as spies, saying, "View the land, especially Jericho." They came into the house of Rahab and lodged there. And it was told to the king.

Then the king of Jericho sent to Rahab, saying, "Bring the men who have come to you. They have come to search out all the land."

Rahab said, "The men came to me, but when the gate was about to be closed at dark, the men went out. I do not know where the men went. Pursue them quickly, for you will overtake them." But she had hid the men with the stalks of flax that she had laid on the roof.

Rahab came up on the roof and said to the men, "I know that the LORD has given you the land. For we have heard how the LORD dried up the water of the Red Sea before you when you came out of Egypt. As soon as we heard it, our hearts melted. The LORD your God, He is God in the heavens above and on the earth beneath. Now, please swear to me by the LORD that, as I have dealt kindly with you, you also will save alive my father and mother, my brothers and sisters, and all who belong to them."

The men said, "If you do not tell this business of ours, then when the LORD gives us the land we will deal kindly and faithfully with you."

Then Rahab let them down by a rope through the window, for her house was built into the city wall. She said, "Go into the hills and hide there three days."

The men said, "When we come into the land, tie this scarlet cord in the window. Gather into your house all your father's household. If anyone goes into the street, his blood shall be on his own head. If a hand is laid on anyone who is with you in the house, his blood shall be on our head. If you tell this business of ours, then we shall be guiltless with respect to your **oath** that you have made us swear."

Rahab agreed, and the men departed. She tied the scarlet cord in the window.

The men went into the hills and remained there three days. Then they came and said to Joshua, "Truly the LORD has given all the land into our hands."

DID YOU KNOW?

- *Joshua* means "the Lord saves" or "the Lord is salvation." Joshua is an Old Testament form of the name Jesus.

- Rahab, a prostitute, is a distant ancestor of Jesus.

- Flat roofs of ancient houses made them practical as work spaces, spare rooms, storage areas, or drying floors for crops.

Israel Enters the Promised Land

Joshua 3–5

Joshua and all the people of Israel came to the Jordan. He said to the people, "Consecrate yourselves. Tomorrow the LORD will do wonders among you."

The LORD said to Joshua, "Command the priests who bear the ark of the covenant, 'Stand still in the Jordan.'"

Joshua said to the people, "The **ark of the covenant** of the Lord is passing before you into the Jordan. When the feet of the priests bearing the ark rest in the Jordan, the waters shall be cut off from flowing and stand in one heap."

As soon as the feet of the priests bearing the ark were in the water (now the Jordan overflows all its banks throughout the harvest), the waters rose up in a heap far away. The priests bearing the ark stood on dry ground in the midst of the Jordan.

When all the people had finished passing over, the ark of the LORD and the priests passed over before the people. About 40,000 ready for war passed over for battle, to the plains of Jericho. When the priests' feet were on dry ground, the waters of the Jordan returned to their place and overflowed all its banks, as before.

The 12 stones Joshua set up at Gilgal. He said, "When your children ask, 'What do these stones mean?' say, 'Israel passed over this Jordan on dry ground.' For the LORD your God dried up the waters of the Jordan as He did to the Red Sea." As soon as all the kings in the land heard that the LORD had dried up the waters of the Jordan, their hearts melted. There was no longer any spirit in them.

The people of Israel kept the Passover on the plains of Jericho. The day after the Passover, they ate of the produce of the land. And the manna ceased the day after.

When Joshua was by Jericho, he saw a man standing before him with his drawn sword in his hand. Joshua said, "Are you for us, or for our **adversaries**?"

He said, "No. I am the commander of the army of the LORD. Now I have come."

Joshua fell on his face and worshiped. He said, "What does my lord say to His servant?"

The commander of the LORD's army said, "Take off your sandals. The place where you are standing is holy." And Joshua did so.

Words to Remember

For the LORD your God dried up the waters of the Jordan for you until you passed over . . . so that all the peoples of the earth may know that the hand of the LORD is mighty, that you may fear the LORD your God forever. *Joshua 4:23–24*

DID YOU KNOW?

- The ark is the focus of the miracle at the Jordan. To follow the ark of the covenant is to follow the Lord.

- Jesus was baptized in the Jordan River, taking upon Himself all the sin of the world for our sake so that He could put it to death on the cross.

- Israel entered the Promised Land exactly forty years after the day they selected lambs for the Passover before their exodus from Egypt. They sacrificed the Passover lambs in the Promised Land four days later, exactly forty years after the first Passover.

The Fall of Jericho

Joshua 6 and 24

Now Jericho was shut up inside and outside because of the people of Israel. And the LORD said to Joshua, "I have given Jericho into your hand. You shall march around the city once a day for six days. Seven priests shall bear seven trumpets of rams' horns before the ark. On the seventh day you shall march around the city seven times, and the priests shall blow the trumpets. When you hear the sound of the trumpet, then all the people shall shout with a great shout. The wall of the city will fall down flat."

Joshua did as the Lord commanded. On the seventh day, the people rose at dawn and marched around the city in the same manner seven times. At the seventh time, when the priests had blown the trumpets, Joshua said, "Shout, for the LORD has given you the city. Only Rahab and all who are with her in her house shall live, because she hid the messengers whom we sent."

So the people shouted, and the trumpets were blown. And the wall fell down flat, so that the people went up into the city. And they captured the city.

To the two men who had spied out the land, Joshua said, "Go into Rahab's house and bring out the woman and all who belong to her." So the spies brought out Rahab and all who belonged to her. They put them outside the camp of Israel. And she has lived in Israel to this day, because she hid the messengers whom Joshua sent to spy out Jericho.

So the LORD was with Joshua, and his fame was in all the land.

After Joshua and the people of Israel had taken all the land, Joshua gathered all the tribes of Israel. He said, "Fear the LORD. Serve Him in sincerity and in faithfulness. Choose this day whom you will serve, but as for me and my house, we will serve the LORD."

Then the people answered, "It is the LORD our God who brought us and our fathers up from the land of Egypt, out of the house of slavery. He did those great signs in our sight and preserved us in all the way that we went. And the LORD drove out before us all the peoples who lived in the land. Therefore we also will serve the LORD, for He is our God."

Words to Remember

As for me and my house, we will serve the LORD.
Joshua 24:15

DID YOU KNOW?

- The city of Jericho is thought to be one of the oldest continuously inhabited cities in the world.

- Jericho was the first city God's people conquered as they entered the Promised Land.

- The names *Joshua* and *Jesus* both mean "the Lord saves."

Judges Rule God's People

When the people of Israel cried out to the LORD, the LORD raised up a deliverer for the people of Israel, who saved them. Judges 3:9

In Joshua's final words to the Israelites, he reminded them of God's covenant. The Lord had kept His promise. The descendants of Abraham and Isaac and Jacob were in the Promised Land. Now the people had a choice: serve the true God or serve the false gods of those who lived around them. If you had crossed the Jordan River on dry ground, if you had watched Jericho's walls tumble because of a shout, what would your choice have been? Joshua said, "As for me and my house, we will serve the LORD" (Joshua 24:15). All of Israel agreed with Joshua's choice.

However, the people of Israel forgot their promise. The people didn't obey God's Law. The Israelites worshiped the false gods of the people of Canaan. They didn't honor their parents. They coveted their neighbors' things. Then their enemies would oppress (hold down) the Israelites. Each time, the people of Israel eventually remembered all that God had done for them. Then they would cry out to God to save them. Because He loved the children of Israel, because He had promised to make them a great nation, because from Abraham's Seed would come great blessing, God would "raise up," or choose, a judge to save the Israelites.

Like the Israelites, you might forget to put God first. You might complain about going to church. You might fight with your brother or sister. You might refuse to do your chores. You might want the phone your friend has and whine about it. But God raises up judges to lead you: parents and pastors and teachers and friends who show you your sin. Through them, God calls you back from following the false god of your own selfish wishes. Jesus' perfect obedience (His righteousness) covers your sinful thoughts and actions. Because Jesus lived, died, and rose again for you, He will deliver you safely to the promised land of heaven.

Making Connections

The word *judge* might make you think of a courtroom or maybe of a person who grades your performance. The judge decides whether you have been good or bad and gives out the punishment or the prize.

Did you know that Jesus is a judge? The Bible tells us that on the Last Day Jesus will judge who is going to heaven and who is going to hell.

That may seem frightening, until you remember that Jesus isn't only a judge. He is also the deliverer who saves (see Judges 3:9). Jesus knew you could never be perfect, as God's Law requires. So He came from heaven and obeyed God's Law in your place. When Jesus heard the judgment of guilty, He went to the cross and suffered the punishment for your sin. God judged Jesus' sacrifice to be perfect, and Jesus rose on Easter. Because you are God's child through the water of Baptism, Jesus' perfect-10 performance becomes yours. And on the Last Day, Jesus will award you the victor's crown in heaven.

Peoples in the Land of Canaan

The people who lived in Canaan worshiped false gods, like Baal and Asheroth. God told the Israelites to clear out these people to avoid temptation. The following are the main groups the Israelites met in Canaan.

Canaanites—descendants of Noah's son Ham; they may have created the first alphabet

Amorites—descendants of Noah's son Ham

Jebusites—their capital city was Jerusalem

Hittites—scholars think these people may have come from Russia; Esau married a Hittite woman

Hivites—these people made a treaty with Joshua

Girgashites—descendants of Noah's son Ham

Perizzites—very little is known about these people

Philistines—originally from the island of Crete, they controlled access to iron

Everyone did what was right in his own eyes.

Judges

1399–1375 BC Deaths of Joshua and the elders • c. 1379–1060 BC Judges lead Israel • 1048–1009 BC Saul reigns over Israel

Tools of War

The era of the Book of Judges is reported through a number of war stories, since judges served as temporary military deliverers. The tools of war depicted here are sized based on the amount of text dedicated to the major stories in the book. Although judges helped to deliver Israel, the accounts also depict them as rogues in many cases. Their examples show how God uses all manner of persons for the good of His people.

Minor Judges:
Othniel, Shamgar, Tola, Jair, Ibzan, Elon, and Abdo

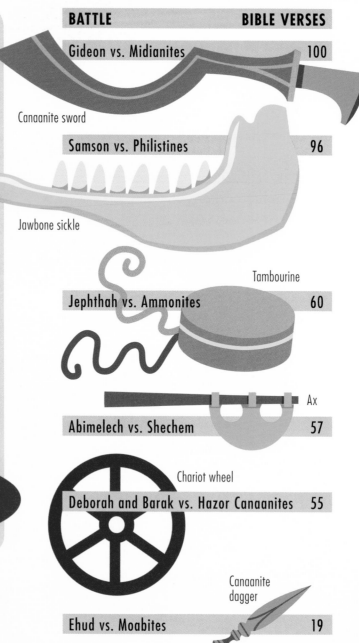

BATTLE	BIBLE VERSES
Gideon vs. Midianites	100
Samson vs. Philistines	96
Jephthah vs. Ammonites	60
Abimelech vs. Shechem	57
Deborah and Barak vs. Hazor Canaanites	55
Ehud vs. Moabites	19

Canaanite sword

Jawbone sickle

Tambourine

Ax

Chariot wheel

Canaanite dagger

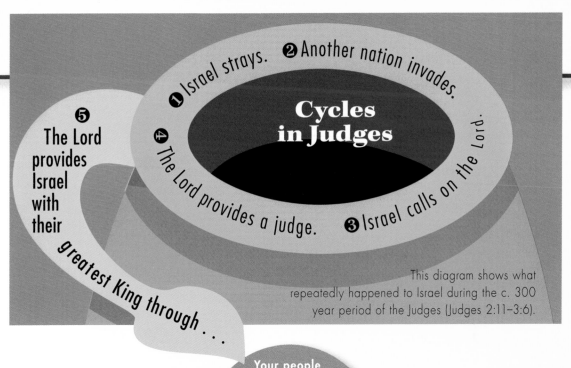

Cycles in Judges

❶ Israel strays.

❷ Another nation invades.

❸ Israel calls on the Lord.

❹ The Lord provides a judge.

❺ The Lord provides Israel with their greatest King through . . .

This diagram shows what repeatedly happened to Israel during the c. 300 year period of the Judges (Judges 2:11–3:6).

Your people shall be my people, your God my God.

1 chapter

Read in 15 minutes

Ruth

1099–1060 BC Eli's priesthood and judgeship • c. 1000 BC Ruth written • 1009–970 BC David's reign

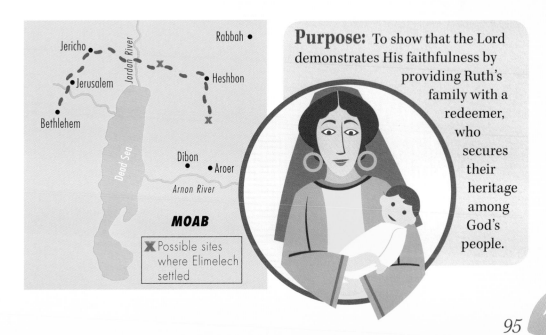

Jericho

Jerusalem

Bethlehem

Jordan River

Rabbah •

✗

• Heshbon

Dead Sea

Dibon •

• Aroer

Arnon River

MOAB

✗ Possible sites where Elimelech settled

Purpose: To show that the Lord demonstrates His faithfulness by providing Ruth's family with a redeemer, who secures their heritage among God's people.

Deborah the Prophetess

Judges 2 and 4–5

The people served the LORD all the days of Joshua, and all the days of the elders who outlived Joshua. And there arose another generation after them who did not know the LORD or the work that He had done for Israel. The people of Israel did what was evil in the sight of the LORD. The LORD sold them into the hand of Jabin king of Canaan. The commander of his army was Sisera. Then the people of Israel cried out to the LORD for help.

Deborah, a **prophetess**, was judging Israel at that time. She summoned Barak and said, "Has not the LORD, the God of Israel, commanded you, 'Gather your men at Mount Tabor. I will draw out Sisera to meet you by the river with his chariots and troops. I will give him into your hand'?"

Barak said to Deborah, "If you will go with me, I will go."

She said, "I will go. But the LORD will sell Sisera into the hand of a woman."

Sisera called out 900 chariots of iron and all the men who were with him. Deborah said to Barak, "Up! For this is the day in which the LORD has given Sisera into your hand. Does not the LORD go before you?" So Barak went down from Mount Tabor with 10,000 men. And the LORD defeated Sisera and all his chariots and army before Barak.

But Sisera fled on foot to the tent of Jael, the wife of Heber the Kenite. Jael said, "Turn aside to me. Do not be afraid." So Sisera turned aside into the tent, and Jael covered him with a rug.

Sisera said, "Please give me a little water to drink." So Jael gave him a drink of milk. He said, "If any man asks, 'Is anyone here?' say, 'No.'" But Jael went softly to Sisera and drove a tent peg into his temple while he was fast asleep from weariness.

As Barak was pursuing Sisera, Jael said to him, "I will show you the man whom you are seeking." So Barak went in to her tent. There lay Sisera dead.

Then sang Deborah and Barak:

> "Hear, O kings. Give ear, O princes.
>> To the LORD I will sing.
>> I will make melody to the LORD, the God of Israel.
> Awake, awake, Deborah!
>> Awake, awake, break out in a song!
> Arise, Barak, lead away your captives."

And the land had rest for 40 years.

DID YOU KNOW?

- The Book of Judges describes more than three hundred years of Israel's history. No one knows for sure who wrote the book, but many scholars have attributed it to Samuel.

- Deborah did not lead the troops herself but fulfilled the prophet's true role by encouraging with the words and promises of God.

- Jael appeared to be showing kindness by offering Sisera something better (goats' or sheep's milk) than he had requested (water). Yet the milk made him sleepy, giving Jael the opportunity to kill him.

Gideon Defeats Midian

Judges 6–8

The people of Israel did what was evil in the sight of the LORD. And the LORD gave them into the hand of Midian. The people of Israel cried out for help to the LORD.

Now the angel of the LORD came to Gideon and said, "The LORD is with you, O mighty man of **valor**."

Gideon said, "Please, sir, if the LORD is with us, where are all His wonderful deeds that our fathers told to us? But now the LORD has forsaken us and given us into the hand of Midian."

And the LORD said, "Save Israel from the hand of Midian. I will be with you, and you shall strike the Midianites as one man." The Spirit of the LORD clothed Gideon, and he sounded the trumpet, and the people were called out to follow him.

Now all the Midianites and the people of the East crossed the Jordan and camped in the valley. The LORD said to Gideon, "The people with you are too many. Israel will boast, saying, 'My own hand has saved me.' Therefore say, 'Whoever is fearful, let him return home.'" Then 22,000 of the people returned, and 10,000 remained.

The LORD said, "The people are still too many. Take them down to the water. Every one who laps the water with his tongue, as a dog laps, you shall set by himself." Those who lapped, putting their hands to their mouths, totaled 300 men. The LORD said, "With the 300 men I will save you. Let all the others go home."

That same night the LORD said to Gideon, "Arise, go down against the camp. I have given it into your hand."

Gideon said, "Arise, for the LORD has given the host of Midian into your hand." He divided the 300 men into three companies. He put trumpets into the hands of all of them and empty jars, with torches inside the jars. He said, "Look at me, and do likewise. When I come to the outskirts of the camp and blow the trumpet, then blow the trumpets also on every side of the camp. Shout, 'For the LORD and for Gideon.'"

So Gideon and the men came to the outskirts of the camp. The three companies blew the trumpets and broke the jars. They cried, "A sword for the LORD and for Gideon!" Every man stood in his place around the camp, and all the army ran. The LORD set every man's sword against his comrade and against all the army. And the army fled, and Gideon and his men pursued after Midian.

So Midian was **subdued** before the people of Israel. They raised their heads no more. And the land had rest 40 years in the days of Gideon.

DID YOU KNOW?

- The Midianites were descendants of Abraham by his wife Keturah, following the death of Sarah (Genesis 25:1–2). Midianites are mentioned as some of the caravan traders that took Joseph as a slave into Egypt (Genesis 37:28–36). Moses' wife was also a Midianite (Exodus 2:15–22).

- According to Deuteronomy 20:8, a man was exempted from military service if he was fearful of battle and would demoralize other soldiers.

- With Gideon's army reduced to 300, they were outnumbered 450 to 1.

God Makes Samson Strong

Judges 13 and 15–16

The people of Israel again did what was evil in the sight of the LORD. So the LORD gave them into the hand of the Philistines for 40 years.

The angel of the LORD appeared to Manoah's wife and said, "You shall give birth to a son. No razor shall come upon his head. He shall begin to save Israel from the Philistines." And the woman bore a son and named him Samson. The young man grew, and the LORD blessed him. He defeated many Philistines.

One day the Philistines said to the men of Judah, "We have come for Samson."

The men of Judah said to Samson, "Do you not know that the Philistines are rulers over us? We have come to bind you, that we may give you to them." Samson let them bind him with two new ropes. When the Philistines came, the Spirit of the LORD rushed upon Samson. The ropes on his arms melted off. Samson found a fresh jawbone of a donkey. With it he struck 1,000 men.

After this, Samson loved a woman named Delilah. The lords of the Philistines said to her, "See where his great strength lies so we may overpower him." Three times Samson told her a false story about what would take away his strength. Each time, Samson broke free and killed his attackers. But Delilah pressed him hard with her words day after day.

Finally, Samson said, "If my head is shaved, then my strength will leave me." So Delilah made him sleep, and she had a man shave Samson's head. The Philistines seized Samson, gouged out his eyes, and bound him with bronze shackles. Samson ground at the mill in the prison. But the hair of his head began to grow again.

Now the lords of the Philistines gathered to offer a great sacrifice to Dagon their god. They said, "Our god has given Samson our enemy into our hand." When their hearts were merry, they called Samson out of the prison to entertain them.

Samson said to the young man who led him, "Let me lean against the pillars on which the house rests." Now the house was full of people, and on the roof there were about 3,000 people. Then Samson called, "O Lord GOD, please strengthen me only this once, that I may be **avenged** on the Philistines for my two eyes." Samson leaned his weight on the pillars. Then he bowed with all his strength, and the house fell upon the lords and all the people who were in it.

All Samson's family buried him. He had judged Israel 20 years.

Words to Remember

Then Samson called to the LORD and said, "O Lord GOD, please remember me and please strengthen me only this once, O God." . . . Then he bowed with all his strength, and the house fell upon the lords and upon all the people who were in it. *Judges 16:28, 30*

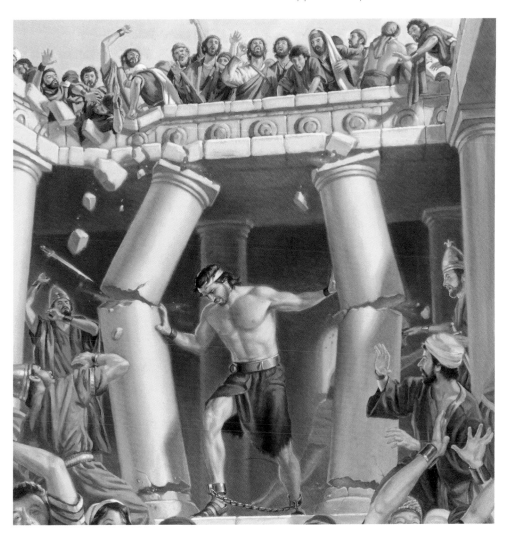

DID YOU KNOW?

- Sarah, Hannah, and Elizabeth were other barren women in the Bible who were visited by the Lord (through the promise of an angel or a priest) and then conceived a child who became an important agent of God (Isaac, Samuel, and John the Baptist).

- The Philistine rulers promised Delilah enough money to support her for fifteen years if she discovered Samson's weakness (Judges 16:5).

- Samson's family showed courage in retrieving his body from the ruins and giving it an honorable burial in the tomb of his now-deceased father.

Ruth's Story

The Book of Ruth

Words to Remember

Blessed be the LORD, who has not left you this day without a redeemer, and may His name be renowned in Israel! *Ruth 4:14*

In the days when the judges ruled, there was a famine. Elimelech, Naomi, and their two sons went into Moab. Elimelech died, and the sons took Moabite wives: Orpah and Ruth. Then both sons died.

Naomi heard that the LORD had given His people food. So she set out with her two daughters-in-law to return to the land of Judah. But Naomi said, "Return home. May the LORD deal kindly with you." Orpah kissed her mother-in-law and went home, but Ruth clung to Naomi.

Ruth said, "Where you go I will go, and where you lodge I will lodge. Your people shall be my people, and your God my God." So the two of them came to Bethlehem at the beginning of barley harvest.

Ruth said to Naomi, "Let me **glean** among the ears of grain." Naomi agreed, and Ruth worked in the field of Boaz.

Boaz said to Ruth, "All that you have done for Naomi has been told to me. A full reward be given you by the LORD, the God of Israel, under whose wings you have come to take **refuge**!" Boaz told his men to let Ruth glean even among the sheaves.

When Naomi saw all that Ruth had gleaned and learned whose field it was, she said, "The man is a close relative of ours, one of our redeemers. Wash and **anoint** yourself. Go down to the threshing floor. Boaz will tell you what to do." So Ruth did as Naomi had commanded her.

When Boaz saw Ruth, she said to him, "Spread your wings over your servant, for you are a **redeemer**."

Boaz said, "I am a redeemer, yet there is one nearer than I. If he is not willing to redeem you, then as the LORD lives, I will redeem you." The next day, Boaz sat at the gate. Behold, the redeemer of whom Boaz had spoken came by. He said to the redeemer, "Naomi is selling the land that belonged to our relative Elimelech. If you will redeem it, redeem it."

The redeemer said, "I cannot redeem it. Take my right of redemption yourself."

Boaz said to the elders and all the people, "You are witnesses this day that I have bought the land from the hand of Naomi. Also Ruth the Moabite I have bought to be my wife."

So Boaz took Ruth, and she became his wife. And the LORD gave her a son. Naomi took the child and laid him on her lap and became his nurse. They named him Obed. He was the father of Jesse, the father of David.

DID YOU KNOW?

- Ruth was King David's great-grandmother.

- Boaz was Naomi's redeemer (the person who could protect her inheritance). He is a picture, or type, of Christ, symbolizing His kindness, care, and deliverance of God's people.

- *Bethlehem* means "the house of bread."

I will raise up
a faithful priest before
My anointed one.

1 & 2 Samuel

1099–1060 BC Eli's priesthood and judgeship • 1009–970 BC Reign of David • 970–931 BC Reign of Solomon

Challenge of the Philistines

House of Eli	**House of Samuel**	**House of Saul**	**House of David**
Judge and priest	Judge	King	King
1099–1060 BC	c. 1060–1048 BC	1048–1009 BC	1009–970 BC and beyond
			In Judah, 21 rulers succeeded David, who founded a great dynasty that lasted 1009–587 BC.

Oaths and Promises: The Books of Samuel record vows or oaths for eleven important characters, including the Lord, who vows judgment on the unfaithful (1 Samuel 3:14). The many vows show how greatly God treasures a promise. The Lord would fulfill His Word concerning David (1 Samuel 16); He would fulfill the promise through David (2 Samuel 7:16), from whose family the Christ would be born.

Ups and Downs in the Life of David

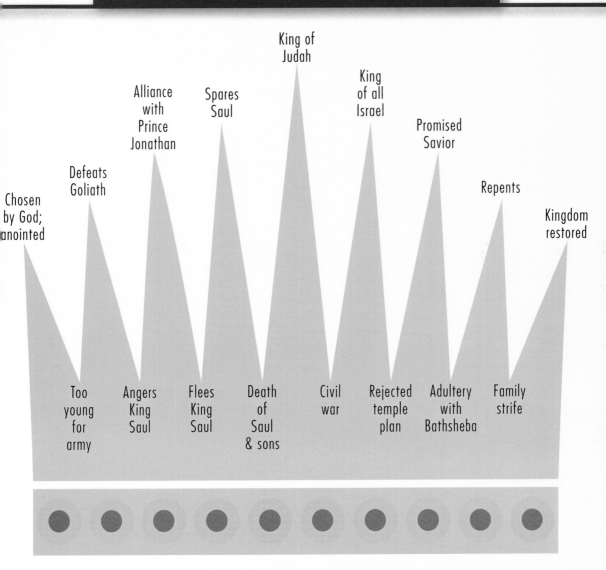

David's life and rule was full of ups and downs as the Lord blessed him and as he faced trials, stumbled and fell, and was restored by God's grace. The high points and low points on the crown above trace events in David's life from left to right. Despite David's weaknesses, God described him as "a man after His own heart" (1 Samuel 13:14).

Hannah and Samuel

1 Samuel 1–2

Elkanah had two wives. Peninnah had children, but Hannah had no children. As often as Hannah went to the house of the Lord, Peninnah used to provoke her because the Lord had closed her womb. Therefore Hannah wept and would not eat. Elkanah said, "Hannah, why do you weep? Why do you not eat? Am I not more to you than 10 sons?"

Now Eli the priest was sitting on the seat beside the door-post of the **temple** of the LORD. Hannah prayed to the LORD and wept bitterly. She vowed a vow and said, "O LORD of hosts, if You will give to your servant a son, then I will give him to the LORD all the days of his life."

Eli took her to be a drunken woman. But Hannah said, "I have drunk neither wine nor strong drink, but I have been pouring out my soul before the LORD."

Eli answered, "Go in peace. The God of Israel grant your **petition**."

Elkanah and his family went back to their house. And the LORD remembered Hannah. She gave birth to a son. She called his name Samuel, for she said, "I have asked for him from the LORD."

When Hannah had weaned Samuel, she brought him to the house of the LORD. They brought the child to Eli. Hannah said, "I am the woman who was standing here, praying to the LORD. The LORD has granted me my petition. Therefore as long as he lives, he is lent to the LORD." Samuel worshiped the LORD. Hannah prayed:

> "My heart **exults** in the LORD.
>> My strength is **exalted** in the LORD.
> There is none holy like the LORD.
>> There is none besides You.
>> There is no rock like our God.
> The LORD makes poor and makes rich.
>> He brings low and He exalts.
> He raises up the poor from the dust.
>> He lifts the needy from the ash heap.
> The LORD will judge the ends of the earth.
>> He will give strength to His king
>> and exalt the power of His anointed."

Then Elkanah and Hannah went home. And Samuel ministered to the LORD in the presence of Eli the priest.

DID YOU KNOW?

- The Books of 1 and 2 Samuel record the history of God's people from the birth of Samuel, the last of Israel's judges, to the death of King David, the second king of Israel.

- Hannah's barrenness called into question God's blessing on her life (Genesis 1:28). Lack of children also put her economic and social status in jeopardy, as Elkanah's future through her seemed to come to an end.

- Samuel would have been about age 3 at the time he was weaned and taken to Eli. Breast-feeding typically lasted much longer than it does today.

God Calls Samuel

1 Samuel 2–4

The sons of Eli were worthless men. They did not know the LORD. The men treated the offering of the Lord with **contempt**. Eli said to them, "Why do you do such things?" But they would not listen to their father. Now the young man Samuel was ministering to the LORD under Eli.

Words to Remember

Speak, for Your servant hears.
1 Samuel 3:10

Eli, whose eyesight had begun to grow dim, was lying down in his own place. The lamp of God had not yet gone out, and Samuel was lying down in the temple of the LORD, where the ark of God was. The LORD called Samuel. He ran to Eli and said, "Here I am, for you called me."

But Eli said, "I did not call. Lie down again." So Samuel went and lay down.

And the LORD called again, "Samuel!"

Samuel went to Eli and said, "Here I am, for you called me."

But Eli said, "I did not call, my son. Lie down again." Now Samuel did not yet know the LORD. The word of the LORD had not yet been revealed to him.

And the LORD called Samuel again the third time. He went to Eli and said, "Here I am, for you called me."

Then Eli **perceived** that the LORD was calling the young man. Therefore Eli said to Samuel, "Go, lie down. If He calls you, you shall say, 'Speak, LORD, for Your servant hears.'" So Samuel went and lay down in his place.

And the LORD came and stood, calling as at other times, "Samuel! Samuel!"

And Samuel said, "Speak, for Your servant hears."

Then the LORD said to Samuel, "Behold, I am about to do a thing in Israel. On that day I will punish Eli's house forever, because his sons were **blaspheming** God, and he did not restrain them."

Samuel lay until morning. Then he opened the doors of the house of the LORD. Eli called Samuel and said, "What was it that He told you? Do not hide it from me." So Samuel told Eli everything.

Eli said, "It is the LORD. Let Him do what seems good to Him."

Samuel grew, and the LORD was with him. All Israel knew that Samuel was a prophet of the LORD.

Now Israel went to battle against the Philistines. And the sons of Eli were there with the ark of the covenant. The Philistines defeated Israel. The ark was captured, and Eli's sons were killed. When word came to Eli, he fell over backward, broke his neck, and died.

DID YOU KNOW?

- Samuel serves God's people as prophet, priest, and ruler, thus foreshadowing the future work of Christ.

- Samuel served and assisted the priests in their duties, living as an apprentice to a teacher. As such, he would have lived among the families of the priests.

- Eli's sons did not "know" the Lord because of their refusal to submit to God. Samuel does not yet "know" God because he lacks experience with God's direct revelation.

Great Prophets and Kings

You, O Lord GOD, have spoken, and with Your blessing shall the house of Your servant be blessed forever. *2 Samuel 7:29*

The people of Israel demanded to be given a king, like all the nations around them. So God told Samuel to anoint Saul to be the first king of Israel. He was tall and handsome—Saul looked like a king. But Saul didn't trust God to defeat the enemies of Israel. Saul disobeyed God's commandments.

God told Samuel to anoint David to be the next king. David loved God and trusted Him to bring victory over his enemies. Most important, David believed that God forgave his sins and would keep His promises of blessing.

David's son Solomon began as a king who trusted God. In fact, God used Solomon to build the temple where the people of Israel worshiped. But just as during the time of the judges, Solomon and his subjects started to worship other gods. And most of the kings who followed Solomon sinned more and more, which made God angry.

God sent prophets to speak His words. Elijah and Elisha, Isaiah and Jeremiah, as well as a prophetess named Huldah, told the kings and the people of Israel and Judah to turn from their evil ways or God would scatter them among the nations. The prophets also did miracles and announced God's promises of forgiveness and salvation and blessing. Their prophecies especially pointed to Jesus, who would come as David's "righteous branch" to save God's people.

As you read about the great kings and prophets, list the times that God promises blessing for following His ways. Like Solomon, ask God to give you a heart and mind that understand the difference between right and wrong. Like Kings Josiah and Hezekiah, ask God to forgive you for the times you don't follow His commands. Like the prophets, pray that God will make you a strong and confident witness for the truth of His Word.

Making Connections

All the kings and prophets and priests you will read about in this section who speak God's words were pointing forward to the perfect Prophet, Priest, and King: Jesus.

When Jesus speaks to us, He isn't only repeating God's words like a prophet—Jesus is God and speaks as God. He has all the power to back up what He says. When Jesus says, "I forgive you" or "Be healed," it happens.

In the Old Testament, the priests made sacrifices daily to ask for God's forgiveness or to praise God or to thank Him. Because the priests sinned, they even made sacrifices for themselves. Jesus lived a perfect life in our place and offered one perfect sacrifice on the cross—Himself. Now you don't have to sacrifice animals to receive forgiveness. You have it right now through Jesus' blood and righteousness.

God promised to establish David's throne forever if he followed all God's commandments. But like all of us, David sinned. In Jesus, David's sinless descendant, God's people are gathered into the kingdom of the Church. On the Last Day, Jesus will bring all who believe in Him into the kingdom of heaven where He will rule as our eternal King.

Prophets Who Spoke for God

God chose special people to share His words of command, comfort, and warning. In this list, the names in bold are mentioned in Bible stories in this section. Names in italic (or bold italic) wrote books in the Bible. Check them out!

Samuel, Gad, **Nathan**, Zadok, Shemaiah, Iddo, Ahijah, Azariah, Hanani, Jehu, Jahaziel, **Elijah**, Micaiah, Eliezer, **Elisha**, **Huldah**, Jehoiada, *Isaiah*, *Jeremiah*, **Daniel**, *Ezekiel*, Hosea, Joel, Amos, Obadiah, **Jonah**, Micah, Nahum, Habakkuk, Zephaniah, Haggai, Zechariah, **Malachi**

Detail of Judah

Saul Becomes King

1 Samuel 8–11

Words to Remember

I have seen My people, because their cry has come to Me. *1 Samuel 9:16*

The elders of Israel said to Samuel, "You are old and your sons do not walk in your ways. Appoint for us a king to judge us like all the nations."

The Lord said, "Obey the voice of the people. They have not rejected you, but they have rejected Me."

There was a wealthy man named Kish who had a son named Saul who was very handsome. Saul and a servant went to look for some lost donkeys. They passed through the lands of Ephraim and of Benjamin, but did not find them.

The servant said, "There is a man of God in this city. Perhaps he can tell us the way we should go." So they went to the city where the man of God was.

Now the Lord had revealed to Samuel: "Tomorrow I will send to you a man from the land of Benjamin. You shall anoint him to be prince over My people Israel. He shall save My people from the Philistines." When Samuel saw Saul, the LORD told him, "Here is the man of whom I spoke to you!"

Samuel said to Saul, "You shall eat with me. As for your donkeys that were lost, they have been found." So Saul ate with Samuel. When they came into the city, a bed was spread for Saul on the roof. The next day, Samuel took a flask of oil and poured it on Saul's head and kissed him. Samuel said, "Has not the LORD anointed you to be prince over His people Israel? You will save them from their enemies."

Later, Samuel called the people together and said, "Thus says the LORD, 'I delivered you from the Egyptians and from all the kingdoms that were oppressing you.' But today you have rejected your God and said, 'Set a king over us.'"

Samuel brought all the tribes near, and Saul the son of Kish was taken by lot. But when they sought him, he could not be found. The LORD said, "He has hidden himself among the baggage." They ran and took him from there. When Saul stood among the people, he was taller than any of the people.

Samuel said, "Do you see him whom the LORD has chosen? There is none like him among all the people."

All the people shouted, "Long live the king!"

The Ammonites threatened the people of Israel. When Saul gathered his army, the people of Israel were 300,000. They came into the midst of the camp in the morning watch and struck down the Ammonites.

Then Samuel said to the people, "Let us renew the kingdom." So the people made Saul king before the LORD. They sacrificed peace offerings before the LORD. Saul and all the men of Israel rejoiced greatly.

DID YOU KNOW?

- Israel's desire to be like other nations and to have a king was a rebuke to Samuel and a rejection of the Lord as their King.

- Donkeys were valued as beasts of burden and for agricultural operations, particularly for threshing and plowing. Wealth was often tied to the number of donkeys owned.

- The exact procedure for "taking by lot" is not clearly known, but it was the method used to determine God's will and required faith that God would indeed guide the choice, as well as a willingness to abide by the choice as being from God.

Samuel Anoints David

1 Samuel 15–16

Samuel said to Saul, "Thus says the LORD of hosts, 'Strike Amalek and destroy all that they have. Do not **spare** them.'" So Saul defeated the Amalekites. But Saul and the people spared Agag and the best of the sheep and oxen and all that was good. All that was worthless they destroyed.

The word of the LORD came to Samuel: "I regret that I have made Saul king. He has turned back from following Me and has not performed My commandments."

Samuel rose early to meet Saul. Samuel said, "Why did you not obey the voice of the LORD?"

Saul said to Samuel, "I have sinned. Please pardon my sin and return with me that I may worship the LORD."

Samuel said to Saul, "I will not return with you. For you have rejected the word of the LORD, and the LORD has rejected you from being king over Israel." Then Samuel went to Ramah, and Saul went up to his house.

The LORD said to Samuel, "Fill your horn with oil. I will send you to Jesse the Bethlehemite. I have provided for Myself a king among his sons." Samuel did what the LORD commanded and came to Bethlehem. He consecrated Jesse and his sons and invited them to the sacrifice. When they came, Samuel looked on Eliab and thought, "Surely the LORD's anointed is before Him."

But the LORD said, "Do not look on his appearance, because I have rejected him. For the LORD sees not as man sees. Man looks on the outward appearance, but the LORD looks on the heart."

Then Jesse called two more sons and made them pass before Samuel, but Samuel said, "Neither has the LORD chosen these."

Jesse made seven of his sons pass before Samuel. And Samuel said to Jesse, "The LORD has not chosen these. Are all your sons here?"

Jesse said, "There remains yet the youngest. He is keeping the sheep."

Samuel said, "Get him, for we will not sit down till he comes here." Jesse sent and brought him in. Now he was ruddy and had beautiful eyes and was handsome.

The LORD said, "Arise, anoint him, for this is he." Then Samuel took the horn of oil and anointed him in the midst of his brothers. And the Spirit of the LORD rushed upon David from that day forward. And Samuel rose up and went to Ramah.

Words to Remember

The LORD sees not as man sees: man looks on the outward appearance, but the LORD looks on the heart.
1 Samuel 16:7

DID YOU KNOW?

- After Samuel and Saul parted, they never saw each other again, even though they lived fewer than five miles apart.

- In the Bible, God often chooses a younger brother over an older (He chose Jacob rather than Esau, Ephraim rather than Manasseh; Genesis 25:23; 48:17–19). He did the same with David, choosing the person who was least likely to succeed to be the instrument of His might and power.

David Fights Goliath

1 Samuel 17

Words to Remember

This day the LORD will deliver you into my hand, . . . that all the earth may know that there is a God in Israel.
1 Samuel 17:46

The Philistines gathered for battle and stood on the mountain on the one side, and Israel stood on the mountain on the other side, with a valley between them. There came from the camp of the Philistines a **champion** named Goliath. He had a helmet of bronze, a coat of mail, bronze armor on his legs, and a javelin of bronze. He shouted, "Choose a man for yourselves. If he is able to kill me, then we will be your servants. But if I kill him, then you shall be our servants." When Saul and all Israel heard these words, they were greatly afraid.

Now the three oldest sons of Jesse had followed Saul to the battle. Jesse said to David, "Take your brothers grain and bread and cheese. See if they are well." David left the sheep with a keeper and took the provisions to the camp. As he talked with his brothers, David heard Goliath.

David said to the men, "Who is this Philistine, that he should **defy** the armies of the living God?" When the words that David spoke were repeated before Saul, he sent for him. David said to Saul, "Your servant used to keep sheep for his father. The LORD who delivered me from the paw of the lion and from the paw of the bear will deliver me from the hand of this Philistine."

Saul said to David, "Go, and the LORD be with you!" Then Saul clothed David with his armor. But David put the armor off. He took his staff and chose five smooth stones from the brook and put them in his shepherd's pouch. His sling was in his hand, and he approached the Philistine.

Goliath came near David and said, "Am I a dog, that you come to me with sticks? I will give your flesh to the birds of the air and to the beasts of the field."

David said, "You come to me with a sword, a spear, and a javelin, but I come to you in the name of the LORD of hosts, whom you have defied. This day the LORD will deliver you into my hand. I will strike you down and cut off your head. Then all the earth may know that there is a God in Israel and that the LORD saves not with sword and spear. For the battle is the LORD's. He will give you into our hand."

David ran quickly toward the battle line to meet the Philistine. He put his hand in his bag and took out a stone and slung it and struck Goliath on his forehead. He fell on his face to the ground. So David killed the Philistine with a sling and with a stone. David stood over the Philistine and took his sword and cut off his head with it. When the Philistines saw that their champion was dead, they fled. And the men of Israel and Judah rose with a shout and pursued the Philistines.

DID YOU KNOW?

- The Philistines were technologically advanced. They smelted iron and jealously guarded their knowledge to maintain their monopoly, giving them advantages both economically and militarily.

- Goliath was over nine feet tall, and his coat of armor weighed around 125 pounds.

- Saul put his own armor on David because wearing someone else's armor gave the owner's essence to the wearer. Also, Saul could claim credit for David's victory.

David and Jonathan

1 Samuel 18 and 20

Words to Remember
David had success in all his undertakings, for the LORD was with him.
1 Samuel 18:14

The soul of Jonathan, Saul's son, was knit to the soul of David. Jonathan loved him as his own soul. Jonathan stripped himself of the robe he wore and gave it to David, and his armor, and even his sword and his bow and his belt.

But as David won battles, Saul sought to kill him. David said to Jonathan, "What is my sin before your father, that he seeks my life?"

Jonathan said, "You shall not die. Why should my father hide this from me? It is not so. Whatever you say, I will do for you."

David said, "Tomorrow I should not fail to sit at table with the king. But let me hide in the field. If your father misses me, then say, 'David asked leave of me to run to Bethlehem, for there is a yearly sacrifice there.' If he says, 'Good!' it will be well with your servant. But if he is angry, then know that he is determined to harm me."

Jonathan said, "When I have sounded out my father, if he is **well disposed** toward you, shall I not tell you? On the third day remain beside the stone heap. I will shoot three arrows and send the young man to find them. If I say, 'The arrows are on this side of you,' then you are to come. For, as the LORD lives, it is safe for you. But if I say, 'The arrows are beyond you,' then go, for the LORD has sent you away."

So David hid in the field. And Saul said to Jonathan, "Why has not the son of Jesse come to the meal, either yesterday or today?"

Jonathan answered, "David asked to go to Bethlehem to make a sacrifice."

Then Saul's anger was kindled against Jonathan. He said, "For as long as the son of Jesse lives on the earth, neither you nor your kingdom shall be established. Bring him to me, for he shall surely die." So Jonathan knew that his father was determined to put David to death.

In the morning, Jonathan went out into the field and with him a little boy. He said to his boy, "Run and find the arrows that I shoot." When the boy came to the place of the arrow that Jonathan had shot, Jonathan called, "Is not the arrow beyond you? Be quick! Do not stay!" Jonathan's boy gathered the arrows, and Jonathan gave his weapons to his boy and sent him to the city.

As soon as the boy had gone, David rose from beside the stone heap and fell on his face and bowed three times. Then Jonathan said, "Go in peace. We have sworn in the name of the LORD, saying, 'The LORD shall be between me and you, and between my offspring and your offspring, forever.'" David rose and departed, and Jonathan went into the city.

DID YOU KNOW?

- The Hebrew word translated as "knit" is the same word used in Genesis 44:30 to express Jacob's love for his son Benjamin.

- By giving David his robes, Jonathan renounces his right to the throne. Jonathan is not afraid of losing his crown to David because he believes it is God's will that David be the next king of Israel.

- By bowing three times to Jonathan, David gives him the triple homage befitting a royal person.

Lift up your heads; declare the Lord's greatness.

Psalms

1009 BC David becomes king • 960 BC Solomon dedicates temple • 931 BC Death of Solomon

Psalms at a Glance

The Psalter presents the largest and, in many respects, the most complex book of Scripture, since Psalms includes the prayers and praises of God's people written over many centuries. This chart allows you to see the collections of psalms and the many types of psalms.

Many psalms were written for specific historical situations. Yet because they describe common human experiences, they still express the (1) prayers and (2) praises of God's people today. Most important, the messianic or royal psalms prophesy about the person and work of the Messiah, Jesus of Nazareth.

BOOK I

BOOK II

BOOK III

BOOK IV

BOOK V

Principal Authors

Intensely personal psalms of David

Psalms of David and the kingdom; nationalistic

Psalms of Asaph and the sons of Korah; nationalistic

Anonymous psalms and laments

Songs of ascents and praise; psalms of David

Historical Contexts

Life of David; 11th century BC; time of the tabernacle

Reigns of David and Solomon; 11th and 10th centuries BC; time of the first temple

---

Reign of Solomon; 10th century BC; some difficult to date

Historical context less clear; from as early as Moses and as late as exile in Babylon in 6th century BC

Key to Psalms Chart:

Red	Individual Laments
Orange	Community Laments
~~Scarlet~~	Curse (Imprecatory) Psalms
Red-violet	Individual Praise Psalms
Violet	Community Praise & Hallel Psalms
Blue	Descriptive Praise Psalms
Green	Liturgical Psalms & Psalms of Ascents
Yel-green	Creation Psalms
Gold	Messianic or Royal Psalms
Black	Trust Psalms
White	Wisdom Psalms
Silver	Zion Psalms

🐑 Shepherd Psalm, 23

🏰 Fortress Psalm, 46

◯ Word Psalm, 119

— Hallel or Ascent Psalms

✤ Mission Psalm, 145

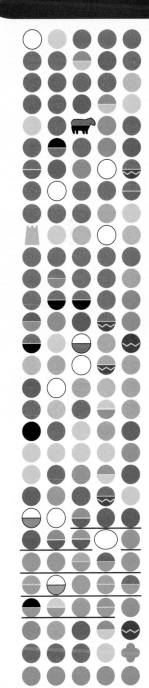

God's Covenant with David

2 Samuel 7

After David became king, and after the LORD had given David rest from all his enemies, he said to Nathan the prophet, "I dwell in a house of cedar, but the ark of God dwells in a tent."

Nathan said to the king, "Do all that is in your heart. The LORD is with you."

That same night the word of the LORD came to Nathan, "Tell my servant David, 'Thus says the LORD: Would you build Me a house? I have not lived in a house since the day I brought up the people of Israel from Egypt. Did I speak a word with any of the judges of Israel, saying, "Why have you not built Me a house of cedar?" ' Say to my servant David, 'Thus says the LORD of hosts, I took you from following the sheep, that you should be prince over My people Israel. I have been with you wherever you went. I have cut off all your enemies from before you. I will make for you a great name. I will appoint a place for My people Israel, so that they may dwell in their own place. I will give you rest from all your enemies. Moreover, the LORD declares to you that the LORD will make you a house. When your days are fulfilled and you lie down with your fathers, I will raise up your offspring. I will establish his kingdom. He shall build a house for My name. I will establish the throne of his kingdom forever. I will be to him a father. He shall be to Me a son. When he commits iniquity, I will discipline him, but My steadfast love will not depart from him. Your throne shall be established forever.' " Nathan spoke all this to David.

Then King David went in the tent and sat before the LORD. He said, "Who am I, O Lord GOD, and what is my house, that You have brought me thus far? Because of Your promise, and according to Your own heart, You have brought about all this greatness. Therefore You are great, O LORD God. For there is none like You. There is no God besides You. You established Your people Israel to be Your people forever. And You, O LORD, became their God. Now, O LORD God, confirm forever the word that You have spoken concerning Your servant and concerning his house. Do as You have spoken. And Your name will be **magnified** forever, saying, 'The LORD of hosts is God over Israel.' The house of Your servant David will be established before You. Now therefore may it please You to bless the house of Your servant, so that it may continue forever before You. For You, O Lord GOD, have spoken. With Your blessing shall the house of Your servant be blessed forever."

Words to Remember

You are great, O LORD God. For there is none like You, and there is no God besides You.
2 Samuel 7:22

DID YOU KNOW?

- David wanted to build a temple for the Lord. David sought God's will by consulting the prophet, but God told David that *He* would do the building.

- David lived about a thousand years before Jesus Christ. Like David, Jesus was born in Bethlehem and was the King of the Jews.

- The word *prophet* comes from the Greek words *pro*, meaning "for," and *phanai*, meaning "to speak" — "to speak for." Prophets preached, exhorted, explained God's Word, and sometimes foretold certain events.

Turn from your evil ways, and keep My Commandments.

1 & 2 Kings

970–931 BC Reign of Solomon • 722 BC Fall of Samaria • 587 BC Fall of Jerusalem

Judah

Faithful Kings	Unfaithful Kings
	Rehoboam
Abijam	
Asa	
Jehoshaphat	
	Jehoram
	Ahaziah
	Athaliah
Joash	
	Amaziah
	Azariah (Uzziah)
	Jotham
	Ahaz
Hezekiah	
	Manasseh
	Amon
Josiah	
	Jehoahaz
	Jehoiakim
	Jehoiachin
	Zedekiah

587 BC Fall of Jerusalem

Israel

Faithful Kings	Unfaithful Kings
None	Jeroboam
	Nadab
	Baasha
	Elah
	Zimri
	Tibni
	Omri
	Ahab
	Ahaziah
	J(eh)oram
	Jehu
	Jehoahaz
	Jehoash
	Jeroboam II
	Zechariah
	Shallum
	Menahem
	Pekah
	Pekahiah
	Hoshea

722 BC Fall of Israel (Samaria)

Purpose: To show that the Lord of history executes the threats and keeps the promises of His holy covenant (2 Kings 17:6–23). Judah and Israel were divided in 931 BC.

Battles of the Old Testament

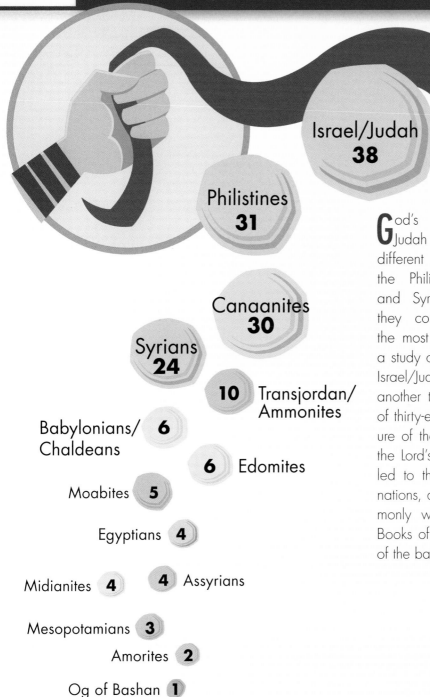

Israel/Judah
38

Philistines
31

Canaanites
30

Syrians
24

10 Transjordan/
Ammonites

Babylonians/ **6**
Chaldeans

6 Edomites

Moabites **5**

Egyptians **4**

Midianites **4**

4 Assyrians

Mesopotamians **3**

Amorites **2**

Og of Bashan **1**

God's people in Israel/
Judah fought against many
different nations, especially
the Philistines, Canaanites,
and Syrians, whose lands
they conquered. However,
the most surprising fact from
a study of their battles is that
Israel/Judah fought with one
another the most, for a total
of thirty-eight battles! The fail-
ure of the Israelites to follow
the Lord's covenant ultimately
led to their defeat by other
nations, as the prophets commonly warned them in the
Books of Kings, where many
of the battles were recorded.

Solomon Becomes King

1 Kings 2–3

Words to Remember

Keep the charge of the LORD your God, walking in His ways and keeping His statutes.
1 Kings 2:3

When David's time to die drew near, he commanded Solomon his son, "Be strong. Show yourself a man. Keep the charge of the LORD your God, walking in His ways and keeping His commandments, as it is written in the Law of Moses."

Then David slept with his fathers and was buried in the city of David. David reigned over Israel 40 years. So Solomon sat on the throne of David his father. Solomon loved the LORD. The LORD appeared to Solomon in a dream by night and said, "Ask what I shall give you."

Solomon said, "You have shown great and steadfast love to Your servant David my father. Now, O LORD my God, You have made Your servant king in place of David, although I am but a little child. Your servant is in the midst of Your people whom You have chosen, a great people, too many to be numbered. Give Your servant an understanding mind to govern Your people, that I may **discern** between good and evil. For who is able to govern this Your great people?"

It pleased the Lord that Solomon had asked this. God said, "Because you have asked for understanding to discern what is right, I give you a wise and discerning mind. I give you also riches and honor. And if you will walk in My ways, as your father David walked, then I will lengthen your days."

Solomon awoke, and behold, it was a dream. Then he came to Jerusalem and stood before the ark of the covenant of the Lord. Solomon offered up offerings.

Two women came to Solomon. One woman said, "This woman and I live in the same house. I gave birth to a child, then on the third day after I gave birth, this woman also gave birth. This woman's son died in the night. She took my son, while I slept, and laid her dead son at my breast. When I rose in the morning, he was dead. But when I looked closely, he was not the child that I had borne."

The other woman said, "No, the living child is mine. The dead child is yours."

Solomon said, "Bring me a sword. Divide the living child in two. Give half to the one and half to the other."

Then the woman whose son was alive said, "Oh, my lord, give her the living child. Do not put him to death."

The other said, "He shall be neither mine nor yours. Divide him."

Solomon said, "Give the living child to the first woman. She is his mother." All Israel heard of the judgment that the king had **rendered**. They stood in **awe** of the king, because they perceived that the wisdom of God was in him to do **justice**.

DID YOU KNOW?

- The Books of 1 and 2 Kings were originally one book in the Hebrew Bible, simply called "Kings." Together, these books record life in Israel during the monarchy from King Solomon to King Jehoiachin.

- Scripture's use of the term *sleep* for death—especially when applied to believers—is a wonderful reminder that we shall awaken from death to life with God in heaven, through the sufferings, death, and resurrection of Jesus Christ.

The fear of the Lord is the beginning of knowledge.

Proverbs

1009–970 BC Reign of David • 970–931 BC Reign of Solomon • 715–686 BC Reign of Hezekiah

The Mind of Solomon and Biblical Proverbs

Solomon and other writers of proverbs described life by contrasting the actions of wise and foolish people. This chart shows many of his favorite expressions.

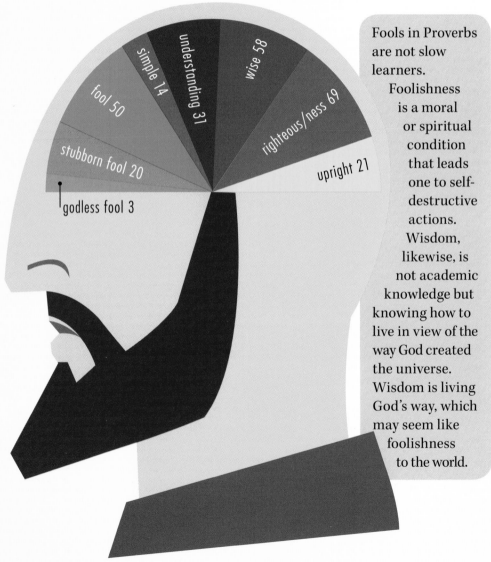

fool 50

simple 14

understanding 31

wise 58

righteous/ness 69

stubborn fool 20

upright 21

godless fool 3

Fools in Proverbs are not slow learners. Foolishness is a moral or spiritual condition that leads one to self-destructive actions. Wisdom, likewise, is not academic knowledge but knowing how to live in view of the way God created the universe. Wisdom is living God's way, which may seem like foolishness to the world.

Wisdom and Folly

As a leader in Israel, Solomon had leisure to pursue wisdom and observe folly in action. In Proverbs 8–9, he describes the dangers of pursuing folly rather than wisdom. However, the Books of Kings tell us that Solomon was more than an observer; he also fell into the same kinds of foolishness as his subjects, demonstrating that wisdom, learning, freedom, wealth, and power do not make one immune to Lady Folly. We need God's eternal Wisdom, which Solomon celebrates in Proverbs 8:12–31, which prophesies the wisdom of Jesus Christ (John 1:1–5, 14–18; 1 Corinthians 1:18–2:16).

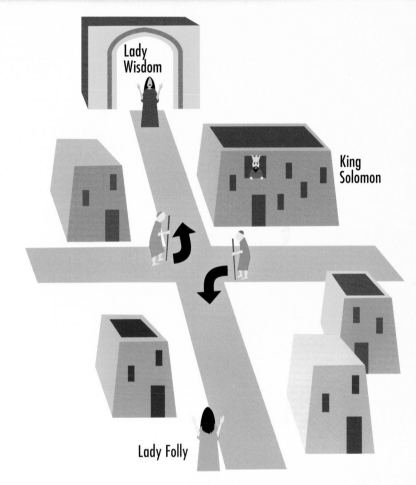

Lady Wisdom

King Solomon

Lady Folly

Other Writers of Proverbs

Although Solomon was the main writer or collector of Proverbs, especially 1:1–22:16, other people contributed. The following are other contributors mentioned in Proverbs.

The Words of Wise People (22:17–24:22)

More Words of Wise People (24:23–34)

Hezekiah's Men, who collected more sayings of Solomon (chs. 25–29)

Agur (ch. 30)

King Lemuel's Mother (31:1–9)

Solomon Builds the Temple

1 Kings 5–6 and 8

Solomon sent word to Hiram, king of Tyre, "I intend to build a house for the name of the LORD my God, as the LORD said to David, 'Your son shall build the house for My name.' Therefore command that cedars of Lebanon be cut for me."

Hiram rejoiced greatly. He said, "Blessed be the LORD this day, who has given to David a wise son to be over this great people. I am ready to do all you desire in the matter of cedar and cypress timber. You shall meet my wishes by providing food for my household." The LORD gave Solomon wisdom, as He promised. And there was peace between Hiram and Solomon.

In the 480th year after the people of Israel came out of the land of Egypt, in the 4th year of Solomon's reign, he began to build the house of the LORD. It was built with stone prepared at the quarry. No tool of iron was heard in the house while it was being built. Solomon lined the walls on the inside with boards of cedar. He covered the floor with boards of cypress. The inner **sanctuary** he prepared in the innermost part of the house, to set there the ark of the covenant of the LORD. He overlaid the whole house with gold. Also the whole altar in the inner sanctuary he overlaid with gold. He was seven years in building the temple.

Then Solomon assembled the elders of Israel and all the heads of the tribes in Jerusalem. The priests brought the ark of the covenant of the LORD to its place in the inner sanctuary of the house. When the priests came out of the Holy Place, a cloud filled the house of the LORD. The priests could not stand to minister because of the cloud, for the glory of the LORD filled the house of the LORD.

Then Solomon stood before the altar of the LORD in the presence of all the assembly of Israel. He said, "O LORD, God of Israel, there is no God like You, keeping covenant and showing steadfast love to Your servants who walk before You with all their heart. Behold, heaven and the highest heaven cannot contain You; how much less this house that I have built! Yet have regard to the prayer of Your servant and to his plea, O LORD my God, that Your eyes may be open night and day toward this house. You have said of this place, 'My name shall be there,' that You may listen to the prayer that Your servant offers toward this place. Listen to the plea of Your servant and of Your people Israel, when they pray toward this place. And listen in heaven Your dwelling place, and when You hear, forgive."

Then the king and all Israel offered a sacrifice before the LORD.

Words to Remember

I will dwell among the children of Israel and will not forsake My people Israel. *1 Kings 6:13*

DID YOU KNOW?

- It took seven years to build "Solomon's temple," but it was later destroyed by King Nebuchadnezzar of Babylon.

- Solomon wrote three thousand proverbs and more than one thousand songs. He is also the author or coauthor of three books in the Bible— Proverbs, Song of Solomon, and Ecclesiastes.

- Prayers can include adoration, confession, thanksgiving, and supplication (ACTS).

Love is the
very flame
of the Lord.

Song of Solomon

1009–970 BC Reign of David • 970–931 BC Reign of Solomon • 931–914 BC Reign of Rehoboam

Solomon most likely wrote his love song about the Shulammite in his younger days. It celebrates love as "the very flame of the LORD," with the king and his bride representing the Lord and the Church.

Fear God and keep
His commandments.

Ecclesiastes

970–931 BC Solomon reigns • 931 BC Israel divided under Rehoboam

Solomon likely wrote Ecclesiastes in his old age. Thirty times he refers to the vanity of a disappointing life, but he concludes by urging his readers to follow "one Shepherd," the Lord.

VANITY VANITY VANITY VANITY
VANITY VANITY VANITY VANITY
VANITY VANITY VANITY VANITY
VANITY VANITY VANITY VANITY
VANITY VANITY VANITY VANITY
VANITY VANITY VANITY VANITY
VANITY VANITY VANITY
VANITY VANITY VANITY

God Provides for Elijah

1 Kings 16–17

Words to Remember
Now I know that you are a man of God, and that the word of the LORD in your mouth is truth. *1 Kings 17:24*

Ahab reigned over Israel in Samaria. He took for his wife Jezebel. He erected an altar for **Baal** and made an **Asherah**. Ahab did more to provoke the LORD to anger than all the kings of Israel who were before him.

Elijah said to Ahab, "As the LORD, the God of Israel, lives, before whom I stand, there shall be neither dew nor rain these years, except by my word."

The word of the LORD came to Elijah: "Hide yourself by the brook Cherith. You shall drink from the brook, and I have commanded the ravens to feed you there." So Elijah did according to the word of the LORD. And the ravens brought Elijah bread and meat in the morning and in the evening, and he drank from the brook. After a while the brook dried up, because there was no rain.

Then the word of the Lord came to Elijah, "Go to Zarephath. I have commanded a widow there to feed you."

So Elijah arose, and when he came to the gate of the city, a widow was there gathering sticks. Elijah called to her and said, "Bring me a little water, that I may drink." As she was going to bring it, he said, "Bring me a morsel of bread."

She said, "As the LORD your God lives, I have nothing baked, only a handful of flour in a jar and a little oil in a jug. I am gathering sticks that I may go in and prepare it for myself and my son, that we may eat it and die."

Elijah said, "Do not fear. Go and do as you have said. But first make me a little cake and bring it to me. Afterward make something for yourself and your son. For thus says the LORD, the God of Israel, 'The jar of flour shall not be spent, and the jug of oil shall not be empty, until the day that the LORD sends rain upon the earth.'" The woman did as Elijah said. And she and he and her household ate for many days.

After this the son of the woman became ill. There was no breath left in him. She said to Elijah, "What have you against me, O man of God? You have come to me to bring my sin to remembrance and to cause the death of my son!"

Elijah carried her son into the upper chamber and laid him on his own bed. He cried, "O LORD my God, have You brought calamity even upon the widow with whom I stay, by killing her son?" Then he stretched himself upon the child three times and cried, "O LORD my God, let this child's life come into him again." The LORD listened to the voice of Elijah. The life of the child came into him again.

Elijah delivered him to his mother. The woman said, "Now I know that you are a man of God, and that the word of the LORD in your mouth is truth."

DID YOU KNOW?———————————————————————————————

- No other prophet achieved as much recognition in the New Testament as the prophet Elijah.

- Ahab was the most notorious of a long line of wicked kings. God raised up the prophet Elijah to counteract the evils of Ahab's reign.

- Elijah prefigured John the Baptist. As Elijah prepared the way for the coming of Elisha, John prepared the way for the coming of Jesus. Both also suffered under a brutal ruler.

Elijah and the Prophets of Baal

1 Kings 18

Elijah said to King Ahab, "Gather all Israel to me at Mount Carmel, and the 450 prophets of Baal and the 400 prophets of Asherah." So Ahab gathered the people and the prophets.

Elijah said to the people, "How long will you limp between two different opinions? If the LORD is God, follow Him. But if Baal is God, then follow him." The people did not answer.

Then Elijah said, "Give us two bulls. Let Baal's prophets cut one bull in pieces and lay it on the wood, but put no fire to it. I will prepare the other bull and lay it on the wood and put no fire to it. You call upon the name of your god. I will call upon the name of the LORD. The God who answers by fire, He is God."

The people answered, "It is well spoken."

The prophets of Baal prepared the bull and called upon the name of Baal from morning until noon. They said, "O Baal, answer us!" But there was no voice, and no one answered.

At noon Elijah **mocked** them, saying, "Perhaps Baal is asleep and must be awakened." As midday passed, they raved on, but there was no voice. No one answered. No one paid attention.

Then Elijah took twelve stones, according to the number of the tribes of the sons of Jacob, and built an altar in the name of the LORD. He made a trench about the altar. He cut the bull in pieces and laid it on the wood. Three times he said, "Fill four jars with water and pour it on the burnt offering and on the wood." The water ran around the altar and filled the trench.

Elijah the prophet said, "O LORD, God of Abraham, Isaac, and Israel, let it be known this day that You are God in Israel, and that I am Your servant, and that I have done all these things at Your word. Answer me, O LORD, that this people may know that You, O LORD, are God, and that You have turned their hearts back." Then the fire of the LORD fell and consumed the burnt offering and the wood and the stones and the dust. It licked up the water that was in the trench.

When all the people saw it, they fell on their faces and said, "The LORD, He is God. The LORD, He is God."

Elijah said to them, "Seize the prophets of Baal. Do not let one of them escape." And they seized them. And Elijah brought them down to the brook Kishon and slaughtered them there.

Words to Remember

The LORD, He is God; the LORD, He is God.
1 Kings 18:39

DID YOU KNOW?_____

- Baal was the principal Canaanite god. He was believed to exercise his power each year in the autumn and winter rains, reviving the dry soil and bringing the mysterious life force to animals and the land.

- When Elijah killed Baal's prophets, he was following the punishment prescribed in Deuteronomy 13:13–16; 17:2–5 for those who worshiped false gods because the New Testament repeal of the old ceremonial and civil law had not yet occurred.

God Takes Elijah to Heaven

1 Kings 19 and 2 Kings 2

Ahab told Jezebel how Elijah had killed all the prophets of Baal. Then Jezebel threatened to kill Elijah. He was afraid and ran a day's journey into the wilderness. He slept under a tree.

Twice, an angel brought Elijah food and water. He ate and drank and went in the strength of that food 40 days and nights to Horeb, the mount of God. And he stayed in a cave.

The LORD said, "Stand on the mount before the LORD." The LORD passed by, and a strong wind tore the mountains, then came an earthquake, and after the earthquake a fire. But the LORD was not in the wind, earthquake, or fire. After the fire came the sound of a low whisper.

When Elijah heard it, he wrapped his face in his cloak and stood at the entrance of the cave. A voice said, "What are you doing here, Elijah?"

Elijah said, "I have been very jealous for the LORD, the God of hosts. And I, even I only, am left, and they seek my life, to take it away."

The LORD said, "Anoint Elisha to be prophet in your place." So Elijah found Elisha and cast his cloak upon him. And Elisha went after Elijah and assisted him.

Now Elijah and Elisha were on their way from Gilgal. Elijah said to Elisha, "Please stay here, for the LORD has sent me as far as Bethel."

But Elisha said, "As the LORD lives, and as you yourself live, I will not leave you." So they went down to Bethel. Two more times, Elijah asked Elisha to stay behind, but Elisha refused. So the two of them came to the Jordan. Elijah rolled up his cloak and struck the water. The water was parted so the two of them could go over on dry ground.

When they had crossed, Elijah said to Elisha, "Ask what I shall do for you, before I am taken from you."

Elisha said, "Please let there be a double portion of your spirit on me."

Elijah said, "If you see me as I am being taken from you, it shall be so for you." As they went on and talked, behold, chariots of fire and horses of fire separated the two of them. And Elijah went up by a whirlwind into heaven.

Elisha saw it and cried, "My father, my father! The chariots of Israel and its horsemen!" He saw him no more. Then Elisha took up the cloak of Elijah and went back and stood on the bank of the Jordan. He took the cloak of Elijah and struck the water, saying, "Where is the LORD, the God of Elijah?" When he had struck the water, the water was parted to the one side and to the other, and Elisha went over.

Words to Remember

Elijah went up by a whirlwind into heaven.
2 Kings 2:11

DID YOU KNOW?

- Mount Horeb is where Moses had received the Ten Commandments centuries earlier.

- Elijah used his cloak as a rod to part the Jordan River just as Moses had stretched out his rod to open a path through the Red Sea. Elisha then demonstrated that he had inherited the spirit of Elijah by performing the same miracle after Elijah had been taken to heaven.

- The appearance of the fiery chariot and Elisha's passionate cry as Elijah ascended into heaven can be seen as a tremendous affirmation of Elijah's importance in Israel's history.

Naaman and Elisha

2 Kings 5

Words to Remember

[Naaman] went down and dipped himself seven times in the Jordan, according to the word of the man of God, and his flesh was restored like the flesh of a little child, and he was clean. *2 Kings 5:14*

Naaman, commander of the army of the king of Syria, was a great man with his master and in high favor. By him the LORD had given victory to Syria. He was a mighty man of valor, but he was a **leper**.

Now the Syrians on one of their raids had carried off a little girl from the land of Israel. She worked for Naaman's wife. She said to her mistress, "Would that my lord were with the prophet who is in Samaria! He would cure him of his **leprosy**."

So Naaman told his lord what the girl had said. The king of Syria said, "Go now, and I will send a letter to the king of Israel."

So Naaman went, taking with him silver, gold, and clothing as gifts. He brought to the king of Israel the letter, which read, "When this letter reaches you, know that I have sent to you Naaman my servant, that you may cure him of his leprosy."

When the king of Israel read the letter, he tore his clothes. He said, "Am I God, to kill and to make alive, that this man sends word to me to cure a man of his leprosy? See how he is seeking a quarrel with me."

But when Elisha the man of God heard that the king had torn his clothes, he sent to the king, saying, "Why have you torn your clothes? Let Naaman come to me, that he may know that there is a prophet in Israel."

So Naaman came with his horses and chariots and stood at the door of Elisha's house. Elisha sent a messenger to him, saying, "Wash in the Jordan seven times, and your flesh shall be restored. You shall be clean."

But Naaman was angry. He said, "I thought that he would come out to me and call upon the name of the LORD his God, and wave his hand over the place and cure the leper. Are not the rivers of Damascus better than all the waters of Israel? Could I not wash in them and be clean?" So Naaman turned and went away in a rage.

But his servants said, "It is a great word the prophet has spoken to you. Will you not do it? Has he actually said to you, 'Wash, and be clean'?"

So Naaman dipped himself seven times in the Jordan, according to the word of Elisha, and his flesh was restored like the flesh of a little child. He was clean.

Then Naaman returned to the man of God and said, "Behold, I know that there is no God in all the earth but in Israel. So accept now a present from your servant."

But Elisha said, "As the LORD lives, before whom I stand, I will receive none."

Naaman urged him to take it, but Elisha refused. Elisha said, "Go in peace."

DID YOU KNOW?

- The wording and request of the king of Syria's letter placed the Israelite king in an awkward position. He feared that the Syrian king would hold him responsible if Naaman was not healed.

- Naaman, an unclean Gentile (Leviticus 13:46), was not invited into Elisha's house, which would have appeared rude to a foreign dignitary.

- Naaman did not understand why he should wash in the Jordan because the rivers of his homeland watered fertile fields, whereas the murky Jordan, rushing into the Salt Sea, had little irrigation value.

Rend your hearts and not your garments.

Joel

873–848 BC Reign of Jehoshophat (Judah) • c. 848–800 BC Joel written • 740 BC Reign of Azariah/Uzziah

Rend here

cutting
swarming
hopping
destroying

Pentecost Prophesied

Joel 2:28–29

Fulfilled about 800 years later

Acts 2:1–18

The prophet Joel describes the Lord sending an army of locusts to chasten His people and drive them to repentance. The locusts may also represent the coming threat of the Assyrian armies, who would later conquer the Northern Kingdom of Israel.

Shall I not pity Nineveh?

Jonah

793–753 BC Reign of Jeroboam II (Israel) • c. 790 BC Jonah written • 722 BC Samaria (Israel) falls to Assyria

Gracious God and Merciful

Nineveh

Slow to Anger

Abounding in Steadfast Love

Relenting from Disaster

120,000
in Nineveh

In Jonah 4:2, the Lord reveals how He cares not just about the chosen people of Israel but also for people of all nations. This mission-minded book anticipates the New Testament's commission to "make disciples of all nations" (Matthew 28:19).

Jonah's Story

The Book of Jonah

The word of the LORD came to Jonah, "Go to Nineveh and call out against it. Their evil has come up before Me." But Jonah found a ship going to Tarshish, away from the presence of the LORD.

The LORD hurled a great wind upon the sea, so that the ship threatened to break up. The mariners were afraid, and each cried out to his god. They hurled the cargo into the sea to lighten the ship. But Jonah was fast asleep. The captain said to him, "Call to your god, that we may not perish."

The sailors cast lots to find out on whose account this evil had come upon them. The lot fell on Jonah. They said, "What is your occupation? Where are you from?"

Jonah said, "I am a Hebrew. I fear the LORD, the God of heaven, who made the sea and the dry land."

The men were very afraid and said, "What is this that you have done!" For the men knew that Jonah was fleeing from the presence of the LORD. "What shall we do to you, that the sea may quiet down for us?"

Jonah said, "Hurl me into the sea. Then the sea will quiet down for you." So they hurled Jonah into the sea, and the sea ceased from its raging. The men offered a sacrifice to the LORD.

The LORD appointed a great fish to swallow up Jonah. And Jonah was in the belly of the fish three days and three nights. Then Jonah prayed to the LORD his God from the belly of the fish:

> "When my life was fainting away,
>> I remembered the LORD.
> Salvation belongs to the LORD!"

The LORD spoke to the fish, and it vomited Jonah out upon the dry land.

So Jonah went to Nineveh. He called out, "Yet 40 days, and Nineveh shall be overthrown!" The people of Nineveh believed God. They **fasted** and put on sackcloth, from the greatest to the least.

The king of Nineveh covered himself with sackcloth and sat in ashes. He issued a proclamation, "Let everyone turn from his evil way. God may relent and turn from His fierce anger, so that we may not perish."

When God saw what they did, God relented of the disaster that He had said He would do to them.

DID YOU KNOW?

- Of all the prophets, Jonah is the only one who did not want his message to succeed. He didn't want Nineveh to repent; he wanted them to go on sinning so that God would punish them. Scripture nowhere reports that any other prophet disobeyed God's call.

- We are not told specifically what kind of sea creature God selected to rescue Jonah. Most often, people think of a whale because the animal would need to be very large. Israelites, like other ancient people, did not use the modern classifications for animals but instead tended to focus on an animal's habitat and locomotion.

Let justice roll down like water.

Amos

793–753 BC Reign of Jeroboam II (Israel) • c. 792–740 BC Amos written • 752–732 BC Reign of Pekah (Israel)

Amos emphasizes how God's people show His justice, or righteousness, in the way they treat one another, revealing the results of the biblical teaching of justification through faith.

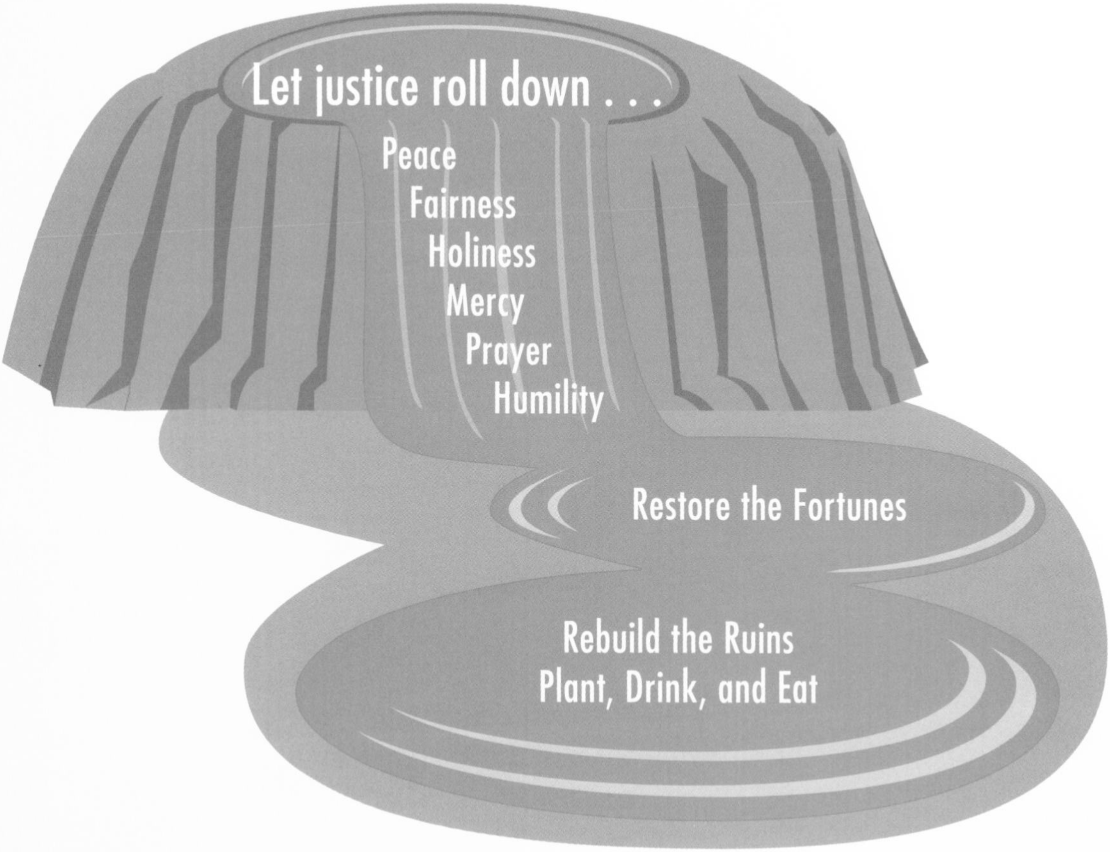

Let justice roll down . . .

Peace
Fairness
Holiness
Mercy
Prayer
Humility

Restore the Fortunes

**Rebuild the Ruins
Plant, Drink, and Eat**

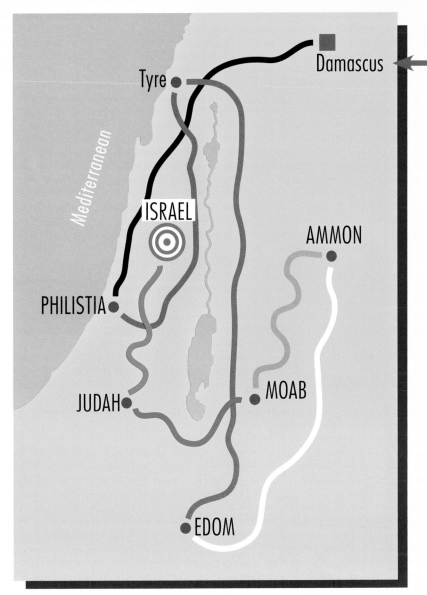

Target: Israel

The path of God's judgment in Amos 1–4.

Early in the Book of Amos, other locations receive as little as a paragraph of rebuke. Israel receives more than two chapters! Amos writes this way to teach Israel that the Lord was most concerned about their sins.

Damascus

Tyre

Mediterranean

ISRAEL

AMMON

PHILISTIA

JUDAH

MOAB

EDOM

66 chapters

Let us go up
to the mountain
of the Lord.

Read in 3 hours, 37 minutes

Isaiah

792–740 BC Reign of Azariah (Uzziah) • 740 BC Call of Isaiah • 715–686 BC Reign of Hezekiah

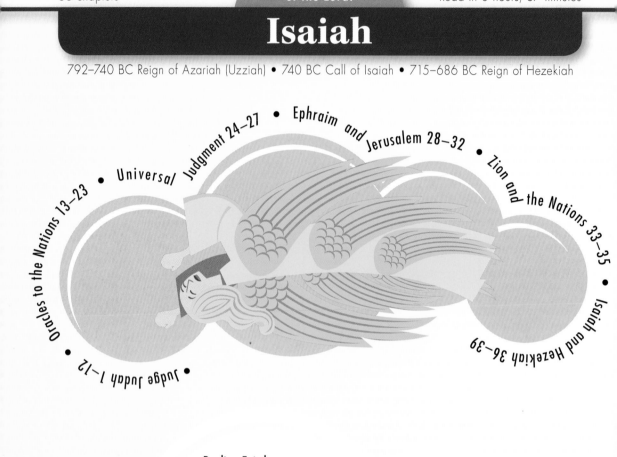

Oracles to the Nations 13–23 • Universal Judgment 24–27 • Ephraim and Jerusalem 28–32 • Zion and the Nations 33–35 • Isaiah and Hezekiah 36–39 • Judge Judah 1–12

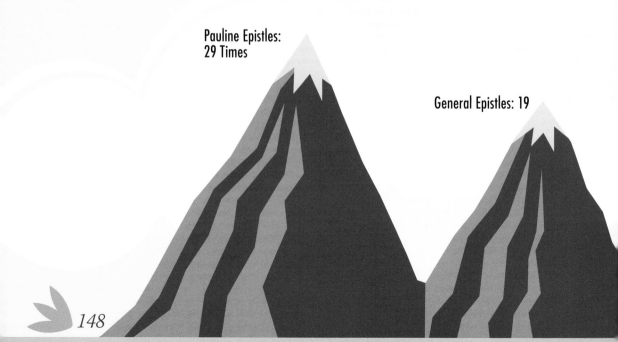

Pauline Epistles:
29 Times

General Epistles: 19

When God called Isaiah to be a prophet, Isaiah saw a vision of God's heavenly throne and six-winged seraphim (angels) flying about it, calling one to another, "Holy, holy, holy is the LORD of hosts; the whole earth is full of His glory!" The holy Lord will judge Judah for its sins, but He will also hallow them through repentance and faith. The first part of his prophecy is more sombre (chs. 1–39). The second part is more joyful (chs. 40–66).

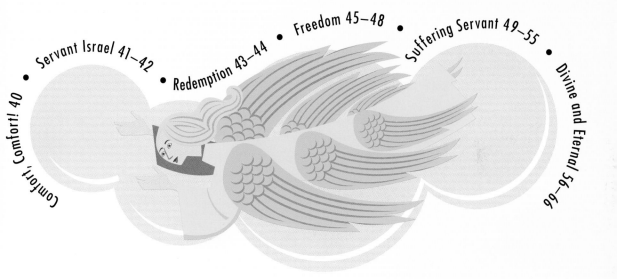

Comfort, Comfort! 40 • Servant Israel 41–42 • Redemption 43–44 • Freedom 45–48 • Suffering Servant 49–55 • Divine and Eternal 56–66

Isaiah Runs throughout the New Testament

Zion, the "mountain of the Lord," is a major topic in Isaiah. Zion is the location of the temple where the Lord hallows His people through the blessings of the covenant, which foreshadowed the coming of Christ the Savior.

No prophet is referenced more in the New Testament than Isaiah: sixteen times in Romans, fifteen times in Matthew, and remarkably, thirteen times in the short letter of 1 Peter. No wonder Isaiah is known as "the fifth Gospel." New Testament writers reference Isaiah a total of 95 times based on studies of the Greek New Testament!

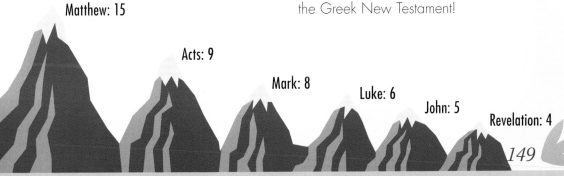

Matthew: 15

Acts: 9

Mark: 8

Luke: 6

John: 5

Revelation: 4

Isaiah Sees the Lord

Isaiah 6–7, 9, and 53

Words to Remember

Holy, holy, holy is the LORD of hosts; the whole earth is full of His glory!
Isaiah 6:3

I saw the Lord sitting upon a throne, high and lifted up. The train of His robe filled the temple. Above Him stood the **seraphim**. Each had six wings: with two he covered his face, with two he covered his feet, with two he flew. He said: "Holy, holy, holy is the LORD of hosts. The whole earth is full of His glory!"

The foundations shook at the voice of him who called. The house was filled with smoke. I said: "Woe is me! For I am lost. I am a man of unclean lips. I dwell in the midst of a people of unclean lips. My eyes have seen the King, the LORD of hosts!"

Then one of the seraphim flew to me. In his hand he had a burning coal that he had taken with tongs from the altar. He touched my mouth and said: "Behold, this has touched your lips. Your guilt is taken away, and your sin **atoned** for."

I heard the voice of the Lord saying, "Whom shall I send, and who will go for Us?" Then I said, "Here am I! Send me."

Here are some of the things God told Isaiah to prophesy about Jesus.

"The Lord Himself will give you a sign. Behold, the virgin shall conceive and bear a son, and shall call His name **Immanuel**."

"The people who walked in darkness
     have seen a great light.
Those who dwelt in a land of deep darkness,
     on them has light shined.
For to us a child is born,
     to us a son is given;
and the government shall be upon His shoulder,
     and His name shall be called
Wonderful Counselor, Mighty God,
     Everlasting Father, Prince of Peace."

"Surely He has borne our griefs
     and carried our sorrows.
Yet we **esteemed** Him stricken,
     smitten by God, and afflicted.
But He was wounded for our **transgressions**;
     He was crushed for our iniquities.
Upon Him was the **chastisement** that brought us peace,
     and with His stripes we are healed."

DID YOU KNOW?

- The name *Isaiah* means "the Lord is salvation." His name was a short version of the message Isaiah preached.

- Isaiah is famous for his detailed predictions, especially his descriptions of the coming Savior.

- Most of Isaiah's book is written as poetry. This made it easier to memorize for the people of his day, who usually weren't wealthy enough to own a scroll of the prophet's writings.

Walk humbly with your God.

Micah

1009 BC David reigns • c. 750–686 BC Micah written • 587 BC Fall of Jerusalem

Purpose: To indict the shepherds of Israel and Judah for exploiting and misleading the people and to prophesy the Lord's work as a shepherd for the remnant.

Leaders Shepherds in the Bible often stand for leaders, whether political or spiritual.

Zion The hill where the Jerusalem temple was built is known as Mount Zion, a spiritual refuge for the people of God. Micah compares the reign of David's dynasty to a tower.

Israel Israel's leaders often took advantage of the people they were leading. Through Micah, the Lord calls the leaders to repent.

 Grace & Gospel

Remnant; Zion; faithful shepherd; God's patience

 Sin & Law

Nakedness and shame; remnant; exile; false prophets

Hosea

752–732 BC Reign of Pekah (Israel) • c. 740–715 BC Hosea written • 722 BC Assyria besieges Samaria

REPRESENTATIONS

| Hosea as God | Gomer as Israel | Price of Redemption |

Gomer
She was unfaithful to Hosea, her husband, as Israel was unfaithful to the Lord.

No Mercy
Hosea and Gomer's firstborn child was named for the judgment Israel would face for its sins.

Not My People
Hosea and Gomer's second child was named for God's rejection of Israel, which was ultimately fulfilled in the 722 BC exile of the northern tribes.

Hosea
Hosea, like the Lord, would not forsake his wife even though she left him.

Barley
Hosea redeemed his wife from prostitution with nine bushels of barley and fifteen shekels of silver, the going price for someone in slavery. His dedication to Gomer represented God's love for Israel.

Shekels

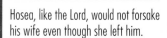

History in Hosea

Patriarchs	Exodus	Judges	Kings
Adam, 6:7	Exodus, 11:1	Gibeah of Benjamin, 10:9	Kingship of David, 3:5
Abraham, 1:10	Wilderness, 9:10		Ephraim's idolatry at Bethel, 10:15
Jacob, 12:12			Tribute to Assyria, 8:9

Hosea, as one of the earliest prophets of the kingdom era, had a broad knowledge of earlier biblical accounts and used them to illustrate his prophecies.

King Hezekiah Prays

2 Kings 18–19

Hezekiah was 25 years old when he began to reign. He reigned 29 years in Jerusalem. He did what was right in the eyes of the LORD. He trusted in the LORD, the God of Israel. He did not depart from following Him, but kept the commandments that the LORD commanded Moses. And the LORD was with him.

In the 14th year of King Hezekiah, Sennacherib king of Assyria took all the fortified cities of Judah. Hezekiah sent to the king, saying, "Withdraw from me. Whatever you **impose** on me I will bear." The king of Assyria required silver and gold. Hezekiah gave it to him.

The king of Assyria sent a great army against Jerusalem. The leaders of the army said to Hezekiah and the people, "In whom do you trust? Thus says the king of Assyria: 'Do not let Hezekiah deceive you. He will not be able to deliver you. Do not let Hezekiah make you trust in the LORD by saying, "The LORD will surely deliver us." Who among all the gods of the lands have delivered their lands out of my hand, that the LORD should deliver Jerusalem?' "

As soon as King Hezekiah heard it, he tore his clothes and covered himself with sackcloth and went into the house of the LORD. When the servants of King Hezekiah came to Isaiah, Isaiah said, "Say to your master, 'Thus says the LORD: Do not be afraid. I will put a spirit in Sennacherib, so that he shall hear a rumor and return to his own land. I will make him fall by the sword in his own land.' "

Hezekiah received another threatening letter from Sennacherib and went up to the house of the LORD and spread it before the LORD. Hezekiah prayed: "O LORD, enthroned above the cherubim, You are the God, You alone, of all the kingdoms of the earth. **Incline** Your ear, O LORD, and hear. Save us, please, that all the kingdoms of the earth may know that You, O LORD, are God alone."

Then Isaiah sent to Hezekiah, saying, "Thus says the LORD concerning the king of Assyria: He shall not come into this city or shoot an arrow there. For I will defend this city to save it, for My own sake and for the sake of My servant David."

That night the angel of the LORD went out and struck down 185,000 in the camp of the Assyrians. Then Sennacherib king of Assyria went home and lived at Nineveh. As Sennacherib was worshiping in the house of his god, his sons struck him down with the sword and escaped into the land of Ararat.

Words to Remember

Incline Your ear, O LORD, and hear; open Your eyes, O LORD, and see.
2 Kings 19:16

DID YOU KNOW?

- Hezekiah was the pious son of wicked King Ahaz. The Lord used Hezekiah to guide Judah through its most challenging moment, facing the great Assyrian Empire.

- To make the tribute payment to Sennacherib, Hezekiah stripped the gold foil off the recently repaired areas of the temple.

- At the time of the exodus, the Lord sent "the destroyer" into every Egyptian home to smite its firstborn. The angel of the Lord executed judgment at David's time by means of a pestilence. It is possible that He slew the Assyrian army by employing the same means.

A stronghold in the day of trouble.

Nahum

722 BC Fall of Israel • c. 663–612 BC Nahum written • 605 BC Nebuchadnezzar besieges Jerusalem

Purpose: To assure that the Lord fights for those who take refuge in Him.

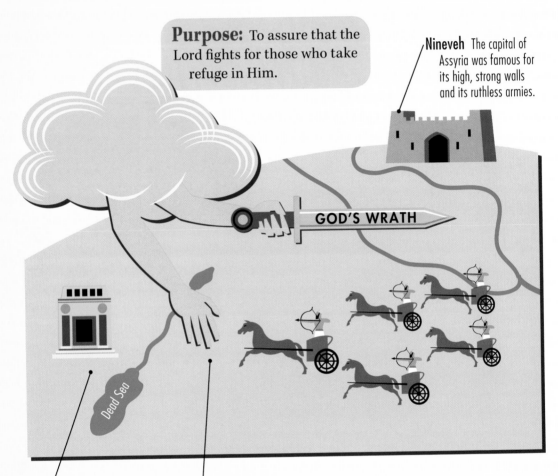

Nineveh The capital of Assyria was famous for its high, strong walls and its ruthless armies.

GOD'S WRATH

Dead Sea

Judah The Assyrians had already conquered the Northern Kingdom of Israel and now sought to conquer the Southern Kingdom, Judah, the location of the temple.

God's Wrath Against all hope, Nahum prophesies that Assyria will be destroyed. The Lord would rescue Judah.

 Grace & Gospel
The Lord frees oppressed Judah; His Word and feasts are for His people

 Sin & Law
The Lord is jealous and avenging; Nineveh is destroyed

Zephaniah

696–642 BC Reign of Manasseh • c. 640–609 BC Zephaniah written • 605 BC Nebuchadnezzer besieges Jerusalem

Through the prophet Zephaniah, the Lord calls Judah to repentance and proclaims that when Judah is restored, the nations will seek refuge in Him there. The dark day of the Lord's wrath will give way to joyful restoration of Zion.

King Josiah

2 Kings 22–23

Words to Remember
Before [Josiah] there was no king like him, who turned to the LORD with all his heart and with all his soul and with all his might, according to all the Law of Moses, nor did any like him arise after him. *2 Kings 23:25*

Josiah was eight years old when he began to reign. He reigned 31 years in Jerusalem. He did what was right in the eyes of the LORD and walked in all the way of David his father.

In the 18th year of King Josiah, the king sent his secretary to the house of the LORD, saying, "Go to Hilkiah the high priest, that he may count the money that has been collected from the people. Give it to the workmen who are at the house of the LORD, repairing the house (that is, to the carpenters, builders, and masons). Let them use it to buy timber and quarried stone."

Hilkiah said to the secretary, "I have found the Book of the Law in the house of the LORD." Hilkiah gave the book to the secretary. He read it and then read it before King Josiah.

When the king heard the words of the Book of the Law, he tore his clothes. The king commanded Hilkiah and other officials, saying, "Inquire of the LORD for me and for all Judah. For great is the **wrath** of the LORD that is kindled against us, because our fathers have not obeyed the words of this book."

So Hilkiah and the other officials went to Huldah the prophetess. She said, "Thus says the LORD, the God of Israel: 'Behold, I will bring disaster upon this place and upon its inhabitants, because they have forsaken Me and have made offerings to other gods. But to the king of Judah, say, Because your heart was **penitent**, and you humbled yourself before the LORD and wept before Me, I also have heard you. Therefore, your eyes shall not see all the disaster that I will bring upon this place.'"

Then the king went to the house of the LORD, and with him all the people, both small and great. He read in their hearing all the words of the Book of the Covenant. And the king made a covenant before the LORD, to keep His commandments with all his heart and all his soul. All the people joined in the covenant.

The king commanded Hilkiah and the priests to bring out of the temple all the vessels made for Baal, for Asherah, and for all the host of heaven. He burned them outside Jerusalem and **defiled** the high places where the priests had made offerings. The king commanded all the people, "Keep the Passover to the LORD your God, as it is written in this Book of the Covenant." For no such Passover had been kept since the days of the judges who judged Israel, or during all the days of the kings of Israel or of the kings of Judah.

DID YOU KNOW?

- Scholars debate the exact contents of the scroll referred to as "the Book of the Law." Many propose that it was Deuteronomy; however, 1 and 2 Kings use expressions similar to "Book of the Law" for Moses's writings generally, and many parallels can be found with Exodus and Leviticus.

- Because of the sincerity of King Josiah's repentance, Jerusalem would remain intact during his lifetime.

- Josiah hoped that the destruction of Jerusalem could still be averted if he and the people complied with the Book of the Law, so he sought to remove all elements of false worship from regions under his rule.

The Lord will make
a new covenant.

Jeremiah

722 BC Samaria (Israel) falls to Assyria • 628 BC Jeremiah called • 587 BC Babylonians take Jerusalem

Chapters
1–29

The Book
of Comfort
Chapters 30–33

Chapters
34–52

Judgment and lamentation are the constant themes of Jeremiah. He may have written or arranged his book to intensify the contrasts between prevailing gloom and the light of hope in the "book of comfort" at the center of his prophecies: God promises restoration and a new covenant in the coming Davidic King, fulfilled in Jesus Christ.

Little Judah

Jeremiah reflects the pressure of mighty empires upon much smaller kingdoms such as Judah and Israel, which never controlled more than 33,000 km² of territory between them. Judah stood at the crossroads of the great continents of Asia, Africa, and Europe. Yet the Lord promised the people of Judah that if they would cling to His Word, they could withstand all threats.

Egyptian empire; about 1,000,000 km²

Assyrian/ Babylonian empires; about 1,400,000 km²

God Calls Jeremiah

Jeremiah 1, 23, and 31

Words to Remember
I have loved you with an everlasting love; therefore I have continued My faithfulness to you. *Jeremiah 31:3*

Now the word of the LORD came to me, saying, "Before I formed you in the womb I knew you, and before you were born I consecrated you. I appointed you a prophet to the nations."

Then I said, "Ah, Lord GOD! I do not know how to speak, for I am only a youth."

But the LORD said to me, "Do not say, 'I am only a youth.' To all to whom I send you, you shall go. Whatever I command you, you shall speak. Do not be afraid of them. I am with you to deliver you, declares the LORD."

Then the LORD put out His hand and touched my mouth. And the LORD said to me, "Behold, I have put My words in your mouth. See, I have set you this day over nations and over kingdoms, to pluck up and to break down, to destroy and to overthrow, to build and to plant."

Here are some of the things God told Jeremiah to prophesy about Jesus and about God's promises to be with His people.

"Behold, the days are coming, declares the LORD, when I will raise up for David a righteous Branch. He shall reign as king and deal wisely. He shall execute justice and righteousness in the land. In His days Judah will be saved, and Israel will dwell securely. This is the name by which He will be called: 'The LORD is our righteousness.'"

"I have loved you with an everlasting love.
    Therefore I have continued My faithfulness to you.
Say, 'He who scattered Israel will gather him,
    and will keep him as a shepherd keeps his flock.'
I will turn their mourning into joy.
    I will comfort them, and give them gladness for sorrow."

"The days are coming, declares the LORD, when I will make a new covenant with the house of Israel and the house of Judah. I will put My law within them, and I will write it on their hearts. I will be their God, and they shall be My people. No longer shall each one teach his neighbor and each his brother, saying, 'Know the LORD.' They shall all know Me, from the least to the greatest, declares the LORD. For I will forgive their iniquity, and I will remember their sin no more."

DID YOU KNOW?

- Jeremiah was only a young man when God's call came to him. Some scholars think he may have been in his early teens!

- Jeremiah was among the most unpopular prophets. At one point, people from his hometown, Anathoth, plotted to assassinate him (11:18–23).

- Jeremiah is often called "the weeping prophet" because of the sad message of judgment he delivered and because so few believed him—or even listened to him.

The righteous shall live by his faith.

Habakkuk

640–609 BC Reign of Josiah (Judah) • c. 605 BC Habakkuk written • 587 BC Fall of Jerusalem

The righteous shall live by his faith.

Galatians 3:11 Romans 1:17 Hebrews 10:38

The little book of Habakkuk provides one of the major themes of the New Testament.

Arrogance   vs. Faith

Through Habakkuk, the Lord contrasted the foolish and the faithful in Judah. The prophet was to write his message on tablets and run to share it (Habakkuk 2:2).

Lamentations

722 BC Samaria (Israel) falls to Assyria • 628 BC Jeremiah called • 587 BC Babylonians take Jerusalem

As in **Jeremiah's** much longer prophecy, he placed his most hopeful passage at the heart of the Book of Lamentations, at 3:22–33. He assured the people that the Lord's "mercies never come to an end; they are new every morning; great is His faithfulness" (3:22–24).

God's People in Exile

The evildoers shall be cut off, but those who wait for the LORD shall inherit the land. Psalm 37:9

Sin is not a joke to God. Throughout the period of the kings, God had sent prophets to announce His anger over the sins of the kings and the people. Like Josiah and Hezekiah, some kings returned to following God's commands. But most became more and more evil.

It may seem odd, but if God didn't keep His promise to take away the kingdoms of Israel and Judah because of their sinfulness, how could we believe that God would keep His promise to send a Savior? So after repeatedly calling for repentance, after famines and wars, after miracles and promises of salvation, God acted. First, the Assyrians took all the people out of the land of Israel and scattered them throughout their empire. Then, about 140 years later, the Babylonians under King Nebuchadnezzar carried away almost all the people of Judah and destroyed the temple and the walls of Jerusalem. God cut the people off from the land in punishment for their sins.

But God did not forget His people. He saved them from death and even made them valuable leaders in their new countries. God promised them "a future and a hope" (Jeremiah 29:11). God kept that promise when Jesus came to restore the kingdom of God.

When you wonder where God is during difficult times, consider that He is preparing you for a better future. Kind of like lifting weights to build muscle, God allows you to be tested for a time to strengthen your faith and trust in Him. Even as God kept His word to destroy and to save, you also know the "Lord will rescue [you] from every evil deed and bring [you] safely into His heavenly kingdom" (2 Timothy 4:18).

Making Connections

"Exile" means to be cut off, to be sent away, to be separated. You might have experienced being in exile if others decided not to talk to you. Or maybe you were separated from family members and had to make new friends because you moved.

Jesus went through an exile. First, He had to leave His heavenly home to come to earth. He had to live as a human being with all of our discomforts and needs, like hunger and thirst. Jesus had to deal with people who didn't like Him. And when Jesus was on the cross, He experienced the absolute worst exile—He was separated from God the Father. Why? Because on the cross Jesus was carrying the sin of the whole world. God accepted Jesus' sacrifice and after three days Jesus came back to life and returned from His exile.

Before you became a child of God, you were in exile. Your sin put you outside the kingdom of God. Because Jesus went through His exile on the cross, He opened the way for you to be brought into God's kingdom. Jesus' death and resurrection won for you the forgiveness of your sins. In Baptism, you have been given the greatest gift—new life as a member of God's family. That means you will be among those worshiping King Jesus on His heavenly throne.

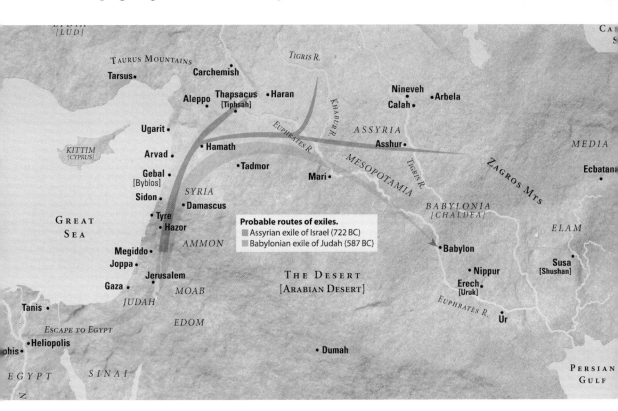

Probable routes of exiles.
- Assyrian exile of Israel (722 BC)
- Babylonian exile of Judah (587 BC)

Israel and Judah in Exile

2 Kings 17 and 24–25

Hoshea reigned over Israel in Samaria nine years. He did what was evil in the sight of the LORD. Against him came Shalmaneser king of Assyria. Hoshea paid him tribute. But the king of Assyria found treachery in Hoshea, bound him in prison, and captured Samaria. He carried the Israelites away to Assyria.

This occurred because the people of Israel had sinned against the LORD their God, who had brought them up out of the land of Egypt. Yet the LORD warned Israel and Judah by every prophet, saying, "Turn from your evil ways and keep My commandments." But they would not listen. They despised the LORD's **statutes** and His covenant. They went after false idols and became false. Therefore the LORD was angry with Israel and removed them out of His sight. Only the tribe of Judah was left.

Jehoiachin was king of Judah three months in Jerusalem. He did what was evil in the sight of the LORD. At that time the servants of Nebuchadnezzar king of Babylon besieged Jerusalem. Jehoiachin gave himself up to the king of Babylon. The king of Babylon took him prisoner and carried off all the treasures of the house of the LORD and of the king's house. He carried away all Jerusalem, all the officials, mighty men of valor, and craftsmen. None remained, except the poorest people of the land. The king of Babylon made Zedekiah king in the place of Jehoiachin.

Zedekiah reigned 11 years in Jerusalem. He did what was evil in the sight of the LORD. And Zedekiah rebelled against the king of Babylon. So Nebuchadnezzar came with all his army against Jerusalem. The army captured Zedekiah. They put out his eyes and bound him in chains and took him to Babylon.

The army burned the house of the LORD, the king's house, and all the houses of Jerusalem. They broke down the walls around Jerusalem. The people who were left in the city and those who had deserted to the king of Babylon, together with the rest of the multitude, the captain of the guard carried into **exile**. He left some of the poorest of the land to be vinedressers and plowmen.

In the 37th year of the exile of Jehoiachin king of Judah, the king of Babylon graciously freed Jehoiachin from prison. He spoke kindly to him and gave him a seat above the seats of the kings who were with him in Babylon. So Jehoiachin put off his prison garments. Every day of his life he dined regularly at the king's table, and the king gave him a regular allowance as long as he lived.

Words to Remember

Turn from your evil ways and keep My commandments and My statutes.
2 Kings 17:13

DID YOU KNOW?

- The Lord allowed Israel to fall and to go into exile as a warning to all generations of believers. The New Testament, too, warns us to guard our doctrine and life lest we fall away from the Lord.

- Jehoiachin was only eighteen years old when he became king.

- In the surrender of Jehoiachin, the Lord allows the dismantling of the temple David had planned and Solomon had built. Thanks be to God, He does not dwell in temples we make, but He dwells instead in the hearts of His people by faith.

Obadiah

587 BC Jerusalem temple destroyed • c. 587–533 BC Obadiah written • 538 BC Cyrus decrees exiles may return

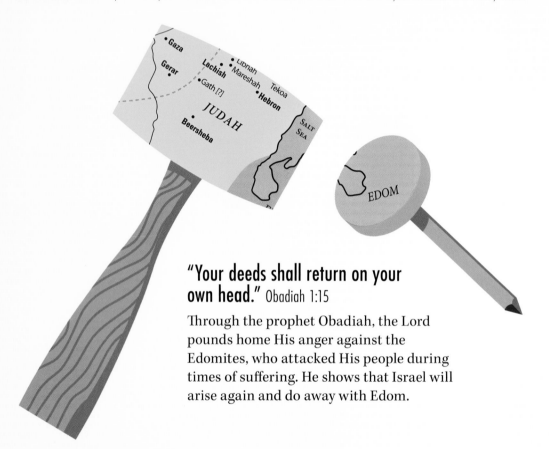

"Your deeds shall return on your own head." Obadiah 1:15

Through the prophet Obadiah, the Lord pounds home His anger against the Edomites, who attacked His people during times of suffering. He shows that Israel will arise again and do away with Edom.

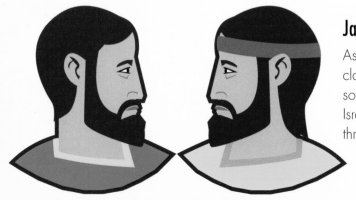

Jacob and Esau

As Jacob and Esau clashed (see page 34), so their descendants, Israel and Edom, clashed throughout their histories.

From the exile of Israel in 722 BC to the restoration of Judah in 537 BC, things were confusing for God's people. There were good kings and bad kings, true prophets and false prophets, Jeremiah 29:31 describes the important influence of false prophets like Abab, Zedekiah, and Shemaiah, who misled the people.

Kings and Events in Judah		Prophets of Judah and Exile	
Good	Hezekiah (715–686 BC)	Nahum	True
Bad	Manasseh (696–642 BC)		
Bad	Amon (642–640 BC)	Habakkuh	True
Good	Josiah (640–609 BC)	Zephaniah Huldah Jeremiah	True True True
Bad	Jehoahaz (609 BC)		
Bad	Jehoiakim (609–598 BC)	Uriah Daniel	True True
	First exiled (605 BC)		
Bad	Jehoiachinh (598–597 BC)	Exekiel	True
Bad	Zedekiah (597–587 BC)	Ahab, son of Koliah Zedekiah, son of Maaseiah Shemaiah the Nehelamite	False False False
	Fall of Jerusalem (587 BC)	Obadiah	
	Restoration of Judah (537 BC)		

Son of man,
I have made you
a watchman.

Ezekiel

593 BC Ezekiel's first vision • 573 BC Ezekiel's vision of new Jerusalem • 538 BC Cyrus decrees exiles may return

Themes in Ezekiel

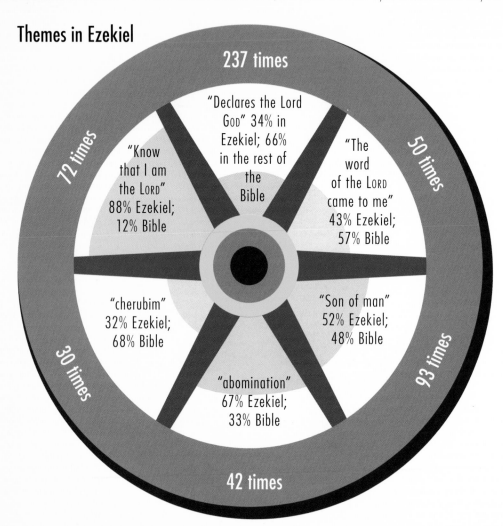

237 times

72 times

50 times

"Declares the Lord GOD" 34% in Ezekiel; 66% in the rest of the Bible

"Know that I am the LORD" 88% Ezekiel; 12% Bible

"The word of the LORD came to me" 43% Ezekiel; 57% Bible

"cherubim" 32% Ezekiel; 68% Bible

"Son of man" 52% Ezekiel; 48% Bible

30 times

93 times

"abomination" 67% Ezekiel; 33% Bible

42 times

Certain words and phrases repeat throughout Ezekiel's descriptions of his visions and prophecies. They illustrate important themes in the book, including the Lord's Word and knowledge about Him (top half of wheel). Characters such as the cherubim support God's throne; Ezekiel as the "son of man" describes the abominations in Judah (bottom of the wheel). In fact, when describing God's throne, Ezekiel refers to wheels more often than other biblical writers—63 percent of all references!

Ezekiel's Vision of the New Israel

The Lord's angel showed Ezekiel the new Israel in a vision of a temple. Under the Lord's inspiration, Ezekiel devoted more than a fourth of his prophecy (chs. 40–48) to describing this vision of an ideal temple. Using Old Testament imagery and setting, he described the wonders of the new covenant. The new Israel he saw in chapters 33–39 would serve the Lord in holiness, as seen in chapters 40–48.

Because of Ezekiel's priestly interest in detail and because of his elaborate visions, his prophecies are among the most challenging to study in the Old Testament.

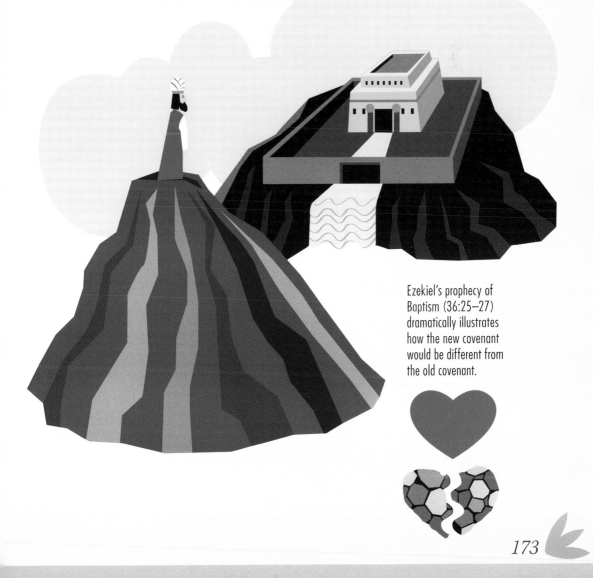

Ezekiel's prophecy of Baptism (36:25–27) dramatically illustrates how the new covenant would be different from the old covenant.

God's Promises to the Exiles

Ezekiel 8 and 36

God said to the prophet Ezekiel, "Son of man, do you see what they are doing, the great **abominations** that the house of Israel are committing, to drive Me far from My sanctuary? Therefore I will act in wrath. My eye will not spare, nor will I have pity. Though they cry in My ears with a loud voice, I will not hear."

Words to Remember

I will give you a new heart, and a new spirit I will put within you.
Ezekiel 36:26

Then the glory of the LORD went out from the temple and stood over the cherubim. The cherubim lifted up their wings and mounted up from the earth before my eyes, with the wheels beside them. They stood at the entrance of the east gate of the house of the LORD, and the glory of the God of Israel was over them.

The Spirit of the LORD fell upon me. He said to me, "Say, Thus says the LORD: I will give you into the hands of foreigners. I will judge you at the border of Israel, and you shall know that I am the LORD. For you have not obeyed My rules, but have acted according to the rules of the nations that are around you."

Later, the word of the LORD came to Ezekiel: "Say to the house of Israel, Thus says the Lord GOD: The nations will know that I am the LORD. I will take you from the nations and gather you from all the countries and bring you into your own land. I will sprinkle clean water on you, and you shall be clean from all your uncleannesses. From all your idols I will cleanse you. I will give you a new heart. A new spirit I will put within you. I will remove the heart of stone from your flesh and give you a heart of flesh. I will put My Spirit within you, and cause you to walk in My statutes and be careful to obey My rules. You shall dwell in the land that I gave to your fathers. You shall be My people, and I will be your God. I will make the fruit of the tree and the increase of the field abundant, that you may never again suffer the disgrace of famine.

"Thus says the Lord GOD: On the day that I cleanse you from all your iniquities, I will cause the cities to be inhabited. The waste places shall be rebuilt. And the land that was **desolate** shall be tilled. They will say, 'This land that was desolate has become like the Garden of Eden. The waste and desolate and ruined cities are now fortified and inhabited.' Then the nations that are left all around you shall know that I am the LORD. I have rebuilt the ruined places and replanted that which was desolate. I am the LORD. I have spoken, and I will do it."

DID YOU KNOW?

- Ezekiel was taken into exile with thousands of other Judeans in 597 BC. The Lord called him as a prophet in 593 BC, and his ministry lasted twenty-two years. He never got to return home.

- Ezekiel's name means "God strengthens." God strengthened Ezekiel for ministry, and He taught His people repentance and patience in captivity.

- The first thirty-two chapters of Ezekiel speak mostly Law to God's people. Once the temple lay in ruins, the people finally began to repent and Ezekiel wrote chapters 33–48 to comfort God's penitent people.

Daniel

605 BC Daniel exiled to Babylon • 538 BC Cyrus decrees exiles may return • 516 BC Second temple completed

Ancient emperors such as Nebuchadnezzar of Babylon and Cyrus of Persia shared a dream of ruling an ideal, everlasting kingdom. But each ruler would in turn lose his kingdom to someone else. Daniel sees in his visions that the Lord would establish an everlasting kingdom not through war but through His Word.

Whereas the Bible as a whole averages three references to kings or kingdoms per chapter, the twelve chapters in the Book of Daniel average more than twenty references per chapter, for a total of 247 references for the book. No other prophet focuses so fully on the kingdoms of the earth and the everlasting Kingdom God will reveal. Note that as Daniel's prophecies focus on the distant future in the later chapters, references to kings and kingdoms diminish, for there will be only one King in the end.

57
37
33
24
26
21
19
16
8
3
3
0

Dreams and Visions in Daniel

This bowl-shaped sundial shows how the Book of Daniel is largely descriptions of **seven dreams and visions** that tell of present (chs. 4–5) and future (chs. 2; 7–12) events. God gives the first dreams and visions to the rulers of Babylon (chs. 2; 4–5). He then inspires Daniel to interpret how these dreams and visions will be fulfilled, demonstrating that Daniel's God is the true God. Then, God provides Daniel with his own dreams and visions, which reveal distant events, including the coming of God's kingdom through the ministry of the Messiah. God's messengers interpret the first dream and vision to Daniel (chs. 7–8). The last two visions (chs. 9–12) are not interpreted, but by this point, the reader has read how Daniel and the Lord's messengers have interpreted the first five dreams and visions, which prepares one for interpreting the last two.

1
2 Great Image
3
4 Great Tree
5 Writing on Wall
6
7 Four Beasts
8 Ram and Goat
9 70 Weeks
10 Kings
11
12

Dreams/Visions of Rulers

Dreams/Visions of Daniel

The Book of Daniel

Three Men in the Fiery Furnace

Daniel 3

King Nebuchadnezzar made an image of gold and gathered all his officials to come to the dedication. As the officials stood before the image, the herald proclaimed, "When you hear the music, you are to fall down and worship the golden image. Whoever does not fall down and worship shall immediately be cast into a burning fiery furnace." As soon as all the people heard the music, they fell down and worshiped the image.

Words to Remember
Blessed be the God of Shadrach, Meshach, and Abednego, who has sent His angel and delivered His servants. *Daniel 3:28*

At that time certain Chaldeans declared to King Nebuchadnezzar, "O king, live forever! There are certain Jews whom you have appointed over the affairs of Babylon: Shadrach, Meshach, and Abednego. These men, O king, pay no attention to you. They do not serve your gods or worship the golden image."

Then Nebuchadnezzar in furious rage asked Shadrach, Meshach, and Abednego, "Is it true that you do not serve my gods or worship the golden image? When you hear the music, if you fall down and worship the image, well and good. But if you do not worship, you shall immediately be cast into a burning fiery furnace. And who is the god who will deliver you out of my hands?"

Shadrach, Meshach, and Abednego said, "Our God whom we serve is able to deliver us from the burning fiery furnace. But if not, O king, we will not serve your gods or worship the golden image."

Nebuchadnezzar ordered the furnace heated seven times more than it was usually heated. He ordered some of the mighty men of his army to bind Shadrach, Meshach, and Abednego. They were bound in their clothes. Because the furnace was overheated, the flame killed those men who took up Shadrach, Meshach, and Abednego. Then King Nebuchadnezzar was astonished. He declared, "Did we not cast three men bound into the fire? I see four men unbound, walking in the midst of the fire. They are not hurt. The appearance of the fourth is like a son of the gods."

Nebuchadnezzar declared, "Shadrach, Meshach, and Abednego, servants of the Most High God, come here!" They came out from the fire. The officials saw that the hair of their heads was not singed, their cloaks were not harmed, and no smell of fire had come upon them. Nebuchadnezzar said, "Blessed be the God of Shadrach, Meshach, and Abednego, who has sent His angel and delivered His servants, who trusted in Him. There is no other god who is able to rescue in this way." Then the king promoted Shadrach, Meshach, and Abednego.

DID YOU KNOW?

- The fiery furnace was probably a smelting kiln with openings on the top and side. Burning was an ancient method of execution (Leviticus 20:14; 21:9).

- The three men were not saved "from" the fire but "in" the fire. Like the burning bush in Exodus 3, they were not consumed.

- There are times when it is not God's will to rescue believers from danger or death. Genuine faith trusts God whether or not He preserves believers when they face trials.

Daniel in the Lions' Den

Daniel 6

It pleased Darius to set over the kingdom 120 satraps and over them 3 presidents, of whom Daniel was one. Daniel became distinguished, because an excellent spirit was in him. The king planned to set Daniel over the whole kingdom. Then the presidents and the satraps sought to find a ground for complaint against Daniel.

Words to Remember

The God of Daniel . . . is the living God, enduring forever; His kingdom shall never be destroyed, and His dominion shall be to the end. *Daniel 6:26*

These presidents and satraps came by agreement to the king and said, "O King Darius, live forever! Establish an **ordinance** that whoever makes petition to any god or man for 30 days, except to you, O king, shall be cast into the den of lions. Sign the document, so that it cannot be changed." Therefore King Darius signed the document.

When Daniel knew that the document had been signed, he went to his house. Three times a day he got down on his knees and prayed and gave thanks before his God, as he had done previously. The men found Daniel praying to God. They said to the king, "O king! Did you not say that anyone who makes petition to any god or man within 30 days, except to you, O king, shall be cast into the den of lions?" The king agreed that he had made the law. The men said, "Daniel pays no attention to you, O king, or the law. He makes his petition three times a day."

The king was much distressed and set his mind to deliver Daniel. He labored till the sun went down to rescue him, but the law could not be changed. So Daniel was cast into the den of lions. The king declared to Daniel, "May your God, whom you serve continually, deliver you!" A stone was laid on the mouth of the den. The king sealed it with his own signet. Then he spent the night fasting.

At break of day, the king went in haste to the den of lions. The king declared, "O Daniel, servant of the living God, has your God, whom you serve continually, been able to deliver you from the lions?"

Daniel said, "O king, live forever! My God sent His angel and shut the lions' mouths. They have not harmed me, because I was found blameless before Him. Also before you, O king, I have done no harm."

The king commanded that Daniel be taken up out of the den. No kind of harm was found on him, because he had trusted in his God. The king commanded, and those men who had maliciously accused Daniel were brought and cast into the den of lions—they, their children, and their wives. Before they reached the bottom of the den, the lions overpowered them and broke all their bones in pieces.

DID YOU KNOW?

- Daniel was taken into exile in Babylon after Nebuchadnezzar's first invasion in 605 BC. He was likely a teenager at the time. He became a high-ranking official in the Babylonian government.

- Daniel is written in both Hebrew and Aramaic.

- The children and wives of Daniel's accusers were thrown into the den as well, probably because of a fear of conspiracy.

Daniel Sees Heaven

Daniel 7

In the first year of Belshazzar king of Babylon, Daniel saw a dream and visions of his head as he lay in his bed. Then he wrote down the dream and told the sum of the matter. Daniel declared, "As I looked,

> thrones were placed,
>> and the **Ancient of Days** took His seat;
> His clothing was white as snow,
>> and the hair of His head like pure wool;
> His throne was fiery flames.
>> Its wheels were burning fire.
> A stream of fire issued
>> and came out from before Him.
>> A thousand thousands served Him,
>> and ten thousand times ten thousand stood
>> before Him.
> The court sat in judgment,
>> and the books were opened.

> "I saw in the night visions,
>> and behold, with the clouds of heaven
>> there came one like a son of man.
> And He came to the Ancient of Days
>> and was presented before Him.
> And to Him was given dominion
>> and glory and a kingdom,
> that all peoples, nations, and languages
>> should serve Him.
> His dominion is an everlasting dominion,
>> which shall not pass away,
> and His kingdom one
>> that shall not be destroyed.

"As for me, Daniel, my spirit within me was anxious, and the visions of my head alarmed me. I approached one of those who stood there and asked him the truth concerning all this. So he told me, 'The **saints** of the Most High shall receive the kingdom and possess the kingdom forever, forever and ever.'"

Words to Remember

With the clouds of heaven there came one like a son of man. . . . And to Him was given dominion and glory and a kingdom, that all peoples, nations, and languages should serve Him. *Daniel 7:13–14*

DID YOU KNOW?

- Most of what the Bible tells us about heaven is conveyed to us in symbolic language, and while we can gain some insight about heaven from this, there are many questions that will be answered only by personal experience when we see it for ourselves.

- Daniel 7–12 is, for the most part, apocalyptic in style. It uses dreamlike images to communicate ideas and emotions, and it tells about the future. Much of what Daniel predicted took place after Daniel died and before Jesus was born.

God's People Return to Judah

For you who fear My name, the sun of righteousness shall rise with healing in its wings. *Malachi 4:2*

After about 70 years in captivity, King Cyrus of Persia announced that he would send the Jewish people back to Jerusalem to rebuild the temple. During the next 100 years or so, the temple and the city of Jerusalem and its walls would be rebuilt. God had kept His promise through the prophets Ezekiel and Jeremiah that the people of God would return to the land of Judah. Their time of testing in exile was over.

Ezra and Nehemiah not only led God's people in rebuilding, they also called the people back to obeying God. At the dedication of the temple and of the city walls, the people pledged to walk in God's commands. The people rejoiced that they were able to worship God in the rebuilt temple, that God granted them safety behind the city's rebuilt walls, and that the nations surrounding them realized that God was watching over them. God was even protecting those Jews who remained in Persia. Through Queen Esther, God kept them safe from the plans of the evil Haman.

God used Malachi to announce once again His plans for sending a Savior. First, there would be a messenger, a second Elijah, to prepare the way. Then, the "messenger of the covenant," the "sun of righteousness" would come to His temple. About 400 years after Malachi, God sent John the Baptist, who announced the coming of the Lamb of God. Then Jesus, King David's descendant, entered the city of Jerusalem and worshiped God in the temple. In Jesus, the Righteous One of God, the whole world has healing from sin.

Making Connections

Waiting is difficult. The Jewish people had to wait in exile, praying to God to return them to Jerusalem. In His own time, God kept His promise, and the city of Jerusalem, the walls, and the temple were rebuilt.

Throughout the Old Testament, God's people waited for the Messiah. For thousands of years—from Adam and Eve to the time of Malachi and for about 400 years after him—people wondered if now was the time that God would keep His promise. But God had a plan, and it wasn't yet the right time to send Jesus.

You may not like to wait either. Sometimes when you have to wait for a long time, you begin to doubt if the "big day" will ever come! But when it finally does, everything is even better than you imagined.

That's how God's plans unfold here on earth. He knows the best time and the best way to keep His promises. He sent Jesus at the perfect time to save you and all people from sin. And God will keep you safely in His care until it's the perfect time to bring you to Himself in heaven.

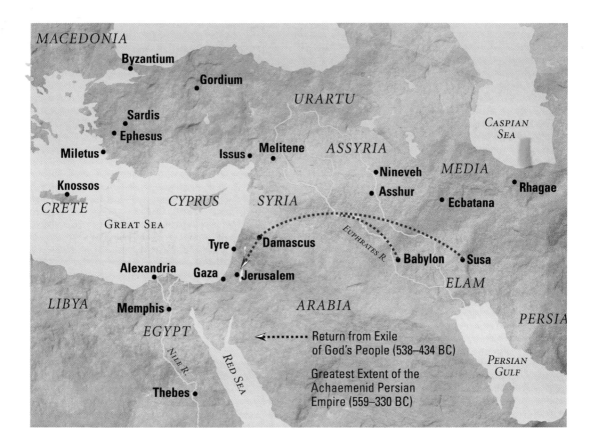

Yours is the kingdom, O Lord.

1 & 2 Chronicles

960 BC Solomon dedicates temple • 538 BC Cyrus's decree • 516 BC Second temple dedication

Chronicles portrays Israel's long succession from the beginning of human history to the dynasty of David, the greatest king of Israel, who received the promise that God would send a Savior to His people. In this way, the writer provided a sense of grand history and comfort to defeated Israel, allowing them to see that the Lord was not done with them yet.

David

Jesse

Boaz

Judah

Jacob (Israel)

Abraham

Noah

Adam

Encouragement through History

The Chronicler elevates David's involvement with the temple, omits many of David's faults, and diminishes Solomon so that David is clearly seen as the ideal leader of Israel (see eraser marks below). Overall, he writes a more positive history to inspire those returning from exile, especially the Levites, who would lead the temple services.

David's Mighty Men
(1 Chronicles 12)

David and Bathsheba
(2 Samuel 11:2–27)

Nathan's Rebuke
(2 Samuel 12:1–15)

Fallout from David's Sin
(2 Samuel 13:1–22)

Absalom's Revenge (2 Samuel 14)

Joab's Scheme (2 Samuel 14)

Absalom's Rebellion
(2 Samuel 15:1–19:8b)

David's Return from Exile
(2 Samuel 19:8c–43)

Sheba's Rebellion
(2 Samuel 20:1–22)

Avenging of Gibeonites
(2 Samuel 21:1–14)

Abishai Rescues David
(2 Samuel 21:15–17)

David's Temple Preparation
(1 Chronicles 22:2–5)

Solomon Charged with Building the Temple (1 Chronicles 22:6–19)

David Organizes the Levites
(1 Chronicles 23)

David Organizes Priests
(1 Chronicles 24)

David Organizes Music
(1 Chronicles 25)

David's Division of Gate Keepers
(1 Chronicles 26:1–19)

David's Treasurers and Officials
(1 Chronicles 26:20–32)

Solomon's Struggles to Gain the Throne (1 Kings 1:5–27; 2:13–46)

Solomon's Wisdom
(1 Kings 3:16–28)

Solomon's Officials
(1 Kings 4:1–19)

Solomon's Projects
(1 Kings 7:1–12)

Solomon's Adversaries and Apostasy (1 Kings 11:1–40)

Abijah's Reign (2 Chronicles 13)

Asa's Reign and Reform
(2 Chronicles 14:1–15:15)

Jehoshaphat's Reign
(2 Chronicles 17)

Jehoshaphat's Reforms and Victory
(2 Chronicles 19:1–20:30)

Joash's Treachery
(2 Chronicles 24:15–22)

Uzziah's War
(2 Chronicles 26:6–15)

Ahaz and Judah Defeated
(2 Chronicles 28:8–15)

Hezekiah's Reforms
(2 Chronicles 29:3–31:21)

The Chronicler ended his books with a prophecy from Jeremiah, which foretold that God's people would return from exile after seventy years. This prophecy was fulfilled when Cyrus, king of Persia, decreed that Israel could rebuild the temple at Jerusalem. The faith and the people would survive!

Return to
the Lord, and He
will gather you.

Ezra & Nehemiah

538 BC Cyrus decrees return to Judah • 516 BC Second temple built • 445 BC Nehemiah repairs Jerusalem walls

Although the Books of Ezra and Nehemiah were probably written independently, they have long stood together and cover the same topics and time in Israel's history.

Altar. After Israel returned from exile, one of their main challenges was to restore worship. They began by building an altar for burnt offerings (Ezra 3).

Second temple. Although Israel started to rebuild the temple, they were delayed due to hostile neighbors. They only completed the temple twenty years later.

Priests. A large number of priests returned to serve at the new altar and temple in Jerusalem: 4,289, according to Nehemiah 7:39–42. However, the Levites were not so excited to return and numbered only 360, plus some other temple servants.

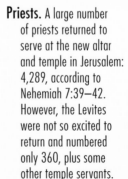

Governor. Nehemiah returned temporarily to become the governor of Judah. His chief task was to inspect the broken-down walls of Jerusalem and to organize the people to rebuild them.

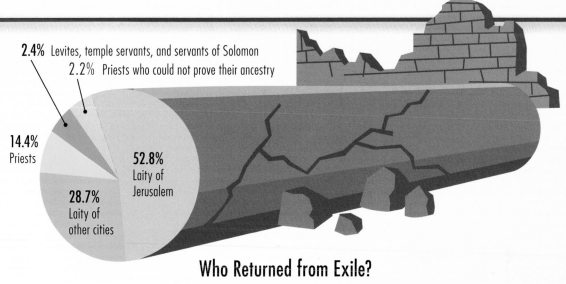

2.4% Levites, temple servants, and servants of Solomon

2.2% Priests who could not prove their ancestry

14.4%
Priests

52.8%
Laity of
Jerusalem

28.7%
Laity of
other cities

Who Returned from Exile?

The persons named and numbered in Ezra 2 give us a picture of who returned from exile in Babylon. (A similar list appears in Nehemiah 7.) Ezra enumerates or names 29,818 people. Most mentioned were from the tribes of Judah, Benjamin, and Levi. A grand total of 42,360 people returned along with 7,337 servants, who were probably not Israelites.

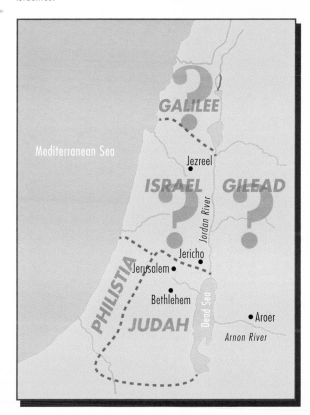

What Happened to the Other Tribes?

The tribe of Simeon settled in Judah much earlier, when Israel entered the Promised Land (Joshua 19:9). We know very little about what happened to the tribes that the Assyrians sent into exile in 722 BC (2 Kings 15:8–17:23). However, 2 Chronicles 30 tells us that some members of Asher, Manasseh, Zebulun, Ephraim, and Issachar attended Passover at Jerusalem in 715 BC. They may have mingled with the southern tribes and so preserved their heritage in Israel (see 1 Chronicles 9:3). Other members of the northern tribes intermarried with foreigners and became the Samaritans (2 Kings 17:24–41). The apocryphal book of Tobit mentions a member of the tribe of Naphtali living in exile (1:1–2), but otherwise we know little else. For that reason, the northern tribes of Israel are often called *"the lost tribes."*

A New Temple and a New Wall

The Books of Ezra and Nehemiah

In the first year Cyrus was king of Persia, he made a proclamation: "The God of heaven has given me all the kingdoms of the earth, and He has charged me to build Him a house at Jerusalem. Whoever is among you of all His people, let him go up to Jerusalem and rebuild the house of the LORD. And let each survivor be assisted by the men of his place with silver and gold, with goods and with beasts, besides freewill offerings for the house of God that is in Jerusalem."

Words to Remember

Do not be grieved, for the joy of the LORD is your strength.
Nehemiah 8:10

Then the heads of Judah and Benjamin, and the priests and the Levites, and everyone whose spirit God had stirred rose up to rebuild the house of the LORD. All around them aided them with vessels of silver, with gold, with goods, with beasts, and with costly goods, besides all that was freely offered. Cyrus also brought out the vessels of the house of the LORD that Nebuchadnezzar had carried away from Jerusalem.

They finished their building by decree of the God of Israel and by decree of Kings Cyrus and Darius and Artaxerxes of Persia. And the people of Israel, the priests and the Levites, and the rest of the returned exiles celebrated the **dedication** of this house of God with joy. The returned exiles kept the Passover with joy, for the LORD had made them joyful.

A little later, Nehemiah learned that the wall of Jerusalem was broken and its gates destroyed by fire. While serving wine to King Artaxerxes, Nehemiah asked, "If it pleases the king, and if your servant has found favor in your sight, send me to Judah, to the city of my fathers' graves, that I may rebuild it." The king agreed.

So Nehemiah went to Jerusalem and inspected the walls and the gates. He said to the people who would do the work, "Come, let us build the wall of Jerusalem, that we may no longer suffer **derision**. The God of heaven will make us prosper, and we His servants will arise and build."

The wall was finished in 52 days. When all the enemies heard of it, all the nations were afraid. They knew that this work had been accomplished with the help of God.

At the dedication of the wall of Jerusalem, two choirs offered praise to God. The people offered great sacrifices that day and rejoiced, for God had made them rejoice with great joy. The women and children also rejoiced. And the joy of Jerusalem was heard far away. On that day they read from the Book of Moses in the hearing of the people.

DID YOU KNOW?

- Cyrus was not likely a believer. He learned the name of Israel's God from the Judean exiles and was tolerant of all religions, letting conquered peoples retain their national gods.

- Ezra and Nehemiah were once combined as one book, titled "Ezra." As a result, the Book of Nehemiah was sometimes named after the prophet Ezra in some translations of the Bible.

- *Nehemiah* means "the Lord has comforted." In this book, we read about the comfort God brought to His people as He restored them to their homeland after exile in Babylon.

Haggai

538 BC Cyrus decrees exiles may return • c. 520 BC Haggai written • 516 BC Second temple completed

Although the Judeans struggled to rebuild the temple and their homes after the exile, the Lord foretold a day when the wealth of the nations would flow into His house, the new temple.

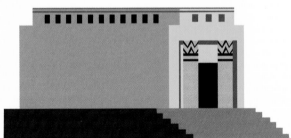

Date

The prophecies of Haggai and Zechariah 1–8 are the most precisely dated in the Bible since they use a calendar rather than just the traditional dating based on kings' reigns.

Not by might nor by power, but by My Spirit.

Zechariah

538 BC Cyrus decrees exiles may return • c. 520 BC Zechariah written • 516 BC Second temple completed

Visions of Zechariah's Day
Chapters 1–8

Visions of the Future Day of the Lord
Chapters 9–14

Through a series of symbolic visions, the Lord showed Zechariah not only His deeds in the present but also His plans for the future restoration of His people, when a Good Shepherd would lead His people.

Deliverance
will arise.

Esther

516 BC Second temple completed • 478 BC Ahasuerus (Xerxes) marries Esther • 445 BC Walls of Jerusalem restored

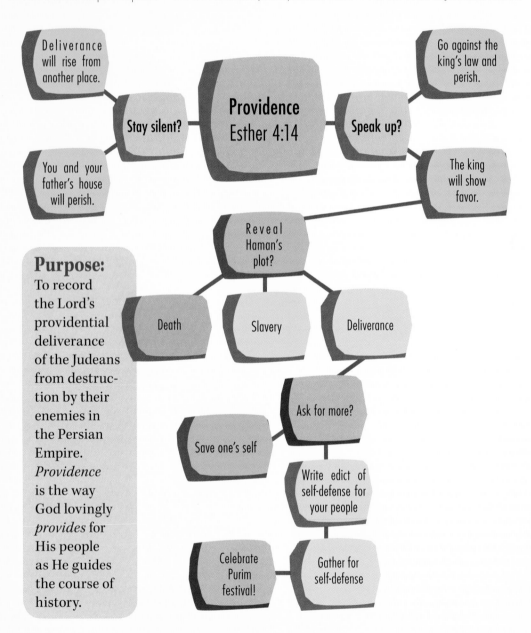

Deliverance will rise from another place.

Stay silent?

Providence
Esther 4:14

Speak up?

Go against the king's law and perish.

You and your father's house will perish.

The king will show favor.

Reveal Haman's plot?

Death

Slavery

Deliverance

Ask for more?

Save one's self

Write edict of self-defense for your people

Gather for self-defense

Celebrate Purim festival!

Purpose:
To record the Lord's providential deliverance of the Judeans from destruction by their enemies in the Persian Empire. *Providence* is the way God lovingly *provides* for His people as He guides the course of history.

Some Old Testament Names for God

Esther never mentions God by name or title but only refers to His providential care. Most Old Testament Books use names and titles like the following.

Almighty *Father*

glory of the LORD

God *God Most High*

God of heaven God of hosts

GOD OF ISRAEL

Holy One of Israel **KING**

living God Lord

LORD LORD God

LORD of hosts Mighty One

Most High REDEEMER

Rock Spirit

Esther and the King

Esther 1–2

In those days when King Ahasuerus sat on his royal throne in Susa, he gave a feast for all his officials and servants. Queen Vashti also gave a feast for the women. The king was merry with wine, and he commanded that Queen Vashti be brought before the king, in order to show the peoples and the princes her beauty. But Queen Vashti refused to come. At this the king became enraged.

The king said, "According to the law, what is to be done to Queen Vashti?"

One of the princes said, "If it please the king, Vashti may never again come before you. And her royal position should be given to another who is better than she." This advice pleased the king and the princes, so all the beautiful young women were gathered so the king could choose a new queen.

Now there was a Jew in Susa whose name was Mordecai. He had been among the captives whom Nebuchadnezzar had carried away. He was bringing up Esther, the daughter of his uncle, for she had neither father nor mother. The young woman was lovely to look at. Esther also was taken into the king's palace and put in custody of Hegai, who had charge of the women. Esther pleased him and won his favor. Esther had not told anyone that she was Jewish because Mordecai told her not to.

When Esther went in to the king, the king loved Esther more than all the women. She won grace and favor in his sight. He set the royal crown on her head and made her queen instead of Vashti. Then the king gave a great feast for all his officials and servants. It was Esther's feast.

Now Mordecai was sitting at the king's gate when two of the king's servants became angry and sought to lay hands on King Ahasuerus. Mordecai told the plot to Queen Esther. Esther told the king in the name of Mordecai. When the affair was investigated and found to be true, the men were both hanged on the gallows. And it was recorded in the book of the chronicles in the presence of the king.

After these things King Ahasuerus promoted Haman above all the officials. All the king's servants bowed down to Haman, for the king had so commanded. But Mordecai did not bow down. When Haman saw that Mordecai did not bow down, Haman was filled with fury. So Haman sought to destroy all the Jews, the people of Mordecai, throughout the whole kingdom of Ahasuerus.

Words to Remember

Esther had not made known her kindred or her people, as Mordecai had commanded her, for Esther obeyed Mordecai just as when she was brought up by him. *Esther 2:20*

DID YOU KNOW?

• The Book of Esther does not mention God's name, nor does it say anything about worship, the temple, or sacrifice. Yet the Lord is clearly at work, preserving His covenant promises in the events Esther records.

• Ahasuerus—better known by his Greek name, Xerxes—was the grandson of Cyrus the Great, who had issued the decree allowing the Judeans in captivity to return to their homeland.

• Esther was taken in to the king and made queen four years after Vashti's rejection.

God Saves His People

Esther 3–8

Words to Remember
The king allowed the Jews who were in every city to gather and defend their lives.
Esther 8:11

Haman convinced King Ahasuerus to support a plan to kill all the Jews in his kingdom. When Mordecai learned of the plan, he asked Esther to go to the king on behalf of her people. Esther said, "All the king's servants know that if any man or woman goes to the king without being called, there is but one law—to be put to death. The only exception is if the king holds out the golden scepter so that he may live."

Mordecai said, "Who knows whether you have not come to the kingdom for such a time as this?"

Esther agreed to talk with the king. She asked Mordecai to gather all the Jews in Susa and fast on her behalf. On the third day, Esther put on her royal robes and stood in the inner court of the king's palace. When the king saw Queen Esther, he held out the golden scepter. The king said, "What is your request? It shall be given you, even to the half of my kingdom." Esther invited the king and Haman to a feast.

On the second day, as the king and Haman were drinking wine after the feast, the king again said to Esther, "What is your wish, Queen Esther? It shall be granted you. Even to the half of my kingdom, it shall be fulfilled."

Then Queen Esther answered, "If I have found favor in your sight, and if it please the king, let my life be granted me for my wish, and my people for my request. For we are to be destroyed, to be killed, and to be annihilated."

King Ahasuerus said, "Who is he, and where is he, who has dared to do this?"

Esther said, "This wicked Haman!"

The king arose in his wrath and went into the palace garden, but Haman stayed to beg for his life from Queen Esther. The king returned as Haman was falling on the couch where Esther was. The king said, "Will he even assault the queen in my presence, in my own house?" So they hanged Haman on the gallows. Then the wrath of the king abated.

On that day King Ahasuerus gave to Queen Esther the house of Haman. And Mordecai came before the king, and the king took off his signet ring and gave it to Mordecai. Esther set Mordecai over the house of Haman. Then Esther fell at the king's feet and wept and pleaded with him to avert the evil plan of Haman. So an edict was written, saying that the king allowed the Jews to defend their lives. In every province and in every city, wherever the king's command and his edict reached, there was gladness and joy among the Jews.

DID YOU KNOW?

- The Book of Esther explains how the Judeans came to celebrate the Feast of Purim. The festival is named *Purim*, which means "lot," because Haman chose the date on which he planned to massacre the Jews by casting lots (a random-selection process like rolling dice).

- Persian law stated that anyone approaching the king unsummoned would be killed unless the king gave immediate pardon. This protected the king from assassination as well as from annoying, petty concerns.

- Even though Haman was dead, his edict lived on. It was impossible for the Persian king to rescind a decree that had gone out in his name, so he issued a second decree to counter the effects of the first.

Behold, I send
My messenger.

Malachi

516 BC Second temple completed • c. 430 BC Malachi written • 334–323 BC Conquests of Alexander the Great

The last book of the Old Testament points directly to God's plans in the New Testament, when John the Baptist would prepare the way of the Lord Jesus, who would cleanse the Jerusalem temple and teach there. God's people would have to wait 400 years for the fulfillment of these prophecies.

The Time between the Testaments

334–323 BC Conquests of Alexander the Great • 167 BC Maccabean Revolt • 516 BC Second temple completed

Alongside the Old Testament and New Testament, Christians may consult a third set of books. They were written during the time between the testaments and are called the "Apocrypha." That name probably comes from a Greek word that means "hidden," because in the early years, they were kept at churches as helpful books to read, but they were not read publicly before the congregations. The persons who wrote the Apocrypha were not prophets, since the prophets had ceased to speak, as 1 Maccabees 9:27; 14:41 explains.

Some Christians may read the books of the Apocrypha privately or in study groups for devotion or edification. They are essential reading if you want to understand what was happening to God's people in the four hundred years between the Old and New Testaments, but books of the Apocrypha do not have the same authority as books of the Old and New Testaments.

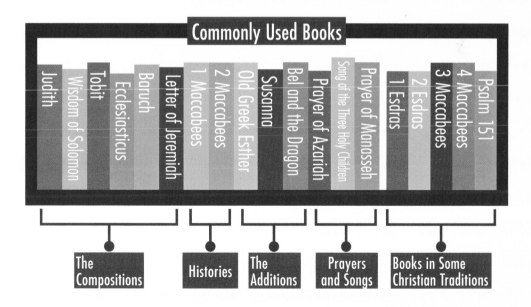

Commonly Used Books

Judith · Wisdom of Solomon · Tobit · Ecclesiasticus · Baruch · Letter of Jeremiah · 1 Maccabees · 2 Maccabees · Old Greek Esther · Susanna · Bel and the Dragon · Prayer of Azariah · Song of the Three Holy Children · Prayer of Manasseh · 1 Esdras · 2 Esdras · 3 Maccabees · 4 Maccabees · Psalm 151

The Compositions | Histories | The Additions | Prayers and Songs | Books in Some Christian Traditions

Waiting for God's Messenger

The Book of Malachi

The word of the LORD to Israel by Malachi:

"From the rising of the sun to its setting My name will be great among the nations. In every place incense will be offered to My name, and a pure offering.

"Behold, I send My messenger. He will prepare the way before Me. The Lord whom you seek will suddenly come to His temple. The messenger of the covenant in whom you delight, behold, He is coming, says the LORD of hosts. But who can endure the day of His coming? Who can stand when He appears? For He is like a **refiner's fire** and like **fullers' soap**. He will sit as a refiner and purifier of silver. He will purify the sons of Levi and refine them like gold and silver. They will bring offerings in righteousness to the LORD. Then the offering of Judah and Jerusalem will be pleasing to the LORD as in the days of old.

"For I the LORD do not change. Therefore you, O children of Jacob, are not consumed. From the days of your fathers you have turned aside from My statutes and have not kept them. Return to Me, and I will return to you, says the LORD of hosts."

Then those who feared the LORD spoke with one another. The LORD paid attention and heard them. A book of remembrance was written before Him of those who feared the LORD and esteemed His name. "They shall be Mine, says the LORD of hosts, in the day when I make up My treasured possession. I will spare them as a man spares his son who serves him. Then once more you shall see the distinction between the righteous and the wicked, between one who serves God and one who does not serve Him.

"For the day is coming, burning like an oven, when all the arrogant and all evildoers will be stubble. The day that is coming shall set them ablaze, says the LORD of hosts. It will leave them neither root nor branch. But for you who fear My name, the sun of righteousness shall rise with healing in its wings. You shall go out leaping like calves from the stall. You shall tread down the wicked. They will be ashes under the soles of your feet, on the day when I act, says the LORD of hosts.

"Remember the law of My servant Moses, the rules that I commanded him at Horeb for all Israel.

"Behold, I will send you Elijah the prophet before the great and awesome day of the LORD comes. He will turn the hearts of fathers to their children and the hearts of children to their fathers."

Words to Remember

Behold, I send My messenger, and he will prepare the way before Me. *Malachi 3:1*

DID YOU KNOW?

- Malachi was the last prophet in Old Testament times. Between Malachi's work and that of John the Baptist lay four hundred years of silence, when no prophetic voice was heard in Israel.

- In the Book of Malachi, the prophet asks twenty-two rhetorical questions in just fifty-five verses. He uses these questions to argue against the Judeans and to accuse them as people who certainly know better than to pursue the sins that were distracting them from true worship.

- When Jews celebrate the Passover, they set an extra place for Elijah to symbolize his return to proclaim the coming of the Savior, as predicted in Malachi 4:5.

The New Testament

Jesus opened His mouth and taught them.

Matthew

2 BC Birth of Jesus • AD 33 Resurrection, Ascension, Pentecost • c. AD 50 Matthew written

Matthew presents about half of Jesus' words in **five major discourses**, or speeches:

- Sermon on the Mount (chs. 5–7)
- Missionary Discourse (10:1–11:1)
- Parables Discourse (13:1–52)
- Forgiveness Discourse (ch. 18)
- End Times Discourse (chs. 24–25).

60 percent words

About 60 percent of the verses in Matthew contain the words of Jesus — more than the other Gospels.

40 percent deeds

Matthew also collected many examples of Jesus' deeds, such as in chapters 8–9.

Key Themes

The birth and background of Jesus; the kingdom of heaven; calling someone to repentance; Baptism

The Four Gospels

Gospels are unique writings that present the words and deeds of Jesus to teach who Jesus is and how He accomplishes our salvation.

Luke
50 percent words
50 percent deeds

Mark
40 percent words
60 percent deeds

Matthew
60 percent words
40 percent deeds

John
50 percent words
50 percent deeds
Unique among the Gospels, John begins by presenting mostly Jesus' deeds, then records Jesus' teaching and prayer on the night He was betrayed (chs. 13–17).

The Son of Man came to give His life as a ransom for many.

Mark

AD 29 Baptism of Jesus • AD 33 Resurrection, Ascension, Pentecost • AD 36 Conversion of Paul

Mark wrote his account of Jesus' life so that it is full of action. He used a special Greek word to highlight this, writing repeatedly that things happened **immediately** or **at once**—especially at the beginning of the Gospel (chs. 1, 4–6). No person acts more dynamically than Jesus. The following chart illustrates how often someone or something acts immediately in Mark's account.

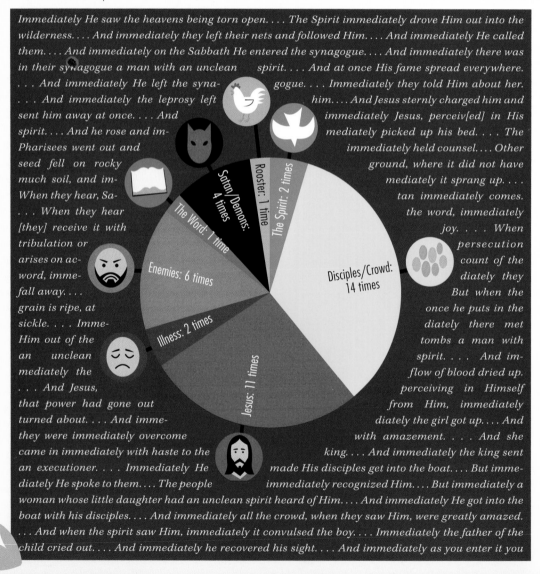

Immediately He saw the heavens being torn open. . . . The Spirit immediately drove Him out into the wilderness. . . . And immediately they left their nets and followed Him. . . . And immediately He called them. . . . And immediately on the Sabbath He entered the synagogue. . . . And immediately there was in their synagogue a man with an unclean spirit. . . . And at once His fame spread everywhere. . . . And immediately He left the synagogue. . . . Immediately they told Him about her. . . . And Jesus sternly charged him and sent him away at once. . . . And immediately the leprosy left him. . . . And Jesus, perceiv[ed] in His spirit. . . . And he rose and immediately picked up his bed. . . . The Pharisees went out and immediately held counsel. . . . Other seed fell on rocky ground, where it did not have much soil, and immediately it sprang up. . . . When they hear, Satan immediately comes. . . . When they hear [they] receive it with the word, immediately tribulation or joy. . . . When arises on ac- persecution word, imme- count of the fall away. . . . diately they grain is ripe, at But when the sickle. . . . Imme- once he puts in the Him out of the diately there met an unclean tombs a man with mediately the spirit. . . . And im- . . . And Jesus, flow of blood dried up. that power had gone out perceiving in Himself turned about. . . . And imme- from Him, immediately they were immediately overcome diately the girl got up. . . . And came in immediately with haste to the with amazement. . . . And she an executioner. . . . Immediately He king. . . . And immediately the king sent diately He spoke to them. . . . The people made His disciples get into the boat. . . . But imme- woman whose little daughter had an unclean spirit heard of Him. . . . And immediately He got into the boat with his disciples. . . . And immediately all the crowd, when they saw Him, were greatly amazed. . . . And when the spirit saw Him, immediately it convulsed the boy. . . . Immediately the father of the child cried out. . . . And immediately he recovered his sight. . . . And immediately as you enter it you

Satan/Demons: 4 times

Rooster: 1 time

The Spirit: 2 times

The Word: 1 time

Enemies: 6 times

Illness: 2 times

Disciples/Crowd: 14 times

Jesus: 11 times

The Unity of the Gospels

Although **each Gospel** presents different words and deeds of Jesus, they also share much in common. The following seventeen events appear in each of the four Gospels. Since fourteen of these events occurred during Holy Week and Easter, they show just how important the Passion and resurrection are for understanding Jesus, the Christian faith, and all of Scripture.

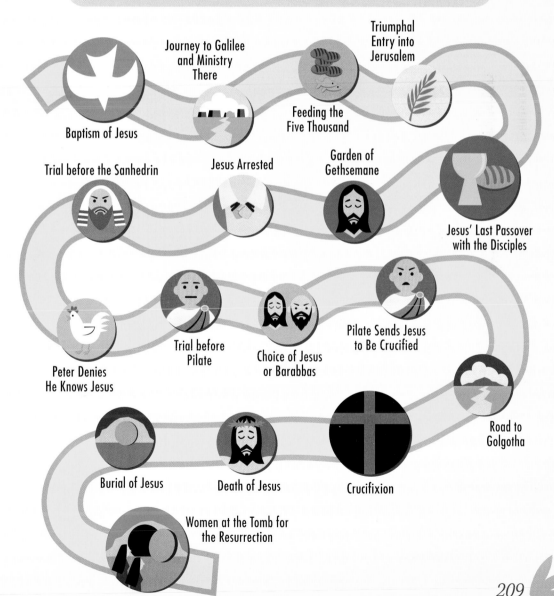

Baptism of Jesus

Journey to Galilee and Ministry There

Triumphal Entry into Jerusalem

Feeding the Five Thousand

Trial before the Sanhedrin

Jesus Arrested

Garden of Gethsemane

Jesus' Last Passover with the Disciples

Peter Denies He Knows Jesus

Trial before Pilate

Choice of Jesus or Barabbas

Pilate Sends Jesus to Be Crucified

Road to Golgotha

Burial of Jesus

Death of Jesus

Crucifixion

Women at the Tomb for the Resurrection

Jesus' Childhood

When the fullness of time had come, God sent forth His Son, born of woman. *Galatians 4:4*

Perfect timing. It's when you walk outside just in time to see an amazing sunset or a colorful hot-air balloon overhead or right as the ice cream truck is coming down the street. Or maybe you want a new video game *and* your parents pay you for helping in the yard *and* your mom has time to take you to the store *and* the store has a great sale on video games. All the pieces of the puzzle fit in place—it's perfect timing.

Think back to all God's promises to send the Savior that are recorded in the Old Testament. Eve thought it would be Cain or Abel or Seth. Throughout the Old Testament, people may have thought, "Now the time is right. God will send the Savior. Maybe it's this person or that one." But God knew exactly what He was going to do and when He was going to do it. Through the prophets He gave the people of Israel promises and clues: a virgin, Bethlehem, a descendant of David, a baby, someone to announce His way.

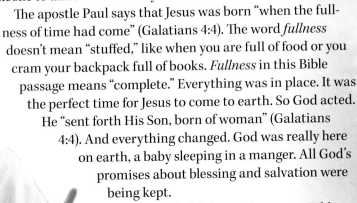

The apostle Paul says that Jesus was born "when the fullness of time had come" (Galatians 4:4). The word *fullness* doesn't mean "stuffed," like when you are full of food or you cram your backpack full of books. *Fullness* in this Bible passage means "complete." Everything was in place. It was the perfect time for Jesus to come to earth. So God acted. He "sent forth His Son, born of woman" (Galatians 4:4). And everything changed. God was really here on earth, a baby sleeping in a manger. All God's promises about blessing and salvation were being kept.

You probably know these next Bible stories very well, but there's still a lot to learn. As you read, think about the fact that God also knew exactly when you would be born. He knew who your parents would be and what color eyes you would have. He knew you would be His much-loved child, a member of His family. God's perfect timing includes your life now and forever!

Making Connections

At home you have to clean the bathrooms and the roof's gutters. At work you may find yourself cleaning up after other people make mistakes. UGH! Those jobs are horrible. You deserve better. There must be someone—anyone—who can take your place.

These examples give you a tiny idea of what it was like for Jesus to come to earth. He is God, yet He became a baby, completely dependent on Mary and Joseph. He slept in a manger, probably filled with scratchy, itchy hay. As a child He lived in a normal house and probably had chores to do—no palace full of servants for our King Jesus.

But Jesus didn't look around for someone to take His place. God had a plan for your salvation, and Jesus knew He was it. Jesus willingly came to earth to live as a human being. He took on the "dirty" work of obeying God's Law perfectly for you. And Jesus suffered and died on the cross in your place so you would receive something way better than you deserve—a place in heaven with Him.

Names for Our Savior

Christ ("Anointed One")

Christ Jesus

Immanuel ("God with us")

Jesus ("Yahweh is salvation")

Jesus Christ

Lord

Savior

Son of David

Son of Man

Son of God

24 chapters

An orderly account
from eyewitness and
ministers of the Word.

Read in 2 hours, 18 minutes

Luke

3 BC Annunciation to Mary • AD 33 Resurrection, Ascension, Pentecost • c. AD 55–60 Luke written

Luke presents an orderly account from the infancy of Jesus to His ascension into heaven. The Jerusalem temple is central to Luke's account of Jesus' life. The story begins at the temple (1:8), climaxes with Jesus teaching at the temple some thirty years later (19:45–21:38), and ends at the temple (24:53) when the disciples gather to worship the ascended Lord.

As you read Luke's carefully researched account of Jesus' life (1:1–4), consider yourself on a journey with Luke to learn more about Jesus of Nazareth, whose body, crucified for the forgiveness of sins, becomes the temple of the living God (22:19).

At five key points in the Gospel of Luke, Jesus teaches at a meal. Although only one of these meals became the meal we call the Lord's Supper, each one is a supper with the Lord, who teaches and has fellowship with disciples and would-be disciples. Over bread and wine, Jesus teaches the true nature of God's kingdom, a central theme in Luke's account of Jesus' life.

Jesus Calls Levi
5:27–39

Jesus Teaches a Pharisee
7:36–50

Jesus' Parables about a Feast and a Banquet
14:1–24

Jesus Institutes the Lord's Supper
22:14–23

Jesus Teaches at Emmaus
24:28–35

The Birth of John Foretold

Luke 1

In the days of Herod, king of Judea, there was a priest named Zechariah. He had a wife named Elizabeth. They were both righteous before God, walking blamelessly in all the commandments of the Lord. But they had no child, because Elizabeth was barren. Both of them were advanced in years.

While Zechariah was serving as priest before God, he was **chosen by lot** to enter the temple of the Lord and burn incense. And the whole multitude of the people were praying outside at the hour of incense.

There appeared to Zechariah an angel of the Lord standing on the right side of the altar of incense. And Zechariah was troubled when he saw him. Fear fell upon him. But the angel said, "Do not be afraid, Zechariah, for your prayer has been heard. Your wife Elizabeth will bear you a son. You shall call his name John. You will have joy and gladness, and many will rejoice at his birth. He will be great before the Lord. He must not drink wine or strong drink. He will be filled with the Holy Spirit, even from his mother's womb. He will turn many of the children of Israel to the Lord their God. He will go before Him in the spirit and power of Elijah, to turn the hearts of the fathers to the children, and the disobedient to the wisdom of the **just**, to make ready for the Lord a people prepared."

Zechariah said to the angel, "How shall I know this? I am an old man, and my wife is advanced in years."

The angel answered, "I am Gabriel. I stand in the presence of God. I was sent to speak to you and to bring you this good news. Behold, you will be silent and unable to speak until the day that these things take place, because you did not believe my words, which will be fulfilled in their time."

The people were waiting for Zechariah. They were wondering at his delay in the temple. When he came out, Zechariah was unable to speak to them. They realized that he had seen a vision in the temple. He kept making signs to them and remained mute. When his time of service was ended, Zechariah went to his home.

After these days his wife Elizabeth conceived. For five months she kept herself hidden, saying, "Thus the Lord has done for me in the days when He looked on me, to take away my **reproach** among people."

Words to Remember

He will turn many of the children of Israel to the Lord their God . . . to make ready for the Lord a people prepared. *Luke 1:16–17*

DID YOU KNOW?

- Luke is one of the three Synoptic Gospels; Matthew and Mark are the others. The term *synoptic* means "seeing together" or "seeing alike." The picture of Jesus' life and ministry presented in each of these three Gospels are quite similar, while John's content is very different.

- John the Baptist's parents were from the priestly line of Aaron.

- John would not be allowed to drink wine or strong drink because, like Samson and Samuel before him, he would live as a Nazirite.

The Birth of Jesus Foretold

Luke 1 and Matthew 1

The angel Gabriel was sent from God to a city of Galilee named Nazareth, to a virgin **betrothed** to a man whose name was Joseph, of the house of David. The angel said, "Greetings, O favored one, the Lord is with you!"

Mary was greatly troubled. The angel said, "Do not be afraid, Mary. You have found favor with God. Behold, you will bear a son. You shall call His name Jesus. He will be great and will be called the Son of the Most High. The Lord God will give to Him the throne of His father David. His kingdom will not end."

Mary said to the angel, "How will this be, since I am a virgin?"

The angel answered, "The Holy Spirit will come upon you, and the power of the Most High will overshadow you. The child to be born will be called holy—the Son of God. Behold, your relative Elizabeth has also conceived a son. For nothing will be impossible with God."

Mary said, "Behold, I am the servant of the Lord. Let it be to me according to your word." And the angel departed from her.

Mary went quickly into the hill country. She entered the house of Zechariah and greeted Elizabeth. When Elizabeth heard Mary, the baby leaped in her womb. Elizabeth was filled with the Holy Spirit and exclaimed, "Blessed are you among women. Blessed is the fruit of your womb! Why is this granted to me that the mother of my Lord should come to me?"

Mary said,

> "My soul magnifies the Lord,
>   and my spirit rejoices in God my **Savior**.
> He has looked on the humble estate of His servant.
>   From now on all generations will call me blessed.
> He who is mighty has done great things for me,
>   and holy is His name.
> His mercy is for those who fear Him
>   from generation to generation."

When Mary told Joseph about the baby, Joseph decided to divorce her. But an angel of the Lord appeared to him in a dream, saying, "Do not fear to take Mary as your wife. That which is conceived in her is from the Holy Spirit. She will bear a son. You shall call His name **Jesus**, because He will save His people from their sins."

Words to Remember

You will conceive in your womb and bear a son, and you shall call His name Jesus. He will be great and will be called the Son of the Most High. *Luke 1:31–32*

DID YOU KNOW?

- Betrothal was a binding contract in Joseph's day, requiring a divorce decree to end it, just as with marriage. When Mary told Joseph that she was pregnant, he set out to divorce her quietly since the typical punishment for being pregnant outside of marriage would have been stoning. But after an angel appeared to him, Joseph took Mary as his wife and prepared to become the earthly father of the Christ Child.

- In contrast to Zechariah's skeptical question, Mary wonders in faith after the angel foretells Jesus' birth.

- *Immanuel* means "God with us."

The Birth of John

Luke 1

The time came for Elizabeth to give birth, and she bore a son. Her neighbors and relatives rejoiced with her. On the eighth day they came to **circumcise** the child. They would have called him Zechariah after his father, but Elizabeth answered, "No. He shall be called John."

They said, "None of your relatives is called by this name." They made signs to Zechariah, inquiring what he wanted him to be called.

Zechariah asked for a writing tablet and wrote, "His name is John." Immediately his mouth was opened and his tongue loosed, and he spoke, blessing God. Zechariah was filled with the Holy Spirit and prophesied, saying:

> "Blessed be the Lord God of Israel.
>> He has visited and redeemed His people
> and has raised up a horn of salvation for us
>> in the house of His servant David,
> as He spoke by the mouth of His holy prophets from of old,
> that we should be saved from our enemies
>> and from the hand of all who hate us;
> to show the mercy promised to our fathers
>> and to remember His holy covenant,
> the oath that He swore to our father Abraham, to grant us
>> that we, being delivered from the hand of our enemies,
> might serve Him without fear,
>> in holiness and righteousness before Him all our days.
> And you, child, will be called the prophet of the Most High;
>> for you will go before the Lord to prepare His ways,
> to give knowledge of salvation to His people
>> in the forgiveness of their sins,
> because of the tender mercy of our God,
>> whereby the sunrise shall visit us from on high
> to give light to those who sit in darkness and in the shadow of death,
>> to guide our feet into the way of peace."

The child grew and became strong in spirit. John was in the wilderness until the day of his public appearance to Israel.

Words to Remember

You, child, will be called the prophet of the Most High; for you will go before the Lord to prepare His ways. *Luke 1:76*

DID YOU KNOW?

- John's name means "the Lord has shown favor"; it emphasizes God's grace in giving Zechariah and Elizabeth a child in their advanced age.

- It was common to name a male child after his grandfather or father.

- The song that Zechariah sings is called the Benedictus (from the Latin translation of the first word, *Blessed*); it is sung as part of the Church's liturgy.

The Birth of Jesus

Luke 2

In those days a decree went out from Caesar Augustus that all the world should be registered. This was the first registration when Quirinius was governor of Syria. And all went to be registered, each to his own town.

Joseph went up from Galilee, from the town of Nazareth, to Judea, to the city of David, which is called Bethlehem, because he was of the house and **lineage** of David. He went to be registered with Mary, his betrothed, who was with child.

While they were there, the time came for Mary to give birth. And she gave birth to her firstborn son. She wrapped Him in **swaddling cloths** and laid Him in a manger, because there was no place for them in the inn.

In the same region there were shepherds out in the field, keeping watch over their flock by night. An angel of the Lord appeared to them. The glory of the Lord shone around them. The shepherds were filled with fear.

The angel said to them, "Fear not, for behold, I bring you good news of great joy that will be for all the people. For unto you is born this day in the city of David a Savior, who is **Christ** the Lord. This will be a sign for you: you will find a baby wrapped in swaddling cloths and lying in a manger."

Suddenly there was a multitude of the heavenly host praising God and saying, "Glory to God in the highest, and on earth peace among those with whom He is pleased!"

When the angels went away into heaven, the shepherds said to one another, "Let us go to Bethlehem and see this thing that has happened, which the Lord has made known to us." They went with haste and found Mary and Joseph, and the baby lying in a manger.

When they saw it, the shepherds told others what the angel said concerning this child. All who heard it wondered at what the shepherds told them. But Mary treasured up all these things, **pondering** them in her heart.

The shepherds returned, glorifying and praising God for all they had heard and seen.

At the end of eight days, when He was circumcised, He was called Jesus. This was the name given by the angel before He was conceived in the womb.

DID YOU KNOW?

- The prophet Micah said that the Savior would be born in Bethlehem (see Micah 5:2). Caesar Augustus's decree set into motion the events of Jesus' birth, thereby bringing to fulfillment Micah's prophecy regarding His place of birth.

- After birth, babies were washed, rubbed with salt (and possibly olive oil), and then wrapped tightly in strips of cloth to warm and secure them.

- The travel caused by the census likely overwhelmed normal arrangements for hospitality, so Joseph and Mary were forced to bed down in a nearby cave or stable, where animals were housed.

The Visit of the Wise Men

Matthew 2

After Jesus was born in Bethlehem in the days of Herod the king, wise men from the east came to Jerusalem. They said, "Where is He who has been born king of the Jews? We saw His star when it rose and have come to worship Him."

When Herod heard this, he was troubled, and all Jerusalem with him. Assembling all the chief priests and scribes of the people, he asked where the Christ was to be born. They told him, "In Bethlehem of Judea, for so it is written by the prophet."

Herod summoned the wise men secretly and learned from them what time the star had appeared. He sent them to Bethlehem, saying, "Go and search diligently for the child. When you have found Him, bring me word, that I, too, may come and worship Him."

The wise men went on their way. The star that they had seen went before them until it came to rest over the place where the child was. Going into the house they saw the child with Mary His mother. They fell down and worshiped Jesus. They offered Him gifts, gold and **frankincense** and **myrrh**. Being warned in a dream not to return to Herod, the wise men departed to their own country by another way.

When they had departed, an angel of the Lord appeared to Joseph in a dream and said, "Take the child and His mother, and flee to Egypt. Remain there until I tell you. Herod is about to search for the child, to destroy Him." He remained in Egypt until the death of Herod. This was to fulfill what the Lord had spoken by the prophet, "Out of Egypt I called My Son."

When he saw that he had been tricked, Herod became furious. He killed all the male children in Bethlehem who were two years old or under. Then was fulfilled what was spoken by the prophet Jeremiah:

> "A voice was heard in Ramah,
> weeping and loud **lamentation**."

When Herod died, an angel of the Lord appeared in a dream to Joseph in Egypt, saying, "Take the child and His mother and go to the land of Israel. Those who sought the child's life are dead." Joseph went to the land of Israel, and being warned in a dream he withdrew to Galilee. He lived in a city called Nazareth, that what was spoken by the prophets might be fulfilled: "He shall be called a Nazarene."

DID YOU KNOW? _____

- The Greek term translated as "Wise Men" loosely referred to a wide variety of people interested in dreams, astrology, and magic. Their kind of wisdom was not always God-pleasing.

- It is unclear whether the Wise Men worshiped Jesus as true God or revered Him only as an earthly king. "Worship" implies they realized that Jesus was more than just a human king.

- Joseph and Mary were to flee to Egypt, which was about 175 miles southwest of Jerusalem, because it was outside Herod's jurisdiction.

The Boy Jesus in the Temple

Luke 2

Jesus' parents went to Jerusalem every year at the Feast of the Passover. When He was twelve years old, they went up according to custom.

When the feast was ended, as they were returning, the boy Jesus stayed behind in Jerusalem. His parents did not know it, but supposing Him to be in the group they went a day's journey. Then they began to search for Jesus among their relatives and acquaintances. When they did not find Jesus, Mary and Joseph returned to Jerusalem, searching for Him.

After three days Mary and Joseph found Jesus in the temple, sitting among the teachers, listening to them and asking them questions. All who heard Him were amazed at His understanding and His answers.

When His parents saw Him, they were astonished. His mother said to Jesus, "Son, why have You treated us so? Your father and I have been searching for You in great distress."

Jesus said to them, "Why were you looking for Me? Did you not know that I must be in My Father's house?"

Mary and Joseph did not understand the saying that Jesus spoke to them.

Jesus went down with them and came to Nazareth and was **submissive** to them. And His mother treasured up all these things in her heart.

Jesus increased in wisdom and in stature and in favor with God and man.

Words to Remember

[Jesus said,] "Why were you looking for Me? Did you not know that I must be in My Father's house?" *Luke 2:49*

DID YOU KNOW? ————————————————

- This is the only New Testament account of Jesus' later childhood.

- An annual pilgrimage to the Passover was required of all Israelite men. Extended families and neighbors often traveled together, singing and picnicking along the way.

- In order to stimulate more profound thinking, the rabbis often responded to people's questions by posing their own questions. Already as a child, Jesus was able to engage the best religious minds in this way.

Jesus' Public Ministry

[Jesus] went throughout all Galilee . . . proclaiming the Gospel of the kingdom and healing every disease. *Matthew 4:23*

Did you hear? He's coming. Come with me, and let's go see!" Imagine your best friend running into your house and telling you the president or your favorite sports hero or movie star was coming down your street. You would probably grab something for an autograph and race away to join the crowd. If you caught a glimpse, you would be thrilled. But what if the president asked you to join his staff as a special consultant? What if the movie star asked you to be part of her next movie? Would you follow?

It may have been a little like trying to see a movie star when Jesus was traveling and teaching throughout Galilee. He had a group of disciples that followed Him everywhere, making sure He had someplace to stay, food to eat, and taking care of crowd control. The people would come from all the villages to see Jesus, listen to Him teach, and especially to receive healing. Sometimes the crowds were so large Jesus taught from boats or on mountainsides.

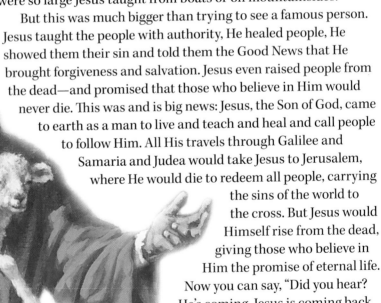

But this was much bigger than trying to see a famous person. Jesus taught the people with authority, He healed people, He showed them their sin and told them the Good News that He brought forgiveness and salvation. Jesus even raised people from the dead—and promised that those who believe in Him would never die. This was and is big news: Jesus, the Son of God, came to earth as a man to live and teach and heal and call people to follow Him. All His travels through Galilee and Samaria and Judea would take Jesus to Jerusalem, where He would die to redeem all people, carrying the sins of the world to the cross. But Jesus would Himself rise from the dead, giving those who believe in Him the promise of eternal life. Now you can say, "Did you hear? He's coming. Jesus is coming back for me!"

Making Connections

When Jesus said, "Follow Me," twelve men left everything familiar. Some of the ways they followed were easy: walking, talking, listening, asking questions. But there were the difficult things too: casting out demons, finding food for thousands, knowing that Jesus' enemies wanted to kill Him (and eventually would want to kill them too). The disciples followed Jesus to the cross and to the empty tomb. Jesus blessed the disciples with the Holy Spirit so they could tell the world about following Him.

You have been called to follow Jesus too. His call to follow doesn't end when you grow tired or when following becomes too difficult or dangerous. So as He did with His disciples, Jesus sends you His Holy Spirit. Every time you read your Bible, each time you go to church, the Holy Spirit is at work in you to keep you following Jesus. And when the world, the devil, and even death try to pull you away, Jesus is with you, announcing His forgiveness and healing your sin-sick soul to bring you to Himself in heaven.

The Twelve Disciples

Jesus called twelve men to follow Him. Several were fishermen, like Andrew and Peter, James and John. Matthew was a tax collector. But to all of them Jesus gave the important job of "catching" others with the Good News of salvation.

Andrew	Judas Iscariot
Bartholomew	Matthew
James the son of Zebedee	Peter
	Philip
James the son of Alphaeus	Simon the Canaanean
John the son of Zebedee	Thaddaeus
	Thomas

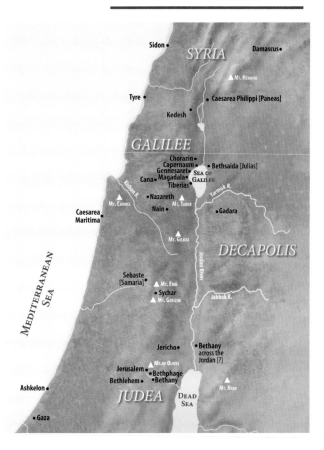

The Word became flesh and dwelt among us.

John

AD 33 Resurrection, Ascension, Pentecost • AD 41 Martyrdom of James, brother of John • AD 90 John written

The Gospel of John divides easily into two major sections: (a) six signs from the beginning of Jesus' ministry (chs. 2–12) and (b) Jesus' last Passover and Passion (chs. 13–20). Yet the apostle John binds his account of Jesus' life together by returning again and again to Jesus' "I am" declarations. They appear throughout the Gospel as a unique way of showing that Jesus is truly divine—the Word become flesh to dwell (literally, "tabernacle" or "tent") among us.

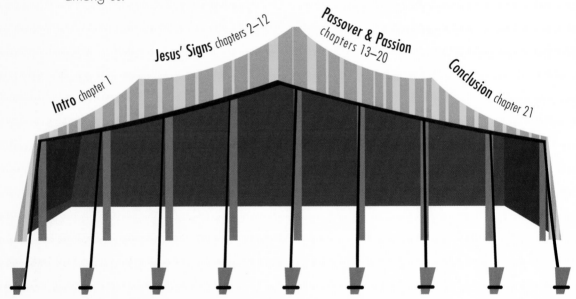

Intro chapter 1

Jesus' Signs chapters 2–12

Passover & Passion chapters 13–20

Conclusion chapter 21

I am He.
chapter 4

I am the living bread. I am the bread of life. It is I.
chapter 6

I am the witness. I am He. Before Abraham was, I am.
chapter 8

I am the Good Shepherd. I am the door.
chapter 10

I am the resurrection and the life.
chapter 11

I am He.
chapter 13

I am the way, and the truth, and the life.
chapter 14

I am the true vine.
chapter 15

I am H
chapter

Jesus' Puzzling Sayings

Whereas Matthew and Luke record Jesus' parables, John records many difficult sayings of Jesus that appear throughout the Gospel and unify its composition.

Blue = Spirit's work
Red = eating sayings
Green = going sayings
Yellow = time sayings
Grey = unique sayings

2:4
My hour
not yet

7:34
Where I am
going

2:19
Destroy this
temple

6:35
Bread
of life

3:3
Unless one is
born again

6:53
Eat
flesh

5:17
Father is
working

6:70
One is a
devil

7:37–38
Rivers of
living water

8:21
Where I am
going

3:8
Born of
the Spirit

8:58
Before
Abraham

7:6
My time
not yet

16:17
You will
not see Me

9:39
Become blind

4:32
I have
food

13:33
Where I am
going

18:36–37
My kingdom

4:10
Living water

6:51
Bread of
My flesh

21:18
Another
will
dress

14:4
Where I am
going

21:22
Remain
until I
come

John Baptizes Jesus

Matthew 3 and John 1

John the Baptist came preaching in the wilderness of Judea, "**Repent**, for the kingdom of heaven is at hand."

When the Jews sent priests and Levites from Jerusalem to ask who he was, John confessed, "I am not the Christ."

They asked him, "Are you Elijah? Are you the Prophet?" John answered, "No."

They said, "Who are you? We need to give an answer to those who sent us. What do you say about yourself?"

John said, "I am the voice of one crying out in the wilderness, 'Make straight the way of the Lord,' as the prophet Isaiah said."

Now John wore a garment of camel's hair and a leather belt around his waist. His food was locusts and wild honey. Jerusalem and all Judea and all the region about the Jordan were going out to him. They were **baptized** by John in the river Jordan, confessing their sins.

But when John saw many of the **Pharisees** and **Sadducees** coming to his **baptism**, he said to them, "You brood of vipers! Who warned you to flee from the wrath to come? Bear fruit in keeping with repentance. Every tree that does not bear good fruit is cut down and thrown into the fire.

"I baptize you with water for repentance, but He who is coming after me is mightier than I. I am not worthy to carry His sandals. He will baptize you with the Holy Spirit and fire. His winnowing fork is in His hand. He will gather His wheat into the barn, but the chaff He will burn with unquenchable fire."

Then Jesus came from Galilee to the Jordan to John, to be baptized by him.

John would have prevented Jesus. John said, "I need to be baptized by You, and do You come to me?"

Jesus answered, "Let it be so, for thus it is fitting for us to fulfill all righteousness." Then John consented.

When Jesus was baptized, immediately He went up from the water. Behold, the heavens were opened to Him. He saw the Spirit of God descending like a dove and coming to rest on Him. Behold, a voice from heaven said, "This is My beloved Son, with whom I am well pleased."

Words to Remember

[John said,] "He who is coming after me is mightier than I. . . . He will baptize you with the Holy Spirit and fire."
Matthew 3:11

DID YOU KNOW?

- To repent means to be converted from unbelief to faith. The exhortation to repent calls for a radical transformation of the entire person, a fundamental turnabout.

- The Pharisees and Sadducees wanted John to baptize them without having repented and confessed their sins.

- John did not want to baptize Jesus because he knew Jesus was without sin. But Jesus submitted to John's Baptism in order to affirm His identity with sinners and to provide them with perfect righteousness.

The Temptation of Jesus

Matthew 4

After His baptism, Jesus was led by the Spirit into the wilderness to be tempted by the **devil**. After fasting forty days and forty nights, Jesus was hungry.

The tempter came and said to Jesus, "If You are the Son of God, command these stones to become loaves of bread."

But Jesus answered, "It is written,

> "'Man shall not live by bread alone,
> but by every word that comes from the mouth of God.'"

Then the devil took Jesus to the holy city and set Him on the pinnacle of the temple. He said to Jesus, "If You are the Son of God, throw Yourself down, for it is written,

> "'He will command His angels concerning You,'

and

> "'On their hands they will bear You up,
> lest You strike Your foot against a stone.'"

Jesus said to him, "Again it is written, 'You shall not put the Lord your God to the test.'"

Again, the devil took Jesus to a very high mountain and showed Him all the kingdoms of the world and their glory. He said to Jesus, "All these I will give You, if You will fall down and worship me."

Then Jesus said to him, "Be gone, **Satan**! For it is written,

> "'You shall worship the Lord your God
> and Him only shall you serve.'"

Then the devil left Jesus, and behold, angels came and were ministering to Him.

Words to Remember

It is written, "Man shall not live by bread alone, but by every word that comes from the mouth of God."
Matthew 4:4

DID YOU KNOW?

- Judea was a place associated with demons because people in Jesus' day believed that evil spirits inhabited desert places.

- God's eternal plan called for the Savior to be tempted and to triumph. He allowed Satan to tempt Jesus.

- An earthly mountain from which one could see "all the kingdoms of the world and their glory" does not exist. The devil was permitted to create for Jesus a spiritual vision of it.

Jesus Calls Disciples

John 1 and Luke 5

After Jesus was baptized, John was standing with two of his **disciples**. He looked at Jesus as He walked by and said, "Behold, the **Lamb of God**!" The two disciples heard him say this, and they followed Jesus.

One of the two who heard John speak and followed Jesus was Andrew, Simon Peter's brother. He first found his own brother Simon and said, "We have found the **Messiah**" (which means Christ). Andrew brought Simon to Jesus.

Jesus said, "So you are Simon the son of John? You shall be called Cephas" (which means Peter).

The next day Jesus decided to go to Galilee. He found Philip and said to him, "Follow Me." Philip was from Bethsaida, the city of Andrew and Peter.

Philip found Nathanael and said, "We have found Him of whom Moses and also the prophets wrote, Jesus of Nazareth, the son of Joseph. Come and see." And Nathanael followed Jesus.

On one occasion, while the crowd was pressing in on Jesus to hear the word of God, He saw two boats by the lake. The fishermen had gone out of them and were washing their nets. Getting into one of the boats, which was Simon's, Jesus asked him to put out a little from the land. Jesus taught the people from the boat.

When Jesus had finished speaking, He said to Simon, "Put out into the deep and let down your nets for a catch."

Simon answered, "Master, we toiled all night and took nothing! But at Your word I will let down the nets." When they had done this, they enclosed a large number of fish, and their nets were breaking. They signaled to their partners in the other boat to help them. They filled both the boats, so that they began to sink.

When Simon Peter saw it, he fell down at Jesus' knees, saying, "Depart from me, for I am a sinful man, O Lord." For he and all who were with him were astonished at the catch of fish that they had taken. So also were James and John, sons of Zebedee, who were partners with Simon.

Jesus said to Simon, "Do not be afraid. From now on you will be catching men." When they had brought their boats to land, they left everything and followed Him.

After this Jesus went out and saw a tax collector named Levi [Matthew], sitting at the tax booth. Jesus said to him, "Follow Me." Leaving everything, he rose and followed Jesus.

Words to Remember

Behold, the Lamb of God, who takes away the sin of the world! *John 1:29*

DID YOU KNOW?

- John knew Jesus because they were cousins. But he did not fully understand that Jesus was the Messiah until He was baptized.

- Fishing often brought an above-average income, so these disciples left behind considerable assets.

- Tradition holds that Andrew was crucified on an X-shaped cross because he did not want to die on a cross that was the same shape as Jesus' cross.

Jesus Changes Water into Wine

John 2

There was a wedding at Cana in Galilee. The mother of Jesus was there. Jesus also was invited to the wedding with His disciples.

When the wine ran out, the mother of Jesus said to Him, "They have no wine."

Jesus said to her, "Woman, what does this have to do with Me? My hour has not yet come."

His mother said to the servants, "Do whatever He tells you."

Now there were six stone water jars there for the Jewish rites of **purification**, each holding twenty or thirty gallons. Jesus said to the servants, "Fill the jars with water." They filled them up to the brim.

Jesus said to them, "Now draw some out and take it to the master of the feast." So they took it.

When the master of the feast tasted the water now become wine, and did not know where it came from (though the servants who had drawn the water knew), the master of the feast called the bridegroom. He said to him, "Everyone serves the good wine first, and when people have drunk freely, then the poor wine. But you have kept the good wine until now."

This, the first of His signs, Jesus did at Cana in Galilee, and **manifested** His glory. And His disciples believed in Him.

> **Words to Remember**
> This, the first of His signs, Jesus did at Cana in Galilee, and manifested His glory. And His disciples believed in Him. *John 2:11*

DID YOU KNOW?

- According to Jewish custom, the wedding feast typically lasted seven days. Many guests would remain the whole week, abstaining from work and sharing the new family's joy.

- Running out of wine or having wine of poor quality at a wedding was a social blunder.

- Jesus' address to Mary as "woman" was a common and respectful greeting, though somewhat unusual for one's mother. Jesus may have been speaking to her as a disciple.

Jesus Clears the Temple

John 2

The Passover of the Jews was at hand, and Jesus went up to Jerusalem.

In the temple Jesus found those who were selling oxen and sheep and pigeons, and the money-changers sitting there. Making a whip of cords, Jesus drove them all out of the temple, with the sheep and oxen. And He poured out the coins of the money-changers and overturned their tables.

Jesus told those who sold the pigeons, "Take these things away. Do not make My Father's house a house of trade."

Jesus' disciples remembered that it was written, "**Zeal** for Your house will consume Me."

The Jews said to Jesus, "What sign do You show us for doing these things?"

Jesus answered, "Destroy this temple, and in three days I will raise it up."

The Jews then said, "It has taken forty-six years to build this temple. Will You raise it up in three days?"

But Jesus was speaking about the temple of His body. When He was raised from the dead, His disciples remembered that He had said this, and they believed the Scripture and the word that Jesus had spoken.

Words to Remember

[Jesus said,] "Destroy this temple, and in three days I will raise it up." *John 2:19*

DID YOU KNOW?

- Merchants were selling animals to travelers who needed them for the sacrifices prescribed by the Levitical code that were to be performed during Passover; it was impractical for travelers to transport animals from their homes.

- Travelers had to exchange their money into the local currency for the temple tax, which required Jewish coins without human images. The money-changers charged an exorbitant exchange fee.

Jesus Teaches Nicodemus

John 3

There was a man of the Pharisees named Nicodemus, a ruler of the Jews. This man came to Jesus by night and said, "**Rabbi**, we know that You are a teacher come from God. For no one can do these signs that You do unless God is with him."

Jesus answered, "Truly, truly, I say to you, unless one is born again he cannot see the **kingdom of God**."

Nicodemus said, "How can a man be born when he is old? Can he enter a second time into his mother's womb and be born?"

Jesus answered, "Truly, truly, I say to you, unless one is born of water and the Spirit, he cannot enter the kingdom of God. That which is born of the flesh is flesh, and that which is born of the Spirit is spirit. Do not marvel that I said to you, 'You must be born again.' The wind blows where it wishes. You hear its sound, but you do not know where it comes from or where it goes. So it is with everyone who is born of the Spirit."

Nicodemus said, "How can these things be?"

Jesus answered, "Are you the teacher of Israel and yet you do not understand these things? Truly, truly, I say to you, We speak of what We know, and bear witness to what We have seen, but you do not receive Our testimony. If I have told you earthly things and you do not believe, how can you believe if I tell you heavenly things? No one has ascended into heaven except He who descended from heaven, the **Son of Man**. As Moses lifted up the serpent in the wilderness, so must the Son of Man be lifted up, that whoever believes in Him may have **eternal life**.

"For God so loved the world, that He gave His only Son, that whoever believes in Him should not perish but have eternal life. For God did not send His Son into the world to **condemn** the world, but in order that the world might be saved through Him. Whoever believes in Him is not condemned, but whoever does not believe is condemned already, because he has not believed in the name of the only Son of God. And this is the judgment: the light has come into the world, and people loved the darkness rather than the light because their works were evil. For everyone who does wicked things hates the light and does not come to the light, lest his works should be exposed. But whoever does what is true comes to the light, so that it may be clearly seen that his works have been carried out in God."

Words to Remember

For God so loved the world, that He gave His only Son, that whoever believes in Him should not perish but have eternal life.
John 3:16

DID YOU KNOW?

- Nicodemus went to Jesus by night so that his colleagues would not know.

- The word *sign* is used seventeen times in chapters 2 through 20 of John. This fact has led many to call this part of the Gospel "The Book of Signs."

- John uses the word *believe* or a variation of it more than fifty times in his Gospel.

Jesus and the Samaritan Woman

John 4

Jesus came to a town of Samaria, near the field that Jacob had given to his son Joseph. Jacob's well was there. So Jesus, wearied as He was from His journey, was sitting beside the well. It was about the sixth hour.

A woman from Samaria came to draw water. Jesus said, "Give Me a drink." (For His disciples had gone into the city to buy food.)

The Samaritan woman said, "How is it that You, a Jew, ask for a drink from me, a woman of Samaria?" (For Jews have no dealings with Samaritans.)

Jesus answered, "If you knew the gift of God, and who it is that is saying to you, 'Give Me a drink,' you would have asked Him, and He would have given you **living water.**"

The woman said, "Sir, You have nothing to draw water with, and the well is deep. Where do You get that living water? Are You greater than our father Jacob? He gave us the well and drank from it himself, as did his sons and his livestock."

Jesus said, "Everyone who drinks of this water will be thirsty again. Whoever drinks of the water that I will give him will never be thirsty again. The water that I will give him will become in him a spring of water welling up to eternal life."

The woman said, "Sir, give me this water, so that I will not be thirsty or have to come here to draw water."

Jesus said, "Go, call your husband, and come here."

The woman answered, "I have no husband."

Jesus said, "You are right. You have had five husbands, and the one you now have is not your husband. What you have said is true."

The woman said, "Sir, I perceive that you are a prophet. I know that Messiah is coming (He who is called Christ). When He comes, He will tell us all things."

Jesus said, "I who speak to you am He."

So the woman left her water jar and went into town and said to the people, "Come, see a man who told me all that I ever did. Can this be the Christ?" They went out of the town and were coming to Jesus.

Many Samaritans from that town believed in Jesus because of the woman's testimony. Jesus stayed there two days. Many more believed because of His word. They said to the woman, "It is no longer because of what you said that we believe, for we have heard for ourselves. We know that this is indeed the Savior of the world."

> **Words to Remember**
>
> [Jesus said,] "Whoever drinks of the water that I will give him will never be thirsty again."
> *John 4:14*

DID YOU KNOW?

- Jesus' weariness reveals His true humanity.

- By requesting a drink from the woman, Jesus ignored traditional hostility between Jews and Samaritans as well as denigrating attitudes toward women.

- "Living water" is a Hebrew expression for flowing water.

Jesus Rejected at Nazareth

Luke 4

Jesus came to Nazareth, where He had been brought up. As was His custom, He went to the **synagogue** on the Sabbath day. Jesus stood up to read. The scroll of the prophet Isaiah was given to Him. He unrolled the scroll and found the place where it was written,

> "The Spirit of the Lord is upon Me,
>> because He has anointed Me
>> to proclaim good news to the poor.
> He has sent Me to proclaim liberty to the captives
>> and recovering of sight to the blind,
>> to set at liberty those who are oppressed,
> to proclaim the year of the Lord's favor."

Jesus rolled up the scroll and gave it back to the attendant and sat down. The eyes of all in the synagogue were fixed on Him. Jesus began to say to them, "Today this Scripture has been fulfilled in your hearing."

All spoke well of Jesus and marveled at the gracious words that were coming from His mouth. They said, "Is not this Joseph's son?"

Jesus said, "Doubtless you will quote to Me this proverb, 'Physician, heal yourself.' What we have heard You did at Capernaum, do here in Your hometown as well."

And Jesus said, "Truly, I say to you, no prophet is acceptable in his hometown. But in truth, I tell you, there were many widows in Israel in the days of Elijah, when the heavens were shut up three years and six months, and a great famine came over all the land. Elijah was sent to none of them but only to Zarephath, to a woman who was a widow. And there were many lepers in Israel in the time of the prophet Elisha. None of them was cleansed, but only Naaman the Syrian."

When they heard these things, all in the synagogue were filled with wrath. They rose up and drove Jesus out of the town. They brought Him to the brow of the hill on which their town was built, so that they could throw Him down the cliff. But passing through their midst, Jesus went away.

Words to Remember

"The Spirit of the Lord is upon Me, because He has anointed Me to proclaim good news to the poor."
Luke 4:18

DID YOU KNOW?

- Any qualified male could read from the Hebrew Scriptures in a synagogue.

- Rabbis typically taught on the Scripture passages just read from the lectionary, like sermons today.

- Jesus' words outraged His audience because they subtly made a case for including Gentiles in the Messiah's salvation. Elijah and Elisha are examples of prophets who previously extended God's grace to Gentiles.

Jesus Heals a Paralyzed Man

Mark 2

When Jesus returned to Capernaum after some days, it was reported that He was at home. Many were gathered together, so that there was no more room, not even at the door. Jesus was preaching the word to them.

And they came, bringing to Jesus a paralytic carried by four men. When they could not get near Jesus because of the crowd, the men removed the roof above Him. When they had made an opening, they let down the bed on which the paralytic lay.

When Jesus saw their **faith**, He said to the paralytic, "Son, your sins are forgiven."

Now some of the scribes were sitting there. They were questioning in their hearts, "Why does this man speak like that? He is blaspheming! Who can forgive sins but God alone?"

Immediately Jesus, perceiving in His spirit that they questioned within themselves, said to the scribes, "Why do you question these things in your hearts? Which is easier, to say to the paralytic, 'Your sins are forgiven,' or to say, 'Rise, take up your bed and walk'? But that you may know that the Son of Man has **authority** on earth to forgive sins"—He said to the paralytic—"I say to you, rise, pick up your bed, and go home."

And the man rose and immediately picked up his bed and went out before them all. They were all amazed and glorified God, saying, "We never saw anything like this!"

Words to Remember

"That you may know that the Son of Man has authority on earth to forgive sins"—[Jesus] said to the paralytic—"I say to you, rise, pick up your bed, and go home."
Mark 2:10–11

DID YOU KNOW?

- Jesus' practice of preaching within a domestic setting, as described here, set a precedent for His followers. For the next three hundred years, Christian worship services usually took place in house churches.

- Jesus' knowledge of His opponents' inner thoughts reveals His supernatural perception and shows His divinity. Ironically, that is the very thing being called into question.

- The healed man would have had to pass through many people in this crowded house, providing incontrovertible confirmation that Jesus had fully healed him.

The Sermon on the Mount

Matthew 5–7

Seeing the crowds, Jesus went up on the mountain and taught them, saying:

"Blessed are the poor in spirit, for theirs is the kingdom of heaven. Blessed are those who mourn, for they shall be comforted. Blessed are the meek, for they shall inherit the earth. Blessed are those who hunger and thirst for righteousness, for they shall be satisfied. Blessed are the merciful, for they shall receive mercy. Blessed are the pure in heart, for they shall see God. Blessed are the peacemakers, for they shall be called sons of God. Blessed are those who are **persecuted** for righteousness' sake, for theirs is the kingdom of heaven. Blessed are you when others persecute you on My account. Rejoice, for your reward is great in heaven.

"You are the light of the world. Let your light shine before others, so that they may see your good works and give glory to your Father who is in heaven.

"Love your enemies and pray for those who persecute you, so that you may be sons of your Father who is in heaven. For He makes His sun rise on the evil and on the good, and sends rain on the just and on the unjust.

"When you pray, do not heap up empty phrases as the **Gentiles** do. Your Father knows what you need before you ask Him. Pray then like this:

> 'Our Father in heaven, **hallowed** be Your name. Your kingdom come, Your will be done,
>> on earth as it is in heaven.
> Give us this day our daily bread, and forgive us our debts,
>> as we also have forgiven our debtors.
> And lead us not into temptation,
> but deliver us from evil.'

"Everyone who hears these words of Mine and does them will be like a wise man who built his house on the rock. The rain fell, the floods came, the winds blew and beat on that house, but it did not fall, because it had been founded on the rock. Everyone who hears these words of Mine and does not do them will be like a foolish man who built his house on the sand. The rain fell, the floods came, the winds blew and beat against that house, and it fell, and great was the fall of it."

When Jesus finished these sayings, the crowds were astonished at His teaching. He was teaching them as one who had authority, and not as their scribes.

Words to Remember

Your Father knows what you need before you ask Him.
Matthew 6:8

DID YOU KNOW?

- The first part of Jesus' sermon is called the Beatitudes, or blessings. Jesus was not making ethical demands of His followers but was describing blessings they would fully enjoy in the new heaven and new earth (Revelation 21:1).

- Light is a universal symbol for what is beneficial to people. Jesus, the light of the world, called on His followers to fulfill that function for the world.

- Christians have been praying the words of the Lord's Prayer for nearly two thousand years.

Jesus Calms a Storm

Mark 4

After He had taught the people by the sea, when evening had come, Jesus said to His disciples, "Let us go across to the other side."

Leaving the crowd, the disciples took Jesus with them in the boat, just as He was. And other boats were with Him.

A great windstorm arose. The waves were breaking into the boat, so that the boat was already filling. But Jesus was in the stern, asleep on the cushion.

The disciples woke Jesus and said to Him, "Teacher, do You not care that we are perishing?"

Jesus awoke and rebuked the wind and said to the sea, "Peace! Be still!" And the wind ceased, and there was a great calm.

Jesus said to the disciples, "Why are you so afraid? Have you still no faith?"

And the disciples were filled with great fear and said to one another, "Who then is this, that even the wind and the sea obey Him?"

Words to Remember

[Jesus] awoke and rebuked the wind and said to the sea, "Peace! Be still!" And the wind ceased, and there was a great calm. *Mark 4:39*

DID YOU KNOW?

- Mark is the shortest of the Gospels.

- Mark's earliest readers were likely Gentiles and probably Romans.

- Fishing boats were typically about twenty-five feet long and seven feet across. They were big enough to have two or three seats that stretched from side to side and a space near the middle for casting nets. At the back of the boat (the stern), there was a raised platform that also served as a seat. Cushions were stored underneath the platform and were used for resting during a long night of fishing.

Jesus Heals Jairus's Daughter

Mark 5

When Jesus had crossed again in the boat to the other side, a great crowd gathered about Him. Then one of the rulers of the synagogue, Jairus, came. Seeing Jesus, he fell at His feet and implored Him earnestly, saying, "My little daughter is at the point of death. Come and lay Your hands on her, so that she may be made well and live." Jesus went with Jairus.

Words to Remember

[Jesus said,] "Do not fear, only believe."
Mark 5:36

A great crowd followed Jesus and thronged about Him. There was a woman who had been sick for twelve years. She had heard the reports about Jesus. She came up behind Him in the crowd and touched His garment. For she said, "If I touch even His garments, I will be made well." Immediately she felt in her body that she was healed of her disease.

Jesus, perceiving in Himself that power had gone out from Him, immediately turned about in the crowd and said, "Who touched My garments?"

Jesus' disciples said, "You see the crowd pressing around You, and yet You say, 'Who touched Me?'"

The woman, knowing what had happened to her, came in fear and trembling. She fell down before Jesus. She told Him the whole truth.

Jesus said to her, "Daughter, your faith has made you well. Go in peace, and be healed of your disease."

While Jesus was still speaking, some people came from Jairus's house. They said, "Your daughter is dead. Why trouble the Teacher any further?"

Overhearing what they said, Jesus said to Jairus, "Do not fear, only believe." And Jesus allowed no one to follow Him except Peter and James and John the brother of James.

They came to the house of Jairus, and Jesus saw a commotion, people weeping and wailing loudly. When He had entered, Jesus said, "Why are you making a commotion and weeping? The child is not dead but sleeping." The people laughed at Jesus.

But Jesus put them all outside. He took the child's father and mother and those who were with Him and went in where the child was. Taking her by the hand Jesus said to her, "Little girl, I say to you, arise."

Immediately the girl got up and began walking (for she was twelve years of age). They were immediately overcome with amazement. Jesus strictly charged them that no one should know this. He told them to give her something to eat.

DID YOU KNOW?

- Jesus' question "Who touched My garments?" was not an accusatory question but an invitation for the woman to confess her faith.

- Mark uses a crisp, fast-paced style of writing; he uses the words *immediately* and *at once* more than forty times in his book. In doing so, he communicates his urgency to proclaim the Good News.

- Jesus wants the girl to eat not only to recover her strength but also to prove that she is bodily alive.

Jesus Feeds Five Thousand

John 6

Jesus went away to the other side of the Sea of Galilee, which is the Sea of Tiberias. A large crowd was following Him, because they saw the signs that He was doing on the sick.

Jesus went up on the mountain. There He sat down with His disciples. Now the Passover, the feast of the Jews, was at hand.

Words to Remember

This is indeed the Prophet who is to come into the world!
John 6:14

Lifting up His eyes, then, and seeing that a large crowd was coming toward Him, Jesus said to Philip, "Where are we to buy bread, so that these people may eat?" Jesus said this to test Philip, for He Himself knew what He would do.

Philip answered Jesus, "Two hundred **denarii** would not buy enough bread for each of them to get a little."

One of Jesus' disciples, Andrew, Simon Peter's brother, said to Him, "There is a boy here who has five barley loaves and two fish, but what are they for so many?"

Jesus said, "Have the people sit down." Now there was much grass in the place. So the men sat down, about five thousand in number.

Jesus then took the loaves, and when He had given thanks, He distributed them to those who were seated. So also the fish, as much as they wanted.

When the people had eaten their fill, Jesus told His disciples, "Gather up the leftover fragments, that nothing may be lost." So they gathered them up and filled twelve baskets with fragments from the five barley loaves left by those who had eaten.

When the people saw the sign that Jesus had done, they said, "This is indeed the Prophet who is to come into the world!"

Perceiving then that they were about to come and take Him by force to make Him king, Jesus withdrew again to the mountain by Himself.

DID YOU KNOW?

- The word *miracle* comes from a Latin word that means "to wonder." Miracles are occurrences that cause wonder because they are unusual and out of the ordinary.

- Two hundred denarii was over half a year's salary.

- The people wanted to make Jesus a king on their terms (political, earthly) rather than accept Him as the King He was and is (heavenly, eternal).

Jesus Walks on Water

Matthew 14

Jesus made the disciples get into the boat and go before Him to the other side while He dismissed the crowds. After He had dismissed the crowds, Jesus went up on the mountain by Himself to pray.

When evening came, Jesus was there alone. The boat by this time was a long way from the land. It was beaten by the waves, for the wind was against them.

In the **fourth watch** of the night Jesus came to the disciples, walking on the sea. But when the disciples saw Him walking on the sea, they were terrified. They said, "It is a ghost!" They cried out in fear.

Immediately Jesus spoke to them, saying, "Take heart; it is I. Do not be afraid."

Peter answered Jesus, "Lord, if it is You, command me to come to You on the water."

Jesus said, "Come."

So Peter got out of the boat and walked on the water and came to Jesus. But when he saw the wind, Peter was afraid. Beginning to sink he cried out, "Lord, save me."

Jesus immediately reached out His hand and took hold of Peter, saying to him, "O you of little faith, why did you doubt?"

When they got into the boat, the wind ceased. And those in the boat worshiped Jesus, saying, "Truly You are the Son of God."

> **Words to Remember**
>
> [Jesus said,] "Take heart; it is I. Do not be afraid."
> *Matthew 14:27*

DID YOU KNOW?

- John 6:19 reports that the disciples had rowed about three to four miles by the time Jesus came to them.

- The fourth watch would be from three to six in the morning. Romans divided nighttime into four segments of three hours each.

- The Greek translated as "It is I" is *ego eimi*. God made Himself known to Moses using similar words: "I AM WHO I AM."

Jesus Is Anointed

Luke 7

One of the Pharisees asked Jesus to eat with him. So Jesus went into the Pharisee's house and took His place at the table.

A woman of the city, who was a sinner, when she learned that Jesus was reclining at table in the Pharisee's house, brought an alabaster flask of ointment. Standing behind Jesus at His feet, weeping, she began to wet His feet with her tears. She wiped them with her hair and kissed His feet and anointed them with the ointment.

Now when the Pharisee who had invited Jesus saw this, he said to himself, "If this man were a prophet, He would have known who and what sort of woman this is who is touching Him. For she is a sinner."

Jesus said to the Pharisee, "Simon, I have something to say to you."

Simon answered, "Say it, Teacher."

Jesus said, "A certain moneylender had two debtors. One owed five hundred denarii, and the other fifty. When they could not pay, he cancelled the debt of both. Now which of them will love him more?"

Simon answered, "The one, I suppose, for whom he cancelled the larger debt."

Jesus said, "You have judged rightly."

Turning toward the woman Jesus said to Simon, "Do you see this woman? I entered your house. You gave Me no water for My feet, but she has wet my feet with her tears and wiped them with her hair. You gave me no kiss, but from the time I came in she has not ceased to kiss My feet. You did not anoint My head with oil, but she has anointed My feet with ointment. Therefore I tell you, her sins, which are many, are forgiven—for she loved much. But he who is forgiven little, loves little."

Jesus said to the woman, "Your sins are forgiven."

Then those who were at table with Jesus began to say among themselves, "Who is this, who even forgives sins?"

And Jesus said to the woman, "Your faith has saved you; go in peace."

Words to Remember

[Jesus] said to the woman, "Your faith has saved you; go in peace." *Luke 7:50*

DID YOU KNOW?

- The sinful woman was likely a prostitute or adulteress.

- If a ceremonially impure person such as this woman touched an observant Jew, the latter would be rendered unclean and would be unable to enter the temple area, celebrate festivals, or offer sacrifice.

- In the ancient East, the kiss of greeting is equivalent to a handshake. This is still common today in parts of the Near East and Europe.

Peter's Confession and Jesus' Transfiguration

Matthew 16 and Mark 9

Jesus asked His disciples, "Who do people say that the Son of Man is?"

They said, "Some say John the Baptist, others say Elijah, and others Jeremiah or one of the prophets."

Jesus said to them, "But who do you say that I am?"

Simon Peter replied, "You are the Christ, the Son of the living God."

Jesus answered him, "Blessed are you, Simon Bar-Jonah! For flesh and blood has not revealed this to you, but My Father who is in heaven. I tell you, you are Peter, and on this rock I will build My Church. The gates of hell shall not prevail against it. I will give you the keys of the kingdom of heaven. Whatever you bind on earth shall be bound in heaven, and whatever you loose on earth shall be loosed in heaven."

Then Jesus strictly charged the disciples to tell no one that He was the Christ.

After six days Jesus took with Him Peter and James and John. He led them up a high mountain by themselves. And Jesus was **transfigured** before them. His clothes became radiant, intensely white, as no one on earth could bleach them.

There appeared Elijah with Moses, and they were talking with Jesus.

Peter said to Jesus, "Rabbi, it is good that we are here. Let us make three tents, one for You and one for Moses and one for Elijah." For Peter did not know what to say, for they were terrified.

A cloud overshadowed them, and a voice came out of the cloud, "This is My beloved Son; listen to Him."

Suddenly, looking around, the disciples no longer saw anyone with them but Jesus only.

As they were coming down the mountain, Jesus charged Peter, James, and John to tell no one what they had seen, until the Son of Man had risen from the dead. So they kept the matter to themselves, questioning what this rising from the dead might mean.

Words to Remember

[God said,] "This is My beloved Son; listen to Him." *Mark 9:7*

DID YOU KNOW?

- Bar-Jonah is Peter's Aramaic family name, meaning "son of Jonah."

- Since many people thought that the Messiah would be a political leader to free them from Roman domination, Jesus likely wanted His disciples to refrain from proclaiming Him as the Christ until after His resurrection.

- Peter would prolong their stay by providing shelter or places of worship.

Jesus Sends the Seventy-Two

Luke 10

The Lord appointed seventy-two others and sent them on ahead of Him, two by two, into every town and place where He Himself was about to go.

Jesus said to them, "The harvest is plentiful, but the laborers are few. Therefore pray earnestly to the Lord of the harvest to send out laborers into His harvest.

"Go your way. Behold, I am sending you out as lambs in the midst of wolves. Carry no moneybag, no knapsack, no sandals, and greet no one on the road.

"Whatever house you enter, first say, 'Peace be to this house!' And if a son of peace is there, your peace will rest upon him. But if not, it will return to you. Remain in the same house, eating and drinking what they provide, for the laborer deserves his wages. Do not go from house to house.

"Whenever you enter a town and they receive you, eat what is set before you. Heal the sick in it. Say to them, 'The kingdom of God has come near to you.' But whenever you enter a town and they do not receive you, go into its streets and say, 'Even the dust of your town that clings to our feet we wipe off against you. Nevertheless know this, that the kingdom of God has come near.'

"The one who hears you hears Me. The one who rejects you rejects Me. The one who rejects Me rejects Him who sent Me."

The seventy-two returned with joy, saying, "Lord, even the demons are subject to us in Your name!"

Jesus said to them, "I saw Satan fall like lightning from heaven. Behold, I have given you authority to tread on serpents and scorpions, and over all the power of the enemy. Nothing shall hurt you. Nevertheless, do not rejoice that the spirits are subject to you, but rejoice that your names are written in heaven."

Words to Remember

The harvest is plentiful, but the laborers are few. Therefore pray earnestly to the Lord of the harvest to send out laborers into His harvest. *Luke 10:2*

DID YOU KNOW?

- The instructions Jesus gives the disciples (not to carry money, sandals, etc.) required them to trust God. Their daily needs were to be met by those who received their ministry and provided hospitality.

- When Jesus tells the Seventy-Two that they are to eat what is set before them, He means they are to share a table with people considered ceremonially unclean and consume what may not be ceremonially clean.

The Good Samaritan

Luke 10

Behold, a lawyer stood up to put Jesus to the test. He said, "Teacher, what shall I do to inherit eternal life?"

Jesus said to the lawyer, "What is written in the Law? How do you read it?"

The lawyer answered, "You shall love the Lord your God with all your heart and with all your soul and with all your strength and with all your mind, and your neighbor as yourself."

Jesus said to him, "You have answered correctly. Do this, and you will live."

But the lawyer, desiring to **justify** himself, said to Jesus, "And who is my neighbor?"

Jesus replied, "A man was going down from Jerusalem to Jericho, and he fell among robbers. They stripped him and beat him and departed, leaving him half dead. Now by chance a priest was going down that road. When he saw the man, he passed by on the other side. So likewise a Levite, when he came to the place and saw the man, passed by on the other side. But a Samaritan, as he journeyed, came to where he was. When he saw the man, he had **compassion**. The Samaritan went to him and bound up his wounds, pouring on oil and wine. Then he set the man on his own animal and brought him to an inn and took care of him. The next day the Samaritan took out two denarii and gave them to the innkeeper. He said, 'Take care of this man. Whatever more you spend, I will repay you when I come back.'"

Jesus asked, "Which of these three, do you think, proved to be a neighbor to the man who fell among the robbers?"

The lawyer said, "The one who showed him mercy."

Jesus said to him, "You go, and do likewise."

Words to Remember

You shall love the Lord your God with all your heart and with all your soul and with all your strength and with all your mind, and your neighbor as yourself. *Luke 10:27*

DID YOU KNOW?

- "The Law" referred to here is Moses' writings, the first five books of the Bible.

- The Greek word for *neighbor* means "whoever happens to be nearby or close at hand," not just people who have homes nearby.

- The amount of money the Samaritan gave to the innkeeper to care for the injured Jew was equivalent to two days' wages.

Jesus Heals a Blind Man

John 9

Jesus saw a man who was blind from birth. His disciples asked, "Rabbi, who sinned, this man or his parents, that he was born blind?"

Jesus answered, "It was not that this man sinned, or his parents, but that the works of God might be displayed in him. We must work the works of Him who sent Me while it is day. Night is coming, when no one can work. As long as I am in the world, I am the light of the world."

Having said these things, Jesus spat on the ground and made mud with the saliva. He anointed the man's eyes with the mud and said, "Go, wash in the pool of Siloam (which means Sent)." The man went and washed and came back seeing.

The neighbors and those who had seen him before as a beggar were saying, "Is this not the man who used to sit and beg? How were your eyes opened?"

The man answered, "The man called Jesus made mud and anointed my eyes and said to me, 'Go to Siloam and wash.' So I went and washed and received my sight."

They said to him, "Where is He?"

The man said, "I do not know."

Now it was a Sabbath day when Jesus made the mud and opened the man's eyes. So the Pharisees asked the man how he had received his sight. He said, "He put mud on my eyes, and I washed, and I see."

Some of the Pharisees said, "This man is not from God, for He does not keep the Sabbath."

Others said, "How can a man who is a sinner do such signs?"

So they said to the blind man, "What do you say about Jesus, since He has opened your eyes?"

The man said, "He is a prophet."

After further questioning about his blindness and his healing, the Jews accused the man of being one of Jesus' disciples and cast him out.

Jesus heard that the Jews had cast the man out. After Jesus found the man, He said, "Do you believe in the Son of Man?"

The man answered, "And who is He, that I may believe in Him?"

Jesus said, "You have seen Him, and it is He who is speaking to you."

The man said, "Lord, I believe," and he worshiped Him.

Words to Remember

[Jesus said,] "I am the light of the world." *John 9:5*

DID YOU KNOW?

- Many people believed that suffering resulted from a specific sin, so they thought this man's blindness was punishment.

- By making mud, Jesus violated rabbinic rules. The rabbis listed kneading dough among thirty-nine forms of work forbidden on the Sabbath, a law thought also to cover the mixing of earth and saliva.

- The age of legal maturity at this time was thirteen years and one day.

The Good Shepherd

John 10 and Psalm 23

Words to Remember

[Jesus said,] I came that they may have life and have it abundantly. I am the good shepherd. The good shepherd lays down His life for the sheep. *John 10:10–11*

Jesus said, "Truly, truly, I say to you, he who does not enter the sheepfold by the door but climbs in by another way, that man is a thief and a robber. But he who enters by the door is the shepherd. The sheep hear his voice, and he calls his own sheep by name and leads them out. The sheep follow him, for they know his voice.

"Truly, truly, I say to you, I am the door of the sheep. If anyone enters by Me, he will be saved. The thief comes only to steal and kill and destroy. I came that they may have life and have it abundantly. I am the good shepherd. The good shepherd lays down his life for the sheep. He who is a hired hand and not a shepherd, who does not own the sheep, sees the wolf coming and leaves the sheep and flees. I am the good shepherd. I know My own and My own know Me, just as the Father knows Me and I know the Father. I lay down My life for the sheep."

Many years before Jesus came to earth, King David wrote these words:

The LORD is my shepherd; I shall not want.
He makes me lie down in green pastures.
He leads me beside still waters.
　　He restores my soul.
He leads me in paths of righteousness
　　for His name's sake.

Even though I walk through the valley of the shadow of death,
　　I will fear no evil,
for You are with me;
　　Your rod and Your staff,
　　they comfort me.

You prepare a table before me
　　in the presence of my enemies;
You anoint my head with oil;
　　my cup overflows.
Surely goodness and mercy shall follow me
　　all the days of my life,
and I shall dwell in the house of the LORD
　　forever.

DID YOU KNOW? _____

- "Truly, truly" is the ESV translation of "Amen, amen." *Amen* comes from the Hebrew word for faith or faithfulness. John is the only Gospel writer to feature this double amen, which Jesus uses to affirm His testimony.

- A sheepfold is a walled enclosure for keeping sheep safe at night. A gatekeeper guards the entrance to the sheep pen.

- Sheep usually recognize the voice of their shepherd and respond to his call. Shepherds in the Middle East typically lead their flocks rather than drive them from behind; they draw the sheep by their word.

Jesus Raises Lazarus

John 11

Now Jesus loved Martha and Mary and Lazarus. So, when He heard that Lazarus was ill, Jesus stayed two days longer in the place where He was. Then He said to the disciples, "Our friend Lazarus has fallen asleep, but I go to awaken him."

The disciples said, "Lord, if Lazarus has fallen asleep, he will recover."

Then Jesus told them plainly, "Lazarus has died. For your sake I am glad that I was not there, so that you may believe. But let us go to him."

Martha met Jesus, but Mary remained in the house. Martha said, "Lord, if You had been here, my brother would not have died. But even now I know that whatever You ask from God, God will give You."

Jesus said, "Your brother will rise again. I am the resurrection and the life. Whoever believes in Me, though he die, yet shall he live. Everyone who lives and believes in Me shall never die. Do you believe this?"

Martha said, "Yes, Lord. I believe that You are the Christ, the Son of God, who is coming into the world."

Martha went and called her sister Mary. When Mary came to where Jesus was, she fell at His feet, saying, "Lord, if You had been here, my brother would not have died."

When Jesus saw Mary weeping, and the Jews who had come with her also weeping, He was greatly troubled. He said, "Where have you laid him?"

They said, "Lord, come and see."

Jesus wept. So the Jews said, "See how He loved him!"

Jesus, deeply moved again, came to the tomb. He said, "Take away the stone."

Martha said, "Lord, there will be an odor, for he has been dead four days."

Jesus said, "Did I not tell you that if you believed you would see the glory of God?" So they took away the stone.

Jesus lifted up His eyes and said, "Father, I thank You that You have heard Me. I knew that You always hear Me, but I said this on account of the people standing around, that they may believe that You sent Me." When He had said these things, Jesus cried out with a loud voice, "Lazarus, come out."

The man who had died came out, his hands and feet bound with linen strips, and his face wrapped with a cloth. Jesus said to them, "Unbind him, and let him go."

Many of the Jews who had seen what Jesus did believed in Him, but some went to the Pharisees and told them what Jesus had done. From that day on the Pharisees made plans to put Jesus to death.

DID YOU KNOW?

- *Lazarus* means "God has helped."

- The expression "fallen asleep" is commonly used of death in the New Testament. It is no mere euphemism; at the hand of Jesus, death is no more serious than sleep.

- Jesus prayed publicly so the crowd would know and believe that He was dependent on and obedient to His Father, who had sent Him.

The Prodigal Son

Luke 15

Jesus said, "There was a man who had two sons. The younger son said to his father, 'Father, give me the share of property that is coming to me.' And the father divided his property between them.

"Not many days later, the younger son gathered all he had and took a journey into a far country. There he squandered his property in reckless living. When he had spent every-thing, a severe famine arose in that country, and he began to be in need. So he went and hired himself out to one of the citizens of that country, who sent him into his fields to feed pigs. And he was longing to be fed with the pods that the pigs ate, and no one gave him anything.

"But when he came to himself, he said, 'How many of my father's hired servants have more than enough bread, but I perish here with hunger! I will go to my father. I will say to him, "Father, I have sinned against heaven and before you. I am no longer worthy to be called your son. Treat me as one of your hired servants."'

"He arose and came to his father. But while he was still a long way off, his father saw him and felt compassion. He ran and embraced his son and kissed him. The son said, 'Father, I have sinned against heaven and before you. I am no longer worthy to be called your son.'

"But the father said to his servants, 'Bring quickly the best robe, and put it on him. Put a ring on his hand, and shoes on his feet. Bring the fattened calf and kill it, and let us eat and celebrate. For this my son was dead, and is alive again; he was lost, and is found.' And they began to celebrate.

"Now his older son was in the field. As he came near to the house, he heard music and dancing. He called one of the servants and asked what these things meant. The servant said, 'Your brother has come. Your father has killed the fattened calf, because he has received him back safe and sound.'

"But the older son was angry and refused to go in. His father came out and **entreated** him. He answered his father, 'These many years I have served you. I never disobeyed your command, yet you never gave me a young goat, that I might celebrate with my friends. But when this son of yours came, who has devoured your property with prostitutes, you killed the fattened calf for him!'

"The father said, 'Son, you are always with me, and all that is mine is yours. It was fitting to celebrate and be glad, for this your brother was dead, and is alive; he was lost, and is found.'"

DID YOU KNOW?

- In this parable, the father represents God, the prodigal represents a sinner, and the older brother represents those who consider themselves to be "righteous persons who need no repentance" (Luke 15:7).

- Feeding pigs, unclean beasts, was the son's lowest step.

- A young goat was the minimal basis for a feast, so the older son is pointing out how exorbitant he thinks the father's feast is for his wayward brother.

Jesus Heals Ten Men

Luke 17

On the way to Jerusalem Jesus was passing along between Samaria and Galilee. As He entered a village, He was met by ten lepers, who stood at a distance and lifted up their voices, saying, "Jesus, Master, have mercy on us."

When He saw them Jesus said to them, "Go and show yourselves to the priests." And as they went they were cleansed.

Then one of them, when he saw that he was healed, turned back, praising God with a loud voice. He fell on his face at Jesus' feet, giving Him thanks. Now this man was a Samaritan.

Then Jesus answered, "Were not ten cleansed? Where are the nine? Was no one found to return and give praise to God except this foreigner?"

Jesus said to the man, "Rise and go your way; your faith has made you well."

Words to Remember

[Jesus said,] "Your faith has made you well." *Luke 17:19*

DID YOU KNOW?

- Leprosy is a disease caused by a germ that discolors patches of skin and causes those areas to lose feeling. After feeling is lost in a certain area, other damage often occurs to that part of the body and can become quite severe before the person even realizes it.

- Leprosy is a contagious disease until treated, so before medicines were developed to treat it, the only way to avoid leprosy was to stay away from people who had it. It wasn't until the 1940s that a successful treatment was discovered.

- The Jews despised the Samaritans because of historic betrayals and heretical beliefs. Yet the Samaritan, who was least expected to associate with Jesus, a Jew, was the only one to return thanks.

Jesus and the Little Children

Mark 9–10

Jesus and His disciples came to Capernaum. When He was in the house He asked them, "What were you discussing on the way?"

But the disciples kept silent. On the way they had argued with one another about who was the greatest.

Jesus sat down and called the twelve. He said to them, "If anyone would be first, he must be last of all and servant of all."

Jesus took a child and put him in the midst of them. Taking the child in His arms, Jesus said to the disciples, "Whoever receives one such child in My name receives Me. And whoever receives Me, receives not Me but Him who sent Me."

Jesus left there and went to the region of Judea and beyond the Jordan. Crowds gathered to Him again. Again, as was His custom, Jesus taught them.

And they were bringing children to Jesus that He might touch them. The disciples rebuked them.

But when Jesus saw it, He was indignant. He said to them, "Let the children come to Me. Do not hinder them, for to such belongs the kingdom of God. Truly, I say to you, whoever does not receive the kingdom of God like a child shall not enter it."

And Jesus took the children in His arms and blessed them, laying His hands on them.

Words to Remember

[Jesus said,] "Let the children come to Me; do not hinder them, for to such belongs the kingdom of God." Mark 10:14

DID YOU KNOW?

- Jesus shows the disciples that true status is found in serving those whom God values. We do not earn God's love and favor by keeping the Law. All people, like helpless children, receive Jesus' blessing and enter the Kingdom through faith in Him.

- The crowds were bringing children to Jesus so "that He might touch them" in order to bless them.

- The disciples thought children were not important and thus limited their access to Jesus.

Jesus and Zacchaeus

Luke 19

Jesus entered Jericho and was passing through. And there was a man named Zacchaeus. He was a chief tax collector and was rich.

Zacchaeus was seeking to see who Jesus was. But on account of the crowd he could not, because Zacchaeus was small of stature. So he ran on ahead and climbed up into a sycamore tree to see Jesus, for He was about to pass that way.

When Jesus came to the place, He looked up and said to him, "Zacchaeus, hurry and come down. I must stay at your house today."

So Zacchaeus hurried and came down and received Jesus joyfully.

When they saw it, they all grumbled, "He has gone in to be the guest of a man who is a sinner."

Zacchaeus stood and said to the Lord, "Behold, Lord, the half of my goods I give to the poor. And if I have defrauded anyone of anything, I restore it fourfold."

Jesus said to Zacchaeus, "Today salvation has come to this house, since he also is a son of Abraham. For the Son of Man came to seek and to save the lost."

Words to Remember

The Son of Man came to seek and to save the lost.
Luke 19:10

DID YOU KNOW?

- The Roman government hired Jews to collect their taxes, and like the Romans they served, the tax collectors were hated by their fellow Jews, who considered them traitors who had turned against their own people. Often, tax officials collected taxes unfairly, asking for more money than the government required and keeping the extra for themselves.

- Some thought that by eating with such a man as Zacchaeus, Jesus would become a partner with him in his sins. Pious Jews, especially Pharisees, would not associate with Gentiles, tax collectors, or openly wicked Jews, let alone eat with them.

Jesus' Passion, Death, and Resurrection

He was wounded for our transgressions; He was crushed for our iniquities . . . with His stripes we are healed. *Isaiah 53:5*

As every book has a beginning, a middle, and an end, so also every book has some great conflict. The main character or characters must make decisions that will determine the outcome of the plot. In the Bible, the true account of God and His love for you, you learn that God made the decision to send a Savior to redeem (to buy back) His creation from slavery to sin. In many Bible stories, you have read about how God redeemed people: God sent a ram for Abraham to sacrifice instead of Isaac. God brought the children of Israel out of Egypt. God sent judges and kings and prophets to call the Israelites back from worshiping other gods. Always, God reminded His people that a Savior was coming. Finally, when the time was right, God sent Jesus to earth.

Now we come to the great conflict, the great battle, between God and the sin that separates you from Him. To redeem you, God's own Son had to die to pay the price for our sin and for the sin of the whole world. Will Jesus do what His Father asks? Will Jesus go through the suffering and the mocking? Will Jesus be separated from His Father and die alone?

The answer is YES. Jesus came to earth and was born in a stable FOR YOU. He grew to be a man and traveled without a home, teaching and preaching and healing FOR YOU. He obeyed God's Law perfectly FOR YOU. He allowed Himself to be arrested and put on trial and beaten and nailed to a cross FOR YOU. Jesus died FOR YOU—because He loves you so much and wanted to end this conflict with Satan and sin and make you part of God's family forever.

But Jesus' suffering and death isn't the end. Jesus came back to life FOR YOU. His resurrection proved that God accepted Jesus' sacrifice for your sin and for the sin of the whole world. When you were baptized, you were "buried with [Christ] in baptism, in which you were also raised with Him through faith in the powerful working of God, who raised Him from the dead" (Colossians 2:12).

Making Connections

The Jewish leaders accused Jesus' disciples of faking His resurrection—or maybe Jesus faked His death. Let's play detective and look at the evidence.

First, Jesus, who is truly man, bled from His beating and from the crown of thorns. He could not carry His cross because He was physically exhausted. He suffered from thirst. He was in agony as His heavenly Father deserted Him. He said, "It is finished." The soldier in charge said Jesus was dead. Water and blood came out from the spear wound in Jesus' side. Joseph and Nicodemus would not have placed a living man in a tomb. Jesus was really dead.

Second, Jesus, who is truly God, came back to life. The women, Peter, and John could not find a body in the tomb. Jesus appeared to the women as they returned to the disciples and also to Mary Magdalene. Jesus appeared to the disciples behind locked doors. He walked and talked with the Emmaus disciples. He ate food. He appeared on many occasions to many different people over forty days. Jesus was really alive.

The Seven Words from the Cross

The four Gospels record seven statements Jesus made while He was on the cross. For almost 2,000 years, Christians have reflected on these statements, especially during the season of Lent and during Holy Week (the week before Easter).

"Father, forgive them, for they know not what they do." (Luke 23:34)

"Truly, I say to you, today you will be with Me in Paradise." (Luke 23:43, said to the thief on the cross)

"Woman, behold, your son! . . . Behold, your mother!" (John 19:26–27, said to Mary and to John)

"My God, My God, why have You forsaken Me?" (Mark 15:34)

"I thirst." (John 19:28)

"It is finished." (John 19:30)

"Father, into Your hands I commit My spirit!" (Luke 23:46)

The Triumphal Entry

Matthew 21, Mark 11, and Luke 19

When they drew near to Jerusalem and came to the Mount of Olives, then Jesus sent two disciples. He said, "Go into the village in front of you. Immediately you will find a donkey tied, and a colt with her. No one has ever sat on the colt. Untie them and bring them to Me. If anyone says anything to you, you shall say, 'The Lord needs them.' Then he will send them at once."

This took place to fulfill what was spoken by the prophet, saying,

> "Say to the daughter of Zion, 'Behold, your king is coming to you,
>   humble, and mounted on a donkey,
>   and on a colt, the foal of a beast of burden.'"

The disciples did as Jesus had directed them. They found a colt tied at a door outside in the street, and they untied it. Some of those standing there said to them, "What are you doing, untying the colt?"

The disciples told them, "The Lord has need of it." The people let the disciples leave with the animals.

The disciples brought the donkey and the colt. They put their cloaks on the animals, and Jesus sat on them.

Most of the crowd spread their cloaks on the road. Others cut branches from the trees and spread them on the road. The crowds that went before Jesus and that followed Him were shouting, "**Hosanna** to the Son of David! Blessed is He who comes in the name of the Lord! Hosanna in the highest!"

Some of the Pharisees in the crowd said to Jesus, "Teacher, rebuke Your disciples."

Jesus answered, "I tell you, if these were silent, the very stones would cry out."

When He entered Jerusalem, Jesus went into the temple. The whole city was stirred up, saying, "Who is this?"

The crowds said, "This is the prophet Jesus, from Nazareth of Galilee."

Words to Remember

Hosanna to the Son of David! Blessed is He who comes in the name of the Lord! Hosanna in the highest!
Matthew 21:9

DID YOU KNOW?

- The fact that no one had ever sat on the colt meant that it was an unbroken colt, which was normally difficult to ride.

- Jesus commanded that the donkey and her colt be brought to Him in order to fulfill the prophecy recorded in Zechariah 9:9.

- Branches, particularly palms, were used to adorn processions, especially religious ones.

The Widow's Coins

Mark 12

Jesus sat down opposite the treasury and watched the people putting money into the offering box. Many rich people put in large sums.

A poor widow came and put in two small copper coins, which make a penny.

Jesus called His disciples to Him and said to them, "Truly, I say to you, this poor widow has put in more than all those who are contributing to the offering box. For they all contributed out of their abundance, but she out of her poverty has put in everything she had, all she had to live on."

Words to Remember

[Jesus said,] "Truly, I say to you, this poor widow has put in more than all those who are contributing to the offering box. For they all contributed out of their abundance, but she out of her poverty has put in everything she had, all she had to live on."
Mark 12:43–44

DID YOU KNOW?

- Jesus highlights the widow in order to teach what God values. Our giving reflects our priorities.

- Copper coins were the smallest coins in use, but they were all the woman had. She gave proportionately more than all the others.

- Jesus wanted to illustrate the character of absolute dependence on God. Wealth and possession can pose a spiritual threat—wealth has a way of owning its possessor. Jesus' love and sacrifice motivate us to offer our whole lives to Him as our daily offering of gratitude. He gave up everything, including His life, on the cross for us.

The Lord's Supper

Luke 22

As the Passover drew near, the chief priests and the scribes were seeking a way to put Jesus to death, for they feared the people.

Then Satan entered into Judas called Iscariot. He talked with the chief priests and officers about how he might **betray** Jesus to them. They were glad and agreed to give Judas money. So he looked for an opportunity to betray Jesus to them in the absence of a crowd.

Then came the day of Unleavened Bread, on which the Passover lamb had to be sacrificed. Jesus sent Peter and John, saying, "Go and prepare the Passover for us, that we may eat it."

They said to Him, "Where will You have us prepare it?"

Jesus said, "Behold, when you have entered the city, a man carrying a jar of water will meet you. Follow him into the house that he enters. Tell the master of the house, 'The Teacher says to you, Where is the guest room, where I may eat the Passover with My disciples?' He will show you a large upper room furnished. Prepare it there."

Peter and John went and found it just as Jesus had told them. They prepared the Passover.

When the hour came, Jesus reclined at table. The **apostles** were with Him. He said, "I have earnestly desired to eat this Passover with you before I suffer. For I tell you I will not eat it until it is fulfilled in the kingdom of God."

Jesus took bread, and when He had given thanks, He broke it and gave it to them, saying, "This is My body, which is given for you. Do this in remembrance of Me." And likewise the cup after they had eaten, saying, "This cup that is poured out for you is the new covenant in My blood. But behold, the hand of him who betrays Me is with Me on the table."

The disciples began to question one another, which of them it could be who was going to do this.

Peter said to Jesus, "Lord, I am ready to go with You both to prison and to death."

Jesus said, "I tell you, Peter, the rooster will not crow this day, until you **deny** three times that you know Me."

Words to Remember

[Jesus said,] "This is My body, which is given for you. Do this in remembrance of Me. . . . This cup that is poured out for you is the new covenant in My blood." *Luke 22:19–20*

DID YOU KNOW?

- The Feast of Unleavened Bread and the Passover were two festivals commemorating God's deliverance. The two festivals were frequently regarded as one and the names used interchangeably.

- Women usually carried water, so the man carrying a jar of water, whom Jesus told the disciples to look for, would be noticeable.

- They reclined at the table because it was customary to eat while lying on one's left side, especially in formal settings.

Jesus in the Garden

Matthew 26, Mark 14, and Luke 22

After the Passover meal, Jesus went with the disciples to a place called Gethsemane. He said, "Sit here, while I go over there and pray."

Taking with Him Peter and James and John, Jesus began to be sorrowful and troubled. He said, "My soul is very sorrowful, even to death. Remain here, and watch with Me."

Words to Remember

[Jesus said,] "All this has taken place that the Scriptures of the prophets might be fulfilled." *Matthew 26:56*

Going a little farther, Jesus fell on His face and prayed. He said, "My Father, if it be possible, let this cup pass from Me. Nevertheless, not as I will, but as You will."

Jesus came to the disciples and found them sleeping. He said to Peter, "Could you not watch with Me one hour? Watch and pray that you may not enter into temptation. The spirit indeed is willing, but the flesh is weak."

For the second time, Jesus went away and prayed, "My Father, if this cannot pass unless I drink it, Your will be done."

Again Jesus came and found the disciples sleeping, for their eyes were heavy. So, leaving them again, He went away and prayed for the third time. An angel from heaven appeared, strengthening Jesus. And being in an agony, Jesus prayed more earnestly. His sweat became like great drops of blood falling down to the ground.

Then Jesus came to the disciples and said, "Sleep and take your rest later on. See, the hour is at hand. The Son of Man is betrayed into the hands of sinners. Rise, let us be going. See, My betrayer is at hand."

While Jesus was still speaking, Judas came. With him was a great crowd with swords and clubs. Now Judas had given them a sign, saying, "The one I will kiss is the man. Seize Him."

Judas came up to Jesus and said, "Greetings, Rabbi!" And Judas kissed Jesus.

Jesus said, "Friend, do what you came to do." Then they seized Him.

One of those who were with Jesus drew his sword. He struck the servant of the high priest and cut off his ear. Jesus said, "Put your sword back into its place. All who take the sword will perish by the sword. Do you think that I cannot appeal to My Father, and He will at once send Me more than twelve **legions** of angels? But how then should the Scriptures be fulfilled?" And Jesus touched the servant's ear and healed him.

Then all the disciples left Jesus and fled.

DID YOU KNOW?

- *Gethsemane* is a Hebrew word that means "oil press," no doubt referring to the pressing of oil from the olive trees in the area. In Jesus' time, the garden was probably an orchard containing various fruit trees.

- Fully human, Jesus experienced the horror and difficulty of death; unlike all others, He had done nothing to deserve this death.

- The Scriptures say that Jesus' "sweat became like great drops of blood." This may be comparing the drops of sweat with globules of blood. However, severe stress may cause the blood vessels of the skin to break, mixing the blood with sweat (hematidrosis)

Peter Denies Jesus

Matthew 26

Those who had seized Jesus led Him to Caiaphas the high priest, where the scribes and the elders had gathered. Peter was following Jesus at a distance. He went as far as the courtyard of the high priest. Going inside, Peter sat with the guards to see the end. Now the chief priests and the whole Council were seeking false testimony against Jesus that they might put Him to death. They found none, though many false witnesses came forward. At last two came forward and said, "This man said, 'I am able to destroy the temple of God, and to rebuild it in three days.'"

The high priest said, "Have You no answer to make?" But Jesus remained silent. The high priest said, "Tell us if You are the Christ, the Son of God."

Jesus said, "You have said so. But I tell you, from now on you will see the Son of Man seated at the right hand of Power and coming on the clouds of heaven."

Then the high priest tore his robes. He said, "What further witnesses do we need? You have now heard His blasphemy. What is your judgment?"

They answered, "He deserves death."

Then they spit in Jesus' face and struck Him. Some slapped Jesus, saying, "Prophesy to us, You Christ! Who is it that struck You?"

Now Peter was sitting outside in the courtyard. A servant girl came up to him and said, "You also were with Jesus the Galilean."

But Peter denied it before them all, saying, "I do not know what you mean."

When Peter went out to the entrance, another servant girl saw him. She said to the bystanders, "This man was with Jesus of Nazareth."

Again Peter denied it with an oath: "I do not know the man."

After a little while the bystanders came up and said to Peter, "Certainly you too are one of them. Your accent betrays you."

Then Peter began to invoke a curse on himself and to swear, "I do not know the man."

Immediately the rooster crowed. And Peter remembered the saying of Jesus, "Before the rooster crows, you will deny Me three times."

Peter went out and wept bitterly.

Words to Remember

[Jesus said,] "From now on you will see the Son of Man seated at the right hand of Power and coming on the clouds of heaven." *Matthew 26:64*

DID YOU KNOW?

- Peter wanted to see what would happen to Jesus, but from a distance. He was close enough to overhear the results of the trial without endangering his life by being inside.

- They were not able to find false testimony about Jesus because the testimony of at least two witnesses had to agree. Because the testimonies were false, they were inconsistent.

- Blasphemy bore the death penalty in Jewish law.

Jesus' Trial

Matthew 27 and John 18

Words to Remember
[Jesus said,] "My kingdom is not of this world. . . . For this purpose I was born and for this purpose I have come into the world—to bear witness to the truth." *John 18:36–37*

They led Jesus from the house of Caiaphas to the governor's headquarters. Pilate entered and said to Jesus, "Are You the King of the Jews?"

Jesus answered, "My kingdom is not of this world. If My kingdom were of this world, My servants would have been fighting, that I might not be delivered over to the Jews. But My kingdom is not from the world."

Pilate said, "So You are a king?"

Jesus answered, "You say that I am a king. For this purpose I was born and for this purpose I have come into the world—to bear witness to the truth. Everyone who is of the truth listens to My voice."

Pilate said to Jesus, "What is truth?"

After he had said this, Pilate went back outside to the Jews and told them, "I find no guilt in Him."

At the feast, the governor was accustomed to release for the crowd any one prisoner whom they wanted. They had then a notorious prisoner called Barabbas. So Pilate said, "Whom do you want me to release for you: Barabbas, or Jesus who is called Christ?" He knew that it was out of envy that they had delivered Jesus to him.

The chief priests and the elders persuaded the crowd to ask for Barabbas. Pilate said, "Then what shall I do with Jesus who is called Christ?"

They all said, "Let Him be crucified!"

Pilate said, "Why, what evil has He done?"

But they shouted all the more, "Let Him be **crucified**!"

When Pilate saw that a riot was beginning, he took water and washed his hands before the crowd. He said, "I am innocent of this man's blood. See to it yourselves."

All the people answered, "His blood be on us and on our children!"

Then Pilate released Barabbas. Pilate had Jesus scourged, then delivered Him to be crucified.

The soldiers of the governor took Jesus into the governor's headquarters. They stripped Him and put a scarlet robe on Him. Twisting together a crown of thorns, they put it on Jesus' head and put a reed in His right hand. Kneeling before Him, they mocked Him, saying, "Hail, King of the Jews!" The soldiers spit on Jesus and took the reed and struck Him on the head. When they had mocked Jesus, they stripped Him of the robe and put His own clothes on Him and led Him away to crucify Him.

DID YOU KNOW? _____

- Pilate was the Roman governor (prefect) of the province of Judea. Only he had the legal authority to put people to death.

- Jesus did not defend Himself because He was willing to be crucified.

- The washing of hands was a symbol of innocence used by both Jews and Gentiles.

The Crucifixion

Matthew 27, Luke 23, and John 19

Words to Remember

Jesus said, "Father, forgive them, for they know not what they do." *Luke 23:34*

Jesus went out, bearing His own cross, to the place called The Place of a Skull, which is called Golgotha. There they crucified Him, and with Him two others, one on either side. Jesus said, "Father, forgive them, for they know not what they do." The soldiers **cast lots** to divide His garments.

Pilate also wrote an inscription and put it on the cross. It read, "Jesus of Nazareth, the King of the Jews."

One of the criminals who were hanged said, "Are You not the Christ? Save Yourself and us!"

The other said, "Jesus, remember me when You come into Your kingdom."

Jesus said, "Truly, I say to you, today you will be with Me in **Paradise**."

Standing by the cross were Jesus' mother and the disciple whom He loved. Jesus said to His mother, "Woman, behold, your son!" Then He said to the disciple, "Behold, your mother!" From that hour, the disciple took Mary to his own home.

About the ninth hour, Jesus cried, "My God, My God, why have You forsaken Me?"

Knowing that all was now finished, Jesus said, "I thirst." So they put a sponge full of sour wine on a hyssop branch and held it to His mouth. When Jesus had received the wine, He said, "It is finished."

Then Jesus called out with a loud voice, "Father, into Your hands I commit My spirit." He bowed His head and gave up His spirit. And the curtain of the temple was torn in two.

So that the bodies would not remain on the cross on the Sabbath, the Jews asked Pilate to break their legs. When the soldiers came to Jesus and saw that He was already dead, they did not break His legs. But one of the soldiers pierced His side with a spear. At once there came out blood and water. These things took place that the Scripture might be fulfilled: "Not one of His bones will be broken." Another Scripture says, "They will look on Him whom they have pierced."

Joseph of Arimathea, who was a disciple of Jesus, but secretly, for fear of the Jews, asked Pilate for the body of Jesus. Pilate gave him permission. Nicodemus also came, bringing a mixture of myrrh and aloes. So they took the body of Jesus and bound it in linen cloths with the spices.

Now in the place where Jesus was crucified, there was a garden. In the garden there was a new tomb in which no one had yet been laid. Since the tomb was close at hand, Joseph and Nicodemus laid Jesus there.

DID YOU KNOW?

- The inscription was written in Aramaic, which was the local language; Latin, the official language; and Greek, the common language of business. Thus everyone would know the crime of the crucified one.

- The "disciple whom [Jesus] loved" was John, the Gospel writer. This was not a boast that the Lord favored him, but a recognition that the Lord chose to love even him.

- Breaking the legs of the crucified would hasten death, since the victim could no longer hold himself up to avoid eventual asphyxiation.

The Resurrection

Luke 24 and John 20

On the first day of the week, at early dawn, the women went to the tomb, taking the spices they had prepared. They found the stone rolled away from the tomb, but when they went in, they did not find the body of the Lord Jesus.

While they were perplexed about this, two men stood by them in dazzling clothing. The men said, "Why do you seek the living among the dead? Jesus is not here, but has risen. Remember how He told you, while He was still in Galilee, that the Son of Man must be delivered into the hands of sinful men and be crucified and on the third day rise."

Words to Remember

Why do you seek the living among the dead? [Jesus] is not here, but has risen. *Luke 24:5–6*

The women remembered Jesus' words. Returning from the tomb, they told all these things to the eleven and to all the rest. It was Mary Magdalene and Joanna and Mary the mother of James and the other women with them who told these things to the apostles, but they did not believe them.

But Peter rose and ran to the tomb. Stooping and looking in, he saw the linen cloths by themselves. He went home marveling at what had happened.

But Mary Magdalene stood weeping outside the tomb. As she wept, she stooped to look into the tomb. She saw two angels in white, sitting where the body of Jesus had lain, one at the head and one at the feet. They said to her, "Woman, why are you weeping?"

Mary said, "They have taken away my Lord, and I do not know where they have laid Him."

Having said this, she turned around and saw Jesus standing, but she did not know that it was Jesus.

Jesus said to Mary, "Woman, why are you weeping? Whom are you seeking?"

Supposing Him to be the gardener, Mary said to Jesus, "Sir, if you have carried Him away, tell me where you have laid Him, and I will take Him away."

Jesus said to her, "Mary."

Mary turned and said to Him in Aramaic, "Rabboni!" (which means Teacher).

Jesus said, "Do not cling to Me, for I have not yet ascended to the Father. But go to My brothers and say to them, 'I am ascending to My Father and your Father, to My God and your God.'"

Mary Magdalene went and announced to the disciples, "I have seen the Lord"— and that He had said these things to her.

DID YOU KNOW? _____

- Graves were often hollowed-out clefts in a rock. Disk-shaped and several feet in diameter, the stone in front of Jesus' tomb was rolled in a hewn channel to seal off the tomb's entrance and would require several men to move it.

- Though Jesus had promised His own death and resurrection and supported these promises from Scripture, the disciples had not understood the true meaning of the promises.

- Even those who knew Jesus best did not recognize Him until His Word made Him known.

Jesus Appears on the Emmaus Road

Luke 24

Two disciples were going to a village named Emmaus. They were talking with each other about all that had happened. Jesus Himself drew near and went with them. But their eyes were kept from recognizing Him.

Jesus said, "What are you talking about as you walk?"

Cleopas answered, "Are You the only visitor to Jerusalem who does not know the things that have happened there?"

Jesus said to them, "What things?"

They said, "Concerning Jesus of Nazareth, a man who was a prophet mighty in deed and word before God and all the people. How our chief priests and rulers delivered Him up to be condemned to death, and crucified Him. But we had hoped that He was the one to redeem Israel. Besides all this, it is now the third day since these things happened. Some women of our company were at the tomb early in the morning. When they did not find His body, they came back saying that they had even seen a vision of angels, who said that Jesus was alive. Some of those who were with us found the tomb just as the women had said, but they did not see Jesus."

Jesus said, "O foolish ones, and slow of heart to believe all that the prophets have spoken! Was it not necessary that the Christ should suffer these things and enter into His glory?" Beginning with Moses and all the Prophets, Jesus interpreted to them in all the Scriptures the things concerning Himself.

They drew near to the village. Jesus acted as if He were going farther, but the disciples urged Him strongly, saying, "Stay with us. The day is now far spent."

So Jesus went in to stay with them. When He was at table with them, Jesus took the bread and blessed and broke it and gave it to them. And their eyes were opened, and they recognized Him. And Jesus vanished from their sight.

The disciples said to each other, "Did not our hearts burn within us while He talked to us on the road, while He opened to us the Scriptures?" They immediately returned to Jerusalem.

They found the eleven and those who were with them gathered together, saying, "The Lord has risen indeed, and has appeared to Simon!"

Then the two disciples told what had happened on the road, and how Jesus was known to them in the breaking of the bread.

Words to Remember

[Jesus said,] "O foolish ones, and slow of heart to believe all that the prophets have spoken! Was it not necessary that the Christ should suffer these things and enter into His glory?"
Luke 24:25–26

DID YOU KNOW?

- This story is unique to Luke; it does not appear in any of the other Gospels.

- Even though Jesus is a guest, He becomes the host. To take, bless, break, and distribute bread ordinarily began a meal. This was not necessarily the Lord's Supper.

- Jesus vanishes because once the disciples realize He is alive, His visible presence is unnecessary.

Jesus Appears to Thomas

John 20

On the evening of the first day of the week, the doors being locked where the disciples were for fear of the Jews, Jesus came and stood among them. He said to them, "Peace be with you."

When He had said this, Jesus showed them His hands and His side. Then the disciples were glad when they saw the Lord. Jesus said to them again, "Peace be with you. As the Father has sent Me, even so I am sending you."

When He had said this, Jesus breathed on them and said to them, "Receive the Holy Spirit. If you forgive the sins of any, they are forgiven them; if you withhold forgiveness from any, it is withheld."

Now Thomas, one of the Twelve, called the Twin, was not with the disciples when Jesus came. So the other disciples told him, "We have seen the Lord."

But Thomas said to them, "Unless I see in His hands the mark of the nails, and place my finger into the mark of the nails, and place my hand into His side, I will never believe."

Eight days later, Jesus' disciples were inside again. Thomas was with them. Although the doors were locked, Jesus came and stood among them. He said, "Peace be with you."

Then Jesus said to Thomas, "Put your finger here, and see My hands. Put out your hand, and place it in My side. Do not disbelieve, but believe."

Thomas answered Him, "My Lord and my God!"

Jesus said to Thomas, "Have you believed because you have seen Me? Blessed are those who have not seen and yet have believed."

Now Jesus did many other signs in the presence of the disciples, which are not written in this book. But these are written so that you may believe that Jesus is the Christ, the Son of God, and that by believing you may have life in His name.

Words to Remember

These are written so that you may believe that Jesus is the Christ, the Son of God, and that by believing you may have life in His name. *John 20:31*

DID YOU KNOW?

- The disciples were afraid of the Jews who handed Jesus over to the authority of imperial Rome for Jesus' alleged conspiracy against the government.

- After His resurrection, Jesus more fully manifested His divine attributes. Thus, though still completely human, He did not allow physical barriers such as a door to keep Him from revealing Himself to His disciples.

- The Greek word for "blessed," *makarios*, occurs only twice in John (cf. 13:17). It denotes not merely happiness but truly receiving God's gracious favor.

Jesus and Peter

John 21

Jesus revealed Himself again to the disciples by the Sea of Tiberias in this way. Simon Peter, Thomas (called the Twin), Nathanael of Cana in Galilee, the sons of Zebedee, and two others of His disciples were together. Simon Peter said, "I am going fishing."

The others said to Peter, "We will go with you." They got into the boat, but that night they caught nothing.

Just as day was breaking, Jesus stood on the shore. The disciples did not know that it was Jesus. Jesus said, "Children, do you have any fish?"

They answered, "No."

Jesus said, "Cast the net on the right side of the boat, and you will find some." So they cast it, and now they were not able to haul it in, because of the quantity of fish.

That disciple whom Jesus loved said to Peter, "It is the Lord!" When Simon Peter heard that it was the Lord, he put on his outer garment, for he was stripped for work, and threw himself into the sea. The other disciples came in the boat, dragging the net full of fish, for they were not far from the land.

When they got out on land, they saw a charcoal fire with fish laid out on it, and bread. Jesus said, "Bring some of the fish that you have just caught." So Simon Peter went aboard and hauled the net ashore, full of large fish, 153 of them. And although there were so many, the net was not torn.

Jesus said, "Come and have breakfast." Jesus came and took the bread and gave it to the disciples, and so with the fish. This was now the third time that Jesus was revealed to the disciples after He was raised from the dead.

When they had finished breakfast, Jesus said to Simon Peter, "Simon, son of John, do you love Me more than these?"

Peter said, "Yes, Lord. You know that I love You."

Jesus said, "Feed My lambs." He said to him a second time, "Simon, son of John, do you love Me?"

Peter said, "Yes, Lord. You know that I love You."

Jesus said, "Tend My sheep." He said to him the third time, "Simon, son of John, do you love Me?"

Peter was grieved. He said, "Lord, You know everything. You know that I love You."

Jesus said, "Feed My sheep."

Words to Remember

[Peter] said to [Jesus], "Lord, You know everything; You know that I love You." Jesus said to him, "Feed My sheep." *John 21:17*

DID YOU KNOW?

- This miraculous catch of fish is reminiscent of the fish caught when Jesus called the first disciples (see Luke 5:1–11).

- "Children" was not a common form of address, but was perhaps equivalent to present-day "boys" or "guys."

- Peter denied the Lord three times, and now the Lord invited him to declare his love for Him three times. The Lord's threefold calling restored Peter for future service to Him and to His Church.

Jesus Ascends to Heaven

Matthew 28 and Acts 1

Jesus presented Himself alive to the disciples after His suffering by many proofs. He appeared to them during forty days and spoke about the kingdom of God. While staying with them, Jesus ordered them not to depart from Jerusalem, but to wait for the promise of the Father.

Now the eleven disciples went to Galilee, to the mountain to which Jesus had directed them. Jesus came and said, "All authority in heaven and on earth has been given to Me. Go therefore and make disciples of all nations, baptizing them in the name of the Father and of the Son and of the Holy Spirit, teaching them to observe all that I have commanded you. And behold, I am with you always, to the end of the age."

They asked Jesus, "Lord, will You at this time restore the kingdom to Israel?"

Jesus said, "It is not for you to know times or seasons that the Father has fixed by His own authority. But you will receive power when the Holy Spirit has come upon you. And you will be My witnesses in Jerusalem and in all Judea and Samaria, and to the end of the earth." When Jesus had said these things, as they were looking on, Jesus was lifted up, and a cloud took Him out of their sight.

While they were gazing into heaven as He went, behold, two men stood by them in white robes. They said, "Men of Galilee, why do you stand looking into heaven? This Jesus, who was taken up from you into heaven, will come in the same way as you saw Him go into heaven."

Then the disciples returned to Jerusalem. They went to the upper room, where they were staying, Peter and John and James and Andrew, Philip and Thomas, Bartholomew and Matthew, James the son of Alphaeus and Simon the Zealot and Judas the son of James. All these with one accord were devoting themselves to prayer, together with the women and Mary the mother of Jesus, and His brothers.

Peter stood up and said, "Brothers, the Scripture had to be fulfilled concerning Judas, who became a guide to those who arrested Jesus. So one of the men who have accompanied us during all the time that the Lord Jesus went in and out among us must become with us a witness to His resurrection."

They put forward Joseph called Barsabbas and Matthias. They prayed, "You, Lord, who know the hearts of all, show which one of these two You have chosen." They cast lots. The lot fell on Matthias, and he was numbered with the eleven apostles.

DID YOU KNOW?

- Luke and Acts form a two-part account, with Acts depicting the growth of the apostolic Church as a consequence of Christ's life, death, and resurrection.

- The cloud is an Old Testament symbol of God's immediate, majestic presence. (See, e.g., Exodus 16:10.)

- Just as they had at the annunciation (Luke 1:26–27) and for Jesus' birth (Luke 2:8–14), ministry (Mark 1:13; Luke 22:43), and resurrection (Matthew 28:2–7), angels also appear here at the ascension. As God's messengers, they explain the significance of these events.

The Holy Spirit Leads God's Church

The Lord added to their number day by day
those who were being saved. *Acts 2:47*

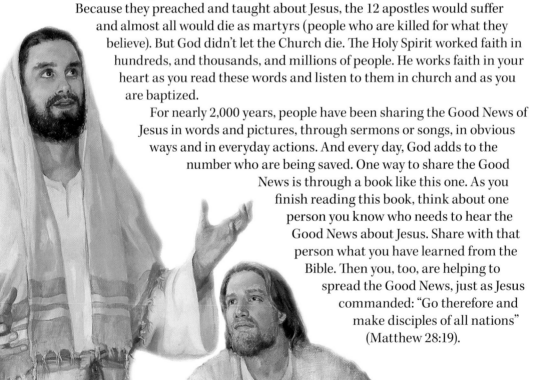

Throughout this entire book, you have been reading parts of God's Word, the Bible. You have learned about the very beginning, how God created the world and everything in it. You have learned about the first people, the first family, and the first sin. You have read about God's people, from Adam to the disciples and so many more in between. You have read about promises God made and how He kept those promises. You have heard the very best news about Jesus, the Savior, and about His life, death, and resurrection. Now what?

In this final section, all the Bible stories describe how God the Holy Spirit worked through the disciples, now called apostles (or "sent ones"), to tell others about Jesus. Because they preached and taught about Jesus, the 12 apostles would suffer and almost all would die as martyrs (people who are killed for what they believe). But God didn't let the Church die. The Holy Spirit worked faith in hundreds, and thousands, and millions of people. He works faith in your heart as you read these words and listen to them in church and as you are baptized.

For nearly 2,000 years, people have been sharing the Good News of Jesus in words and pictures, through sermons or songs, in obvious ways and in everyday actions. And every day, God adds to the number who are being saved. One way to share the Good News is through a book like this one. As you finish reading this book, think about one person you know who needs to hear the Good News about Jesus. Share with that person what you have learned from the Bible. Then you, too, are helping to spread the Good News, just as Jesus commanded: "Go therefore and make disciples of all nations" (Matthew 28:19).

Making Connections

What do you do when you hear good news? You tell someone, of course!

You know that Jesus lived, died, and rose again for you. You know that Jesus has forgiven you and made you part of God's family, the Church. What do you do with this Good News? You tell a friend, a cousin, a neighbor. You tell everyone!

If you feel like you don't know the right words, that's okay. You tell people about Jesus by how you act. Do you treat others with respect? Do you always do your best? Do you have a smile on your face and in your heart? People wonder why you act like this. When they ask, you can say, "I act this way because Jesus loves me and I love Jesus. Do you know that Jesus loves you too?" Witnessing is that simple.

PAUL'S MISSIONARY JOURNEYS AND TRIP TO ROME

Acts

AD 33 Resurrection, Ascension, Pentecost • AD 49 Jerusalem Council • AD 70 Romans destroy Jerusalem

Acts tells the story of how God's witnesses spread the Gospel from Israel, at the boundaries of three continents, to the ends of the earth.

Africa

Acts describes the early spread of the Gospel to distant Ethiopia, but oddly does not include any history of how the Gospel first reached Egypt.

Asia

Christianity is an Asian religion. The region of Syria became a vital early center of Christianity, which spread ever further east.

Europe

Roman Europe viewed Christianity as a form of Judaism until the Jews protested that Christianity was truly different.

Jerusalem & Judea,
    chapters 1–7, 12, 15
Samaria, chapter 8
Ethiopia, chapter 8
Antioch & Asia,
    chapters 11, 13–20
Rome, chapters 21–28

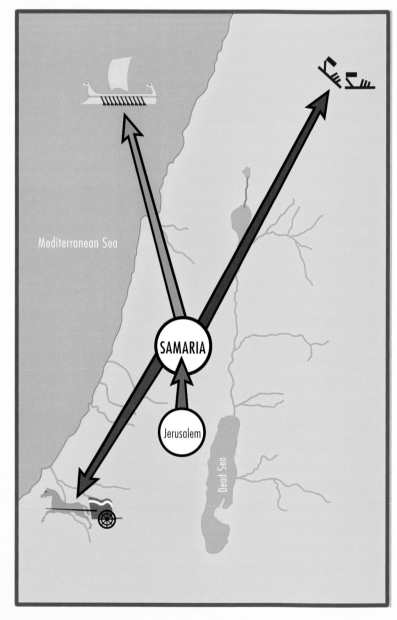

Mediterranean Sea

SAMARIA

Jerusalem

Dead Sea

The Holy Spirit, Peter, and Paul

Two main characters in Acts are the apostles Peter and Paul, whom the Holy Spirit moves to spread the Gospel from Jerusalem to Rome.

Acts ends with Paul at Rome under house arrest. According to church tradition, both Peter and Paul died as martyrs in Rome in AD 68.

Peter's route (Acts 1–15)

- Jerusalem
- Temple
- Sanhedrin
- Samaria
- Lydda
- Joppa
- Caesarea
- Jerusalem

Paul's route (Acts 9–28)

- Damascus
- Antioch
- Iconium
- Lystra
- Antioch
- Jerusalem
- Macedonia
- Athens
- Corinth
- Antioch
- Ephesus
- Jerusalem
- Temple
- Sanhedrin
- Caesarea
- Crete
- Malta

Rome

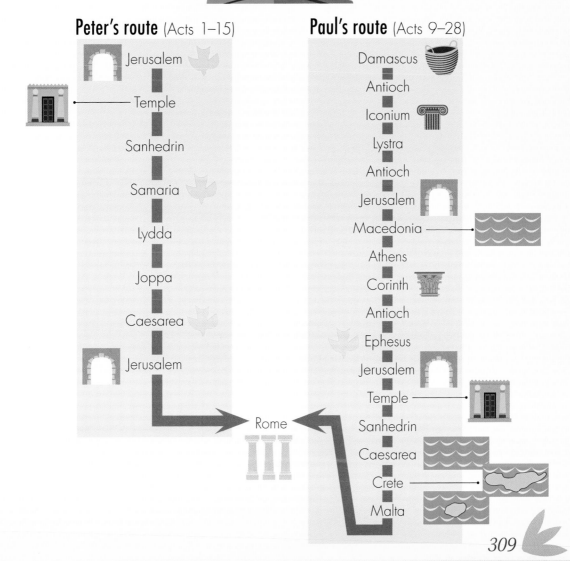

Pentecost

Acts 2

When the day of Pentecost arrived, all the disciples were together in one place. Suddenly there came from heaven a sound like a mighty rushing wind, and it filled the entire house. Divided tongues as of fire appeared to them and rested on each one of them. They were all filled with the Holy Spirit and began to speak in other **tongues** as the Spirit gave them utterance.

There were dwelling in Jerusalem Jews, **devout** men from every nation under heaven. At this sound the multitude came together. They were amazed and said, "Are not all these who are speaking Galileans? How is it that we hear them telling in our own tongues the mighty works of God?"

But others mocked the disciples and said, "They are filled with new wine."

Peter, standing with the eleven, addressed the crowd: "Men of Judea and all who dwell in Jerusalem, these people are not drunk. But this is what was said through the prophet Joel:

> "'And in the last days it shall be, God declares, that I will pour out My Spirit on all flesh. Your sons and your daughters shall prophesy,
>> and your young men shall see visions,
>> and your old men shall dream dreams.'

"Men of Israel, hear these words: Jesus of Nazareth, a man attested to you by God with mighty wonders and signs that God did through Him in your midst— this Jesus, delivered up according to the definite plan of God, you crucified and killed by the hands of lawless men. This Jesus God raised up. Of that we all are witnesses. Being therefore exalted at the right hand of God, and having received from the Father the promise of the Holy Spirit, He has poured out this that you are seeing and hearing. God has made Him both Lord and Christ, this Jesus whom you crucified."

When the crowd heard this, they were cut to the heart. They said to Peter and the rest of the apostles, "Brothers, what shall we do?"

Peter said, "Repent and be baptized every one of you in the name of Jesus Christ for the forgiveness of your sins, and you will receive the gift of the Holy Spirit. The promise is for you and for your children and for all who are far off, everyone whom the Lord our God calls to Himself."

Those who received Peter's word were baptized. There were added that day about three thousand souls.

Words to Remember

Repent and be baptized every one of you in the name of Jesus Christ for the forgiveness of your sins, and you will receive the gift of the Holy Spirit. *Acts 2:38*

DID YOU KNOW?

- The word *Pentecost* means "fiftieth." Jews celebrated the Feast of the Pentecost on the fiftieth day after the Passover Sabbath (Leviticus 23:15–21). It was also called "the Feast of Weeks" or "the Feast of Harvest" and marked the completion of the harvest season.

- Christians today celebrate Pentecost fifty days after Easter, remembering that Jesus kept His promise to send the Holy Spirit on that day.

- Peter is the spokesman for the Twelve; he is always named first in lists of the apostles.

Peter and John Heal a Lame Man

Acts 3

Peter and John were going up to the temple at the hour of prayer. A man lame from birth was being carried, whom they laid daily at the gate of the temple that is called the Beautiful Gate. The man would ask **alms** of those entering the temple. Seeing Peter and John, he asked to receive alms.

Peter looked at the man, as did John, and said, "Look at us." The man looked at them, expecting to receive something. But Peter said, "I have no silver and gold. What I do have I give to you. In the name of Jesus Christ of Nazareth, rise up and walk!" And Peter took the man by the right hand and raised him up.

Immediately the man's feet and ankles were made strong. Leaping up, he stood and began to walk. The man entered the temple with Peter and John, walking and leaping and praising God.

While the man clung to Peter and John, all the people, utterly astounded, ran to them in the portico called Solomon's. When Peter saw it, he addressed the people: "Men of Israel, why do you wonder at this? Why do you stare at us, as though by our own power or **piety** we have made this man walk? The God of Abraham, the God of Isaac, and the God of Jacob, the God of our fathers, glorified His servant Jesus, whom you delivered over and denied in the presence of Pilate. You killed the Author of life, whom God raised from the dead. To this we are witnesses. Jesus' name—by faith in His name—has made this man strong. The faith that is through Jesus has given the man this perfect health in the presence of you all.

"Now, brothers, I know that you acted in ignorance, as did also your rulers. But what God foretold by the mouth of all the prophets, that His Christ would suffer, He fulfilled. Repent therefore, and turn again, that your sins may be blotted out, that times of refreshing may come from the presence of the Lord, and that He may send the Christ appointed for you, Jesus. Moses said, 'The Lord God will raise up for you a prophet like me from your brothers.' All the prophets who have spoken, from Samuel and those who came after him, also proclaimed these days. You are the sons of the prophets and of the covenant that God made, saying to Abraham, 'In your offspring shall all the families of the earth be blessed.' God, having raised up His servant, sent Jesus to you first, to bless you by turning every one of you from your wickedness."

DID YOU KNOW?

- Jesus' holy name works not by magic but through trust, or faith. Faith in Jesus completes the people's existing faith in the God of Israel and His promised Messiah.

- Peter says the men acted in ignorance because, since Christ rarely showed His divine majesty on earth, the people did not fully understand who He was.

- Repentance is God's work that leads a person to renounce sin — requesting God's mercy and returning to His way.

God's Servant Stephen

Acts 6–7

Words to Remember

Behold, I see the heavens opened, and the Son of Man standing at the right hand of God. *Acts 7:56*

When the disciples were increasing in number, a complaint arose because some widows were being neglected. The Twelve summoned all the disciples and said, "It is not right that we should give up preaching the Word of God to serve tables. Pick seven men of good **repute**, full of the Spirit and of wisdom, whom we will appoint to this duty." The whole gathering chose Stephen and six other men. These they set before the apostles, and they prayed and laid their hands on them.

Stephen, full of grace and power, was doing great wonders and signs among the people. Some members of the synagogue of the Freedmen and other Jews disputed with Stephen. But they could not withstand the wisdom and the Spirit with which Stephen was speaking. So they stirred up the people, who seized Stephen and brought him before the council. False witnesses said, "We have heard this man say that Jesus of Nazareth will destroy this place and will change the customs that Moses delivered to us."

Stephen spoke to the assembly, reminding the people of the call of Abraham, how Joseph saved his family during the famine, the call of Moses, and how God brought the children of Israel out of Egypt. Stephen said: "Our fathers had the tent of witness in the wilderness. So it was until the days of David, who asked to find a dwelling place for the God of Jacob. But it was Solomon who built a house for Him. Yet the Most High does not dwell in houses made by hands. You stiff-necked people, you always resist the Holy Spirit. As your fathers did, so do you. They killed those who announced beforehand the coming of the **Righteous One**, whom you have now betrayed and murdered."

When they heard these things, they were enraged. But Stephen, full of the Holy Spirit, gazed into heaven and saw the glory of God. He said, "Behold, I see the heavens opened, and the Son of Man standing at the right hand of God."

But they cried out with a loud voice and stopped their ears and rushed together at him. Then they cast Stephen out of the city and stoned him. The witnesses laid down their garments at the feet of a young man named Saul.

As they were stoning Stephen, he called out, "Lord Jesus, receive my spirit." And falling to his knees he cried out with a loud voice, "Lord, do not hold this sin against them." And when Stephen had said this, he fell asleep.

DID YOU KNOW?

- By instituting the separate office of deacon, the Church's practical affairs (especially relief of the poor) were entrusted to different office bearers. Though Christ alone had authority to establish the apostolic ministry, the apostles could establish other offices according to the Church's needs.

- The "Freedmen" were likely Jews from Italy, freed from slavery.

- Luke (the author of Acts) wrote that Stephen "fell asleep" because, since Christ conquered sin, death, and the power of the devil, when believers die, their death leads to everlasting life.

Philip and the Ethiopian

Acts 8

An angel of the Lord said to Philip, "Rise and go toward the south to the road that goes down from Jerusalem to Gaza." This is a desert place. And Philip rose and went.

There was an Ethiopian, a eunuch, a court official of Candace, queen of the Ethiopians, who was in charge of all her treasure. He had come to Jerusalem to worship and was returning, seated in his chariot. He was reading the prophet Isaiah.

> **Words to Remember**
> Like a sheep He was led to the slaughter and like a lamb before its shearer is silent, so He opens not His mouth.
> *Acts 8:32*

The Spirit said to Philip, "Go over and join this chariot."

So Philip ran to the eunuch. He heard him reading Isaiah the prophet. Philip asked, "Do you understand what you are reading?"

The eunuch said, "How can I, unless someone guides me?" And he invited Philip to come sit with him. Now the passage of Scripture that he was reading was this:

> "Like a sheep He was led to the slaughter
> and like a lamb before its shearer is silent,
> so He opens not his mouth.
> In His humiliation justice was denied Him.
> Who can describe His generation?
> For His life is taken away from the earth."

The eunuch said to Philip, "About whom does the prophet say this, about himself or about someone else?"

Then Philip opened his mouth, and beginning with this Scripture he told the eunuch the Good News about Jesus.

As they were going along the road, they came to some water. The eunuch said, "See, here is water! What prevents me from being baptized?"

He commanded the chariot to stop, and they both went down into the water. Philip baptized the eunuch. When they came up out of the water, the Spirit of the Lord carried Philip away. The eunuch saw Philip no more, and went on his way rejoicing.

Philip found himself at Azotus. As he passed through, he preached the **Gospel** to all the towns until he came to Caesarea.

DID YOU KNOW?

- Judeans fled to Egypt during the Babylonian exile and settled in Upper Egypt. They likely spread the faith southward into Nubia and Ethiopia.

- Although the term *eunuch* sometimes refers to a castrated man, that was not always the case. In the Israelite kingdom period, eunuchs were minor officials, but in other nations, they served in more important administrative roles.

- The Ethiopian must have been a man of considerable means and education to be able to afford such a large scroll as Isaiah.

The Conversion of Saul

Acts 9

Words to Remember

The Lord said, . . . "[Saul] is a chosen instrument of Mine to carry My name before the Gentiles and kings and the children of Israel." *Acts 9:15*

Saul asked the high priest for letters to the synagogues at Damascus, so that if he found any belonging to **the Way** he might bring them bound to Jerusalem.

As he approached Damascus, suddenly a light from heaven flashed around Saul. Falling to the ground, he heard a voice saying to him, "Saul, Saul, why are you persecuting Me?"

Saul said, "Who are You, Lord?"

He said, "I am Jesus, whom you are persecuting. But rise and enter the city, You will be told what you are to do."

The men who were traveling with Saul stood speechless, hearing the voice but seeing no one. Saul rose from the ground. Although his eyes were opened, he saw nothing. So they led him by the hand and brought him into Damascus. For three days, Saul was without sight. He neither ate nor drank.

There was a disciple at Damascus named Ananias. The Lord said to him in a vision, "Rise and go to the street called Straight. At the house of Judas, look for a man of Tarsus named Saul. He is praying, and he has seen in a vision a man named Ananias come in and lay his hands on him so that he might regain his sight."

But Ananias answered, "Lord, I have heard from many about this man, how much evil he has done to Your saints at Jerusalem."

But the Lord said, "Go, for he is a chosen instrument of Mine to carry My name before the Gentiles and kings and the children of Israel. For I will show him how much he must suffer for the sake of My name."

Ananias departed and entered the house. Laying his hands on Saul, Ananias said, "Brother Saul, the Lord Jesus who appeared to you on the road by which you came has sent me so that you may regain your sight and be filled with the Holy Spirit." Immediately, something like scales fell from Saul's eyes, and he regained his sight. Then Saul rose and was baptized. Taking food, he was strengthened.

Immediately Saul proclaimed Jesus in the synagogues, saying, "He is the Son of God." All who heard him were amazed. Saul confounded the Jews who lived in Damascus by proving that Jesus was the Christ.

When Saul had come to Jerusalem, he attempted to join the disciples. They were all afraid, for they did not believe that he was a believer. But Barnabas brought Saul to the apostles. So Saul went in and out among them at Jerusalem, preaching boldly in the name of the Lord.

DID YOU KNOW?

- This is the same Saul who was present at Stephen's stoning.

- "The Way" is a name for Christianity used only in the Book of Acts.

- Some interpreters treat Saul's experience as a model for Christian conversion, as though every person has to experience a crisis in order to become a Christian. However, although God can and does work in people's lives through crises, conversion is always the work of the Holy Spirit through the Means of Grace.

- The Lord often calls those least likely to serve His plans of salvation.

Peter and Cornelius

Acts 10

Words to Remember
God shows no partiality, but in every nation anyone who fears Him and does what is right is acceptable to Him. *Acts 10:34–35*

At Caesarea there was a man named Cornelius, a centurion of what was known as the Italian Cohort. He was a devout man who feared God with all his household. He saw clearly in a vision an angel of God say to him, "Your prayers and your alms have ascended as a memorial before God. Now send men to Joppa and bring one Simon who is called Peter." So Cornelius sent two servants and a devout soldier to Joppa.

The next day, Peter went up on the housetop to pray. He became hungry and wanted something to eat, but while food was being prepared, he fell into a trance. He saw the heavens opened and something like a great sheet descending, being let down by its four corners upon the earth. In it were all kinds of animals and reptiles and birds of the air. A voice said: "Rise, Peter; kill and eat. What God has made clean, do not call common." This happened three times.

While Peter was pondering the vision, the Spirit said to him, "Three men are looking for you. Accompany them without hesitation, for I have sent them." So Peter went away with the men.

Cornelius was expecting them and had called together his relatives and close friends. When Peter entered, Cornelius fell down at his feet and worshiped him. But Peter said, "Stand up. I, too, am a man. You know how unlawful it is for a Jew to associate with or to visit anyone of another nation, but God has shown me that I should not call any person common or unclean. So I came without objection. Why have you sent for me?"

Cornelius explained to Peter about his vision. He said, "We are all here in the presence of God to hear all that you have been commanded by the Lord."

Peter said: "Truly I understand that God shows no partiality, but in every nation anyone who fears Him and does what is right is acceptable to Him. Jesus commanded us to preach to the people and to testify that He is the one appointed by God to be judge of the living and the dead. To Him all the prophets bear witness that everyone who believes in Him receives forgiveness of sins through His name."

While Peter was still speaking, the Holy Spirit fell on all who heard the word. The believers from among the circumcised who had come with Peter were amazed, because the gift of the Holy Spirit was poured out even on the Gentiles. Then Peter declared, "Can anyone withhold water for baptizing these people, who have received the Holy Spirit just as we have?" And Peter commanded them to be baptized in the name of Jesus Christ.

DID YOU KNOW?

- A centurion was a Roman officer in command of one hundred soldiers. The Roman legion, nominally six thousand men, was divided into ten cohorts, or regiments, each of approximately six hundred soldiers.

- Although Cornelius was pious and generous, he did not yet know Jesus as his Savior from sin. He would have known there was a coming Messiah.

- Some homes had a flat roof reached by an external stairway. Peter likely went up to the housetop for solitude to pray.

Peter's Escape from Prison

Acts 12

Herod the king killed James the brother of John with the sword. When he saw that it pleased the Jews, Herod arrested Peter also. When he had seized Peter, he put him in prison, delivering him over to four squads of soldiers to guard him. After the Passover, Herod intended to bring Peter out to the people. Peter was kept in prison, but earnest prayer for him was made to God by the church.

Words to Remember

[Peter] said, "Now I am sure that the Lord has sent His angel and rescued me." *Acts 12:11*

Now when Herod was about to bring him out, on that very night, Peter was sleeping between two soldiers. He was bound with two chains, and sentries before the door were guarding the prison. Behold, an angel of the Lord stood next to Peter, and a light shone in the cell. The angel struck Peter on the side and woke him, saying, "Get up quickly." The chains fell off Peter's hands.

The angel said to Peter, "Dress yourself and put on your sandals." He did so. The angel said, "Wrap your cloak around you and follow me." Peter went out and followed the angel. He did not know that what was being done by the angel was real, but thought he was seeing a vision.

When they had passed the first and the second guard, Peter and the angel came to the iron gate leading into the city. It opened for them of its own accord, and they went out and went along one street. Immediately the angel left Peter.

When Peter came to himself, he said, "Now I am sure that the Lord has sent His angel and rescued me from the hand of Herod and from all that the Jewish people were expecting."

When he realized this, Peter went to the house where many were gathered together and were praying. When he knocked at the door, a servant girl named Rhoda came to answer. Recognizing Peter's voice, in her joy she did not open the gate but ran in and reported that Peter was standing at the gate. They said to her, "You are out of your mind." But she kept insisting that it was so.

Peter continued knocking, and when they opened, they saw him and were amazed. But motioning to them with his hand to be silent, he described to them how the Lord had brought him out of the prison.

Peter said, "Tell these things to James and to the brothers." Then he departed and went to another place.

DID YOU KNOW?

- The leaders showed fearful respect for the crowds and their festivals, as shown by the fact that Herod waited until after the Passover to punish Peter.

- The angel told Peter to dress himself because the guards had likely deprived him of warm clothing as a means of punishment.

- Later tradition suggested that the house Peter went to was the site of the Upper Room, where Jesus instituted the Lord's Supper.

Paul's First Missionary Journey

Acts 13–14

The Holy Spirit said, "Set apart for Me Barnabas and Saul for the work to which I have called them." After fasting and praying they laid their hands on them and sent them off.

When Barnabas and Saul, who was also called Paul, arrived at Salamis, they proclaimed the Word of God in the synagogues. Then they set sail and came to Antioch. On the Sabbath day, they went into the synagogue and sat down. After the reading from the Law and the Prophets, the rulers of the synagogue said, "Brothers, if you have any word of encouragement for the people, say it."

Words to Remember

God raised [Jesus] from the dead . . . and by Him everyone who believes is freed from everything from which you could not be freed by the Law of Moses. *Acts 13:30, 39*

Paul stood up and said: "Men of Israel and you who fear God, listen. The God of this people Israel chose our fathers and made the people great during their stay in the land of Egypt. With uplifted arm He led them out of it. For about forty years He put up with them in the wilderness. He gave them their land as an inheritance. After that He gave them judges until Samuel the prophet. Then God gave them Saul. When He had removed Saul, He raised up David. Of this man's offspring, God has brought to Israel a Savior, Jesus, as He promised.

"Brothers, sons of the family of Abraham, and those among you who fear God, to us has been sent the message of this salvation. We bring you the Good News that what God promised to the fathers, this He has fulfilled to us their children by raising Jesus. Let it be known to you therefore, brothers, that through this man forgiveness of sins is proclaimed to you. By Him everyone who believes is freed from everything from which you could not be freed by the Law of Moses."

As Barnabas and Paul went out, the people begged to hear these things the next Sabbath. The next Sabbath, almost the whole city gathered to hear the Word of the Lord. But when the Jews saw the crowds, they were filled with jealousy. They began to contradict what was spoken by Paul. Paul and Barnabas spoke out boldly, saying, "It was necessary that the Word of God be spoken first to you. Since you thrust it aside and judge yourselves unworthy of eternal life, behold, we are turning to the Gentiles."

When the Gentiles heard this, they began rejoicing and glorifying the Word of the Lord. As many as were appointed to eternal life believed. And the Word of the Lord was spreading throughout the whole region.

DID YOU KNOW?

- Antioch was the political, military, and commercial center for Roman Syria and the Persian frontier; it was one of the most important cities of the empire.

- It was Paul's pattern to begin his mission work in a city's synagogue, preaching the Gospel first to the Jews and then to the Gentiles. His first missionary journey took place over a decade after his conversion.

- Qualified visitors to the synagogue were normally invited to give the message, like guest preachers.

Paul's Letters

Paul wrote letters that encouraged the churches to grow in faith and love and sometimes corrected problems. In each letter, Paul shared the Good News of Jesus Christ.

From Paul's Letter to the Romans

Paul, a servant of Christ Jesus, called to be an apostle, set apart for the Gospel of God.

To all those in Rome who are loved by God and called to be saints:

I am eager to preach the Gospel to you also who are in Rome. For I am not ashamed of the Gospel, for it is the power of God for salvation to everyone who believes, to the Jew first and also to the Greek. For in it the righteousness of God is revealed from faith for faith, as it is written, "The righteous shall live by faith."

Therefore, since we have been justified by faith, we have peace with God through our Lord Jesus Christ.

Words to Remember

By grace you have been saved through faith. And this is not your own doing; it is the gift of God. *Ephesians 2:8*

From Paul's Letter to the Ephesians

Paul, an apostle of Christ Jesus by the will of God,

To the saints who are in Ephesus, and are faithful in Christ Jesus:

God, being rich in mercy, because of the great love with which He loved us, even when we were dead in our trespasses, made us alive together with Christ. For by grace you have been saved through faith. And this is not your own doing; it is the gift of God, not a result of works, so that no one may boast. For we are His workmanship, created in Christ Jesus for good works, which God prepared beforehand, that we should walk in them.

From Paul's First Letter to the Thessalonians

Paul, Silvanus, and Timothy,

To the church of the Thessalonians in God the Father and the Lord Jesus Christ:

We give thanks to God always for all of you, constantly mentioning you in our prayers, remembering before our God and Father your work of faith and labor of love and steadfastness of hope in our Lord Jesus Christ.

We also thank God constantly for this, that when you received the Word of God, which you heard from us, you accepted it not as the word of men but as what it really is, the Word of God, which is at work in you believers.

May the Lord establish your hearts blameless in holiness before our God and Father, at the coming of our Lord Jesus with all His saints.

DID YOU KNOW?

- The reformer Martin Luther thought so highly of Romans that he recommended all Christians memorize the entire book (see *Luther's Works*, American Edition, 35:365).

- Paul wrote Ephesians, Philemon, Philippians, and Colossians while he was imprisoned in Rome. Paul founded the Church in Ephesus and served as its pastor for nearly three years.

- Together, the two Thessalonian letters contain more about Jesus' second coming than any of Paul's other writings.

Faith growing, love increasing.

1 & 2 Thessalonians

AD 33 Resurrection of Jesus • c. AD 51–52 Paul writes to the Thessalonians • AD 68 Martyrdom of Paul

Purpose: To restore relations with the Thessalonian Christians and answer their questions about the return of Christ.

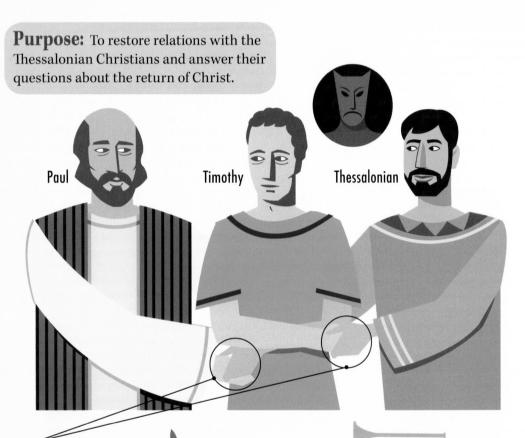

Paul

Timothy

Thessalonian

Restoration Persecution prevented the apostle Paul from visiting the congregation, but he sent Timothy, who was unknown to the persecutors.

Growth Paul praised God and the Thessalonians because, despite persecution, the congregation grew in both faith and love.

Return of Christ In both letters, Paul answers questions about the return of Jesus. He describes a future persecution by "the man of lawlessness," whom the Lord will overcome.

 Sin & Law

Imitation; affliction; God's wrath; sanctification; idleness; steadfastness; eternal destruction; man of lawlessness

 Grace & Gospel

Deliverance; God's Word at work; established blameless; resurrection of the dead; complete sanctification; God's faithfulness and righteousness; Jesus gathers us; the Spirit sanctifies us

Steadfast under trial.

James

AD 49 Jerusalem Council • AD 62 Martyrdom of James, brother of our Lord • AD 70 Romans destroy Jerusalem

Faith brings forth works.

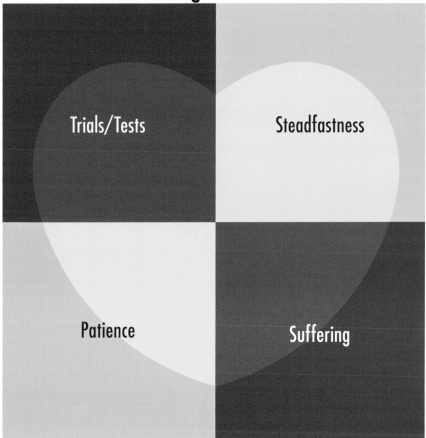

Trials/Tests

Steadfastness

Patience

Suffering

The Book of James begins with themes of trials and steadfastness. It ends with patience and suffering. The heart of the book ponders the relationship between faith and good works, emphasizing that both are necessary for the Christian life.

Paul and Timothy

Acts 16, and 1 and 2 Timothy

Paul and Silas came also to Derbe and to Lystra. A disciple was there, named Timothy. He was the son of a Jewish woman who was a believer, but his father was a Greek. He was well spoken of by the brothers.

Paul wanted Timothy to accompany him. As they went on their way through the cities, they delivered to the people the decisions that had been reached by the apostles and elders who were in Jerusalem. So the churches were strengthened in the faith, and they increased in numbers daily.

Paul's young friend and trusted co-worker Timothy became a minister of the Word. Two of Paul's last letters were written to Timothy. They show Paul's trust that Timothy would continue to preach the Gospel. More important, the letters show Paul's trust in the Lord.

Paul, an apostle of Christ Jesus by command of God our Savior and of Christ Jesus our hope,

To Timothy, my true child in the faith:

Grace, mercy, and peace from God the Father and Christ Jesus our Lord.

The saying is trustworthy and deserving of full acceptance, that Christ Jesus came into the world to save sinners, of whom I am the foremost. But I received mercy for this reason, that in me, as the foremost, Jesus Christ might display His perfect patience as an example to those who were to believe in Him for eternal life.

Fight the good fight of the faith. Take hold of the eternal life to which you were called and about which you made the good confession. O Timothy, guard the deposit entrusted to you.

I thank God whom I serve as I remember you constantly in my prayers night and day. I remind you to fan into flame the gift of God, for God gave us a spirit not of fear but of power and love and self-control.

Continue in what you have learned and have firmly believed, knowing from whom you learned it and how from childhood you have been acquainted with the sacred writings, which are able to make you wise for salvation through faith in Christ Jesus.

I have fought the good fight, I have finished the race, I have kept the faith. There is laid up for me the crown of righteousness, which the Lord, the righteous judge, will award to me on that Day, and not only to me but also to all who have loved His appearing.

DID YOU KNOW?

- Paul mentored several young men, teaching and encouraging them as pastors of God's people. Timothy and Titus were the most prominent of Paul's protégés. When he couldn't be with them in person, Paul wrote them letters of advice and encouragement.

- The word choice in 1 Timothy differs somewhat from that in Paul's other Letters, so many critics have concluded that Paul did not write it. However, authors often adapt their writing style based on the recipient, and Paul also typically worked through a scribe, which could affect the Letter's style.

Paul Tells Lydia about Christ

Acts 16

A vision appeared to Paul in the night: a man of Macedonia was standing there. The man urged Paul, saying, "Come over to Macedonia and help us."

When Paul had seen the vision, immediately we planned to go to Macedonia. We believed that God had called us to preach the Gospel there.

So we set sail from Troas and arrived in Philippi, which is a leading city of the district of Macedonia and a Roman colony. We remained in this city some days.

On the Sabbath day, we went outside the gate to the riverside, where we supposed there was a place of prayer. We sat down and spoke to the women who had come together.

One of the women who heard us was named Lydia. She was from the city of Thyatira, a seller of purple goods, and she worshiped God. The Lord opened her heart to pay attention to what Paul said. After Lydia was baptized, and her household as well, she urged us, saying, "If you have judged me to be faithful to the Lord, come to my house and stay."

Words to Remember

The Lord opened her heart to pay attention to what was said by Paul.
Acts 16:14b

DID YOU KNOW?

- Acts 16 contains the first of the so-called "we" sections of the book. Here, Luke is writing as a companion of Paul.

- Blue and purple dyes were derived from mollusk shells and were expensive to produce. These colors were therefore associated with wealth and royalty and made a profitable trade.

The righteousness of God through faith in Jesus.

Romans

AD 36 Conversion of Paul • AD 55 Paul writes Romans • AD 58–60 Paul imprisoned at Rome

Romans includes a twofold revelation (1:17–18). Paul describes the wrath of God against all unrighteousness but also reveals the righteousness of God through faith in Jesus Christ. Jesus bore God's wrath against our sins and revealed God's righteousness to save us through His blood. Paul unveils these truths to the Romans while requesting support for his mission work.

Righteousness of God

Wrath

Questions	Chapter	Quotations
1	1	0
5	2	3
14	3	8
5	4	4
0	5	0
7	6	0
5	7	2
5	8	1
10	9	14
7	10	11
7	11	13
0	12	3
0	13	3
2	14	3
0	15	7
0	16	0

Paul's Great Doctrinal Treatise

Unlike Paul's other letters, much of Romans reads like a carefully crafted doctrinal treatise (chs. 1–11). The apostle presents a seamless body of teaching that shows how the practice of the Church is tightly bound to its teachings so that the two are inseparable. To accomplish this, Paul anticipates his readers' questions and then answers them, often quoting directly from the Old Testament Scriptures to make his point. The letter includes 67 questions and 73 quotations (depending on how one counts). Below are some of Paul's key questions and answers, which are foundational to the Christian faith.

Question	Answer
What if some were unfaithful? Does their faithlessness nullify the faithfulness of God? (3:3)	By no means! Let God be true though everyone were a liar. (3:4)
What then? Are we Jews any better off? (3:9a)	No, not at all. For we have already charged that all, both Jews and Greeks, are under sin, as it is written, "None is righteous, no, not one." (3:9b–10)
How then was [righteousness] counted to [Abraham]? Was it before or after he had been circumcised? (4:10)	[Abraham] received the sign of circumcision as a seal of the righteousness that he had by faith while he was still uncircumcised. (4:11)
Are we to continue in sin that grace may abound? (6:1)	By no means! . . . We were buried therefore with [Christ] by baptism into death, in order that, just as Christ was raised from the dead by the glory of the Father, we too might walk in newness of life. (6:2, 4)
What then shall we say? That the law is sin? (7:7a)	By no means! Yet if it had not been for the law, I would not have known sin. (7:7b)
Who shall separate us from the love of Christ? (8:35)	I am sure that neither death nor life, nor angels nor rulers, nor things present nor things to come, nor powers, nor height nor depth, nor anything else in all creation, will be able to separate us from the love of God in Christ Jesus our Lord. (8:38–39)
What shall we say then? Is there injustice on God's part? (9:14a)	By no means! For He says to Moses, "I will have mercy on whom I have mercy, and I will have compassion on whom I have compassion." (9:14b–15)
Why do you pass judgment on your brother? Or you, why do you despise your brother? (14:10a)	For we will all stand before the judgment seat of God. . . . So then each of us will give an account of himself to God. (14:10b, 12)

Christ, our wisdom and reconciler.

1 & 2 Corinthians

AD 52–55 Paul's 3rd journey • AD 55 Paul writes 1 & 2 Corinthians • AD 68 Martyrdom of Peter and Paul

The cross of Christ draws together God and man, church and individuals to reconcile all in God's household. While writing to the Corinthians, the apostle Paul explains that the cross is weakness and foolishness to the world but is in fact the power and wisdom of God to save. Paul shows that the **ministry of reconciliation** forms the heart of Christian faith and life.

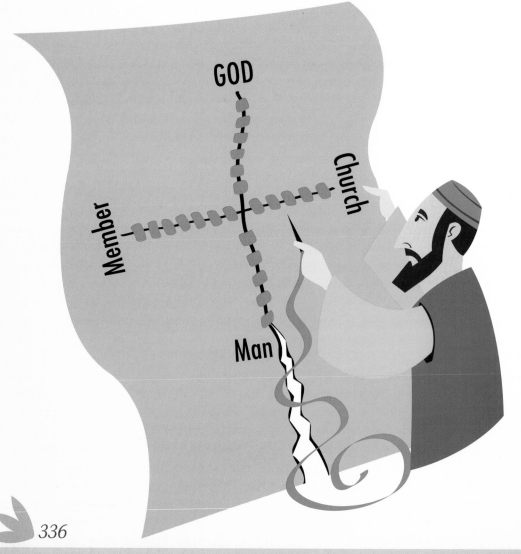

GOD

Church

Member

Man

Images and Titles for Church(es)

Judges	1
Betrothed	1
Partnership	1
Letter	1
Building	1
Field	1
Chosen	1
Dwelling	2
Temple	2
Fellowship	3
Children	5
Kings/Kingdom	6
Saints	11
Body	18
Church(es)	32
Brothers	51

The apostle Paul's letters to the congregations at Corinth focus on ministering to a divided church. As a result, Paul describes churches and church life in numerous ways. As is typical in his letters, he begins with Christian teaching (doctrine) before addressing specific problems at the church (practice). The graph at left shows the many titles and images he uses for the church. The chart below arranges these titles and images into four categories Paul uses most often. They will give you a clearer sense of what the Bible teaches about our lives together in Christ.

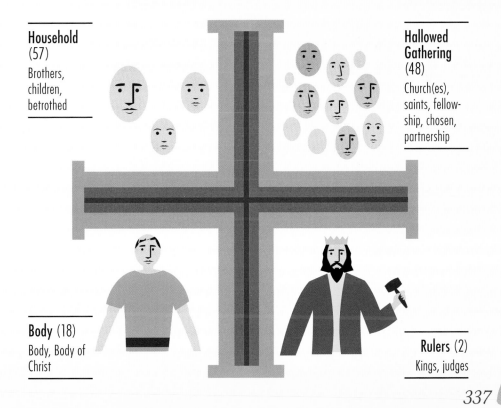

Household (57)
Brothers, children, betrothed

Hallowed Gathering (48)
Church(es), saints, fellowship, chosen, partnership

Body (18)
Body, Body of Christ

Rulers (2)
Kings, judges

Paul and Silas in Prison

Acts 16

As we were going to the place of prayer, we were met by a slave girl who brought her owners much gain by fortune-telling. She followed Paul and us, crying out, "These men are servants of the Most High God, who proclaim to you the way of salvation." She kept doing this for many days.

> **Words to Remember**
> Believe in the Lord Jesus, and you will be saved.
> *Acts 16:31*

Paul, having become greatly annoyed, said to the spirit, "I command you in the name of Jesus Christ to come out of her." And it came out that very hour.

But when her owners saw that their hope of gain was gone, they seized Paul and Silas and dragged them into the marketplace before the rulers. They said, "These men are Jews, and they are disturbing our city. They speak about customs that are not lawful for us as Romans to accept or practice."

The crowd joined in attacking Paul and Silas. The magistrates tore the garments off them and gave orders to beat them with rods. When they had inflicted many blows, they threw Paul and Silas into prison, ordering the jailer to keep them safely. So the jailer put Paul and Silas into the inner prison and fastened their feet in the stocks.

About midnight, Paul and Silas were praying and singing hymns to God. The prisoners were listening, and suddenly there was a great earthquake. The foundations of the prison were shaken. Immediately all the doors were opened, and everyone's bonds were unfastened.

When the jailer woke and saw that the prison doors were open, he drew his sword and was about to kill himself, supposing that the prisoners had escaped. But Paul cried, "Do not harm yourself, for we are all here."

The jailer called for lights and rushed in. Trembling with fear, he fell down before Paul and Silas. He brought them out and said, "Sirs, what must I do to be saved?"

They said, "Believe in the Lord Jesus, and you will be saved, you and your household." Paul and Silas spoke the word of the Lord to the jailer and to all who were in his house.

The jailer took them and washed their wounds. He was baptized at once, he and all his family. Then he brought Paul and Silas up into his house and set food before them. The jailer rejoiced along with his entire household that he had believed in God.

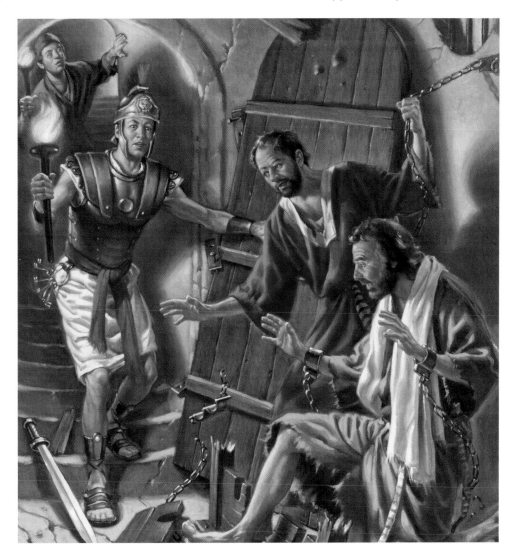

DID YOU KNOW?

- As in Jesus' ministry, the demons who possessed the girl recognized God's presence at work in the apostles and were driven to respond (cf. Luke 4:34, 41).

- The magistrates could punish noncitizens without proper legal proceedings, but since Paul and Silas were Roman citizens, it was illegal for the magistrates to strip them of their clothes and beat them.

- If a Roman guard lost his prisoner, the penalty was death, so the jailer was about to carry out what he assumed was inevitable before Paul stopped him.

Paul Sails to Rome

Acts 27–28

Paul was arrested in the temple, but he requested a trial before Caesar, which was his right as a Roman citizen. So Paul was sent to Rome.

The Roman officials delivered Paul and some other prisoners to a centurion named Julius so that he could take them to Rome. Julius treated Paul kindly and allowed some friends to sail with him to take care of him.

As everyone prepared to board the ship, Paul said, "Sirs, I perceive that the voyage will be with injury and much loss, not only of the cargo and the ship, but also of our lives." But Julius paid more attention to the pilot and to the owner of the ship than to what Paul said.

Soon a tempestuous wind, called the northeaster, struck down from the land. When the ship was caught and could not face the wind, it was driven along. The sailors began to throw the cargo overboard. When neither sun nor stars appeared for many days, all hope of our being saved was at last abandoned.

Since no one had eaten for a long time, Paul said, "I urge you to take heart, for there will be no loss of life among you, but only of the ship. For this very night an angel said, 'Do not be afraid, Paul. God has granted you all those who sail with you.' So take heart, men, for I have faith in God that it will be exactly as I have been told. But we must run aground on some island."

As day was about to dawn, Paul urged everyone to take some food. When it was day, they noticed a bay with a beach, on which they planned if possible to run the ship ashore. But striking a reef, they ran the vessel aground. The soldiers' plan was to kill the prisoners so no one could swim away and escape. But Julius, wishing to save Paul, ordered those who could swim to jump overboard first and make for the land. Those who could not swim would come to shore on planks or on pieces of the ship. So it was that all were brought safely to land.

The island was called Malta. The native people showed us unusual kindness, for they kindled a fire and welcomed us all. When Paul had gathered a bundle of sticks and put them on the fire, a viper came out because of the heat and fastened on his hand. He shook off the creature into the fire and suffered no harm.

After three months, we set sail in a ship that had wintered in the island. So we came to Rome. The brothers there, when they heard about us, came to meet us. On seeing them, Paul thanked God and took courage.

DID YOU KNOW?

- When Paul speaks before boarding the ship, he is most likely offering advice based on his experience as a seasoned traveler; he had already endured three shipwrecks (2 Corinthians 11:25).

- The guards wanted to kill the prisoners because they would be punished if the prisoners escaped.

- "Brothers" (*adelphoi* in Greek) is a general term Paul used for fellow Christians and co-workers in Christ's mission, whether male or female. However, Paul also used the term specifically for men who led congregations.

Justified through faith in Jesus Christ.

Galatians

AD 49–51 Paul's 2nd journey • c. AD 51–53 Paul writes Galatians • AD 52–55 Paul's 3rd journey

In Galatians, the apostle Paul sets aside a misunderstanding of the Old Testament. A group he calls the Judaizers argued that **righteousness** before God came through doing the works of the Old Testament Law. Paul reveals instead that the preaching of the Gospel leads to faith or trust in God, who declares us **righteous** through Jesus Christ.

LAW + WORKS ≠ RIGHTEOUSNESS through Jesus Christ

FAITH

GOSPEL

Chosen in Christ.

Ephesians

AD 52–55 Paul's 3rd journey • c. AD 60 Paul writes Ephesians • AD 65 Paul assigns Timothy to Ephesus

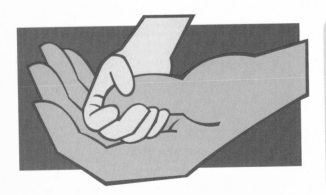

In love He predestined us for adoption as sons through Jesus Christ, according to the purpose of His will, to the praise of His glorious grace, with which He has blessed us in the Beloved.
(Ephesians 1:4–6)

Philippians

AD 52–55 Paul's 3rd journey • c. AD 60 Paul writes Philippians • AD 68 Martyrdom of Peter and Paul

REJOICE•JOY•GLAD•GLORY

In his little Letter to the Philippians, Paul celebrates the cross and the Christian life. While writing from prison, he refers eighteen times to the joy God gives His people in Christ.

Paul Writes to the Philippians

Philippians 1 and 4

Paul wrote the Letter to the Philippians while in prison. Yet, despite the frustrations and other hardships Paul was enduring as he wrote, the letter overflows with joy.

I thank my God in all my remembrance of you, always in every prayer of mine for you all making my prayer with joy, because of your partnership in the Gospel from the first day until now. And I am sure of this, that He who began a good work in you will bring it to completion at the day of Jesus Christ.

Rejoice in the Lord always. Again I will say, Rejoice. Let your reasonableness be known to everyone. The Lord is at hand. Do not be anxious about anything, but in everything by prayer and **supplication** with thanksgiving let your requests be made known to God. And the peace of God, which surpasses all understanding, will guard your hearts and your minds in Christ Jesus.

All the
fullness of God
dwells in Christ.

Colossians

AD 52–55 Paul's 3rd journey • c. AD 60 Paul writes Colossians • AD 68 Martyrdom of Peter and Paul

In Colossians, Paul writes Christ "is the image of the invisible God" (1:15), who renews us in God's image (cf. Genesis 1:27) and warns against false teachers who preach a counterfeit gospel.

**Image of God
Renewed in Christ**

1 chapter

Receive your
brother.

Read in 1 minute

Philemon

AD 57–58 Paul journeys to Rome • c. AD 60 Paul writes Philemon • AD 68 Martyrdom of Peter and Paul

Paul wrote to Philemon on behalf of Onesimus, a slave who ran away from Philemon. In the letter, Paul asks Philemon to welcome Onesimus back not as a slave but as a brother in Christ. This little letter shows how Christian beliefs undermined slavery in the Roman Empire.

Dating Events in Acts and the Epistles

AD 36	Paul's conversion (Acts 9:1–31)
AD 41	Martyrdom of James the brother of John (late March; Acts 12:2); Peter in prison (April; Acts 12:3–4); Passover (May 4; Acts 12:4); Peter leaves Jerusalem (May; Galatians 2:11)
AD 42	Peter in Antioch (May 41–April 42; Galatians 2:11); Peter on mission in Asia Minor (Spring/Summer; 1 Peter 1:1–2); Peter in Corinth (Fall); Peter at Rome (mid November)
AD 44	Herod Agrippa at festival in Caesarea (March 5; Acts 12:19); death of Herod Agrippa (March 10; Acts 12:21–23)
AD 47–48	Paul's first missionary journey (Acts 13:1–14:28)
AD 49	Conference in Jerusalem (Acts 15:1–35); Peter goes to Antioch (February; Galatians 2:11); Paul confronts Peter (April; Galatians 2:11); Paul goes to Macedonia; Barnabas and John Mark go to Cyprus (mid May; Acts 15:36–16:10)
AD 49–51	Paul's second missionary journey (Acts 15:39–18:22)
AD 49–56	Peter likely in Antioch seven years
AD 52–55	Paul's third missionary journey (Acts 18:23–21:17)
AD 55–57	Paul imprisoned in Caesarea (Acts 23:23–26:32)
AD 57–58	Paul's journey to Rome (Acts 27:1–28:16)
AD 58–60	Paul in custody in Rome (Acts 28:17–31)
AD 62	Martyrdom of James, the Lord's brother
AD 64-65	Paul assigns Titus at Crete (Titus 1:5)
AD 65	Paul in Ephesus, where he leaves Timothy (Spring to Summer; 1 Timothy 1:3)
AD 68	Peter and Paul martyred in Rome

This timeline will help you read Acts together with the many New Testament Epistles, which often overlap in time. (From the research of Andrew E. Steinmann, *From Abraham to Paul: A Biblical Chronology* [St. Louis: Concordia, 2011].)

Godly contentment and purpose.

1 & 2 Timothy

AD 65 Paul writes 1 Timothy • AD 68 Paul writes 2 Timothy • AD 68 Martyrdom of Peter and Paul

In the Pastoral Letters, Paul lists twenty-two qualifications for pastors and deacons in the Church: twenty-one for pastors and eight for deacons (see 1 Timothy 3:1–13; Titus 1:6–9). Nearly all the qualifications for deacons are also listed for pastors (with variations in wording). The chart shows how much the offices overlap and how much more was expected of pastors as leaders.

Qualifications for Church Workers

Pastors

Holy
Loving toward what is good
Hospitable
Self-controlled, gentle
Disciplined
Upright
Well thought of
Able to teach
Sober-minded
Not violent
Not quarrelsome

Not arrogant
Not quick-tempered
Above reproach

Deacons

Dignified
Husband of one wife
Manages children well
Holds the mystery of the faith
Not addicted to much wine
Not greedy for dishonest gain
Tested; proved blameless

Not double-tongued

Titus

c. AD 64 Paul assigns Titus to Crete • AD 68 Titus written • AD 68 Martyrdom of Peter and Paul

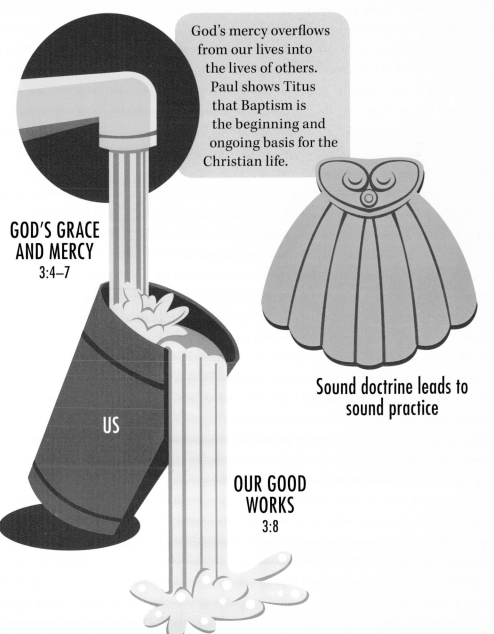

God's mercy overflows from our lives into the lives of others. Paul shows Titus that Baptism is the beginning and ongoing basis for the Christian life.

GOD'S GRACE AND MERCY
3:4–7

US

OUR GOOD WORKS
3:8

Sound doctrine leads to sound practice

**Called into
His marvelous light.**

1 & 2 Peter

AD 49 Jerusalem Council • AD 68 Martyrdom of Peter and Paul • AD 70 Romans destroy Jerusalem

In Peter's letters, he reminds suffering Christians that the Lord called, or summoned, them from the dark ways of the world into His heavenly light.

More than 1/5 of New Testament mentions of suffering occur in these two short letters of Peter.

1 & 2 Peter

Rest of the New Testament

Jesus, the
founder and perfecter
of our faith.

Hebrews

AD 49 Jerusalem Council • AD 70 Romans destroy Jerusalem • AD 96 Clement of Rome cites Hebrews

In Hebrews 11,
the author lists 34 examples of
faith from the Old Testament—a
great cloud of witnesses who
believed God's promises.

Hebrews
emphasizes the faithfulness of
Jesus, our one great High Priest,
whose one sacrifice on the cross
fulfilled the Old Testament.

God
is love.

1, 2 & 3 John

AD 70 Romans destroy Jerusalem • AD 85–95 1, 2 & 3 John written • AD 132 Bar Kokhba revolt begins

No other portion of the Scriptures discusses God's love more intensely than the letters of John. They include sixty-two uses of the word *love*—more than any other portion of Scripture except the much, much longer Gospel of John.

Built up in your most holy faith.

Jude

AD 68 Martyrdom of Peter and Paul • AD 70 Romans destroy Jerusalem • AD 132 Bar Kokhba revolt begins

Jude warns us against the threat of false teachers and encourages congregations to support and uplift one another through faith.

Jesus is
coming soon.

Revelation

AD 70 Romans destroy Jerusalem • AD 95 Revelation written • AD 132 Bar Kokhba revolt begins

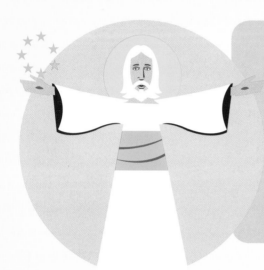

As the last book of the Bible, Revelation draws on all that has gone before and depicts the ascended and heavenly Jesus in the splendor God the Father promised to Him and to those who trust in Him (Revelation 1:12–16).

The apostle John recorded brilliant colors in the visions of Revelation. The following color bars illustrate the appearance of colors mentioned throughout the book. In this array of colors, gold and white appear most often as the brilliant heavenly colors.

Gold 1:12–13	White 4:4	Gold 9:13	Purple 17:4	Pearl 18:16	Onyx 21:20
White 1:14	Gold 4:4	Fire 9:17	Scarlet 17:3–4	White 19:8	Carnelian 21:20
Fire 1:14	Crystal 4:6	Sapphire 9:17	Gold 17:4	White 19:11	Chrysolite 21:20
Bronze 1:15	White 6:2	Sulfur 9:17	Pearl 17:4	Fire 19:12	Beryl 21:20
White 2:17	Red 6:4	Red 9:17	Gold 18:12	White 19:14	Topaz 21:20
Fire 2:18	Black 6:5	Gold 9:20	Silver 18:12	White 20:11	Chrysoprase 21:20
Bronze 2:18	Pale 6:8	Silver 9:20	Pearl 18:12	Jasper 21:11	Jacinth 21:20
White 3:4–5	White 6:11	Bronze 9:20	Purple 18:12	Crystal 21:11	Amethyst 21:20
Gold 3:18	Black 6:12	Red 12:3	Scarlet 18:12	Gold 21:15	Pearl 21:21
Fire 3:18	Red 6:12	White 14:14	Ivory 18:12	Gold 21:18	Gold 21:21
White 3:18	White 7:9	Gold 14:14	Bronze 18:12	Jasper 21:18–19	Crystal 22:1
Jasper 4:3	White 7:13–14	White 15:6	Purple 18:16	Sapphire 21:19	
Carnelian 4:3	Green 9:4	Gold 15:6–7	Scarlet 18:16	Agate 21:19	
Emerald 4:3	Gold 9:7	Fire 16:8	Gold 18:16	Emerald 21:19	

GOD WINS!

First Vision (4:1–8:1)	The Heavenly Court and the Seven Seals
Second Vision (chs. 8–11)	The Seven Trumpets
Third Vision (chs. 12–14)	Satan Overthrown
Fourth Vision (chs. 15:1–16:21)	The Seven Censers
Fifth Vision (chs. 17–19)	Babylon Overthrown
Sixth Vision (chs. 20:1–22:5)	Satan Bound and Condemned

The visions of Revelation show that God's people will face suffering in this sinful world, Christ will return in judgment, and He will rescue all who call on His name. Therefore, repent of all that would hinder this clear, simple confession of Christ and His return. Then pray joyfully and confidently for His return—He is coming as your Savior.

John's Vision of Heaven

Revelation 21–22

Words to Remember

Death shall be no more, neither shall there be mourning, nor crying, nor pain anymore, for the former things have passed away. *Revelation 21:4*

I saw a new heaven and a new earth. And I saw the holy city, new Jerusalem, coming down out of heaven from God, prepared as a bride adorned for her husband. I heard a loud voice from the throne saying, "Behold, the dwelling place of God is with man. He will dwell with them, and they will be His people. God Himself will be with them as their God. He will wipe away every tear from their eyes. Death shall be no more, neither shall there be mourning, nor crying, nor pain anymore, for the former things have passed away."

He who was seated on the throne said, "Behold, I am making all things new. I am **the Alpha and the Omega**, the beginning and the end. To the thirsty I will give from the spring of the water of life without payment. The one who conquers will have this heritage, and I will be his God and he will be My son."

Then came one of the seven angels. He said, "Come, I will show you the Bride, the wife of the Lamb." He carried me away in the Spirit to a great, high mountain. He showed me the holy city Jerusalem coming down out of heaven from God, having the glory of God. It had a great, high wall, with twelve gates, and at the gates twelve angels. On the gates, the names of the twelve tribes of the sons of Israel were inscribed. The wall of the city had twelve foundations. On them were the twelve names of the twelve apostles of the Lamb.

I saw no temple in the city, for its temple is the Lord God the Almighty and the Lamb. The city has no need of sun or moon to shine on it, for the glory of God gives it light, and its lamp is the Lamb. By its light will the nations walk. The kings of the earth will bring their glory into it. Its gates will never be shut by day—and there will be no night there.

Then the angel showed me the river of the water of life, bright as crystal, flowing from the throne of God and of the Lamb through the middle of the street of the city. On either side of the river, the tree of life. The leaves of the tree were for the healing of the nations. Night will be no more. They will need no light of lamp or sun, for the Lord God will be their light, and they will reign forever and ever.

I, John, am the one who heard and saw these things.

The Spirit and the Bride say, "Come." Let the one who hears say, "Come." Let the one who is thirsty come; let the one who desires take the water of life without price.

He who testifies to these things says, "Surely I am coming soon."

Amen. Come, Lord Jesus!

DID YOU KNOW?

- John wrote Revelation using an approach called "apocalyptic" style. The word *apocalypse* means "unveiling" or "revealing."

- Scripture repeatedly underscores that one of the greatest blessings of the new heavens and new earth is that restored mankind will again behold God face-to-face and live in His immediate presence.

- The new creation has already begun to appear through the preaching of the Gospel and the work of the Spirit. However, it will not be completed until the day of Christ's return.

Index

Artwork Credits